SELECTED
PASSAGES
FROM
CORRESPONDENCE
WITH
FRIENDS

SELECTED PASSAGES FROM CORRESPONDENCE WITH FRIENDS

~*by*
NIKOLAI GOGOL

Translated by
Jesse Zeldin

VANDERBILT UNIVERSITY PRESS · NASHVILLE · 1969

69–09294

CONTENTS

INTRODUCTION

Between 1842, when *Dead Souls* was published, and 1847, when he brought out *Selected Passages from Correspondence with Friends*, Nikolai Gogol was occupied with two things: the continuation of *Dead Souls* (a task that plagued him until his death in 1851) and the clarification of his religious, moral, and aesthetic views. The latter forms the content of *Selected Passages*, the last of Gogol's works to be published during his lifetime.

We do not know exactly when Gogol decided that he must publicly expose his convictions on these topics. His first mention of the book is April 2, 1845, in a letter to A. O. Smirnova,[1] at which time he appears to have been much concerned about the effect his fictional works had produced. He thought this new effort would set the record straight. At the end of April he wrote to the Minister of Education, S. S. Uvarov, to thank him for a pension Uvarov had just approved for him, to inform Uvarov that his new book would be much more useful to Russia than anything he had done previously, and that "its subject would not be foreign to your [Uvarov's] own convictions."[2] This letter to Uvarov marks

1. Gogol's long and intimate friendship with Smirnova dates from 1831, when he sent her a copy of his first book, *Evenings on a Farm near Dikanka*. She was at that time well known at court as well as in literary circles and she often intervened with the Emperor when the censors gave her friends trouble. Indeed, she was to approach Nicholas I on several occasions on Gogol's behalf. She also became one of Gogol's more frequent correspondents and one of his closest confidantes.
2. Translated by Carl R. Proffer in *Letters of Nikolai Gogol* (Ann Arbor: The University of Michigan Press, 1967), p. 157.

the beginning of the controversy over *Selected Passages,* for Uvarov promptly publicized it in an attempt to prove that Gogol was a supporter of the status quo in Russia. Gogol's friends, both Westernizers and Slavophiles, thought it a pity at best that Gogol had written such a letter; at worst, they were disgusted by what seemed to them to be toadying on Gogol's part to the government of Nicholas I. Indeed, Belinsky was to refer to this letter some two years later in his famous "Letter to Gogol" when he said,

your letter to Uvarov became known in Saint Petersburg, in which you lament that your works have been misinterpreted in Russia, and subsequently you express dissatisfaction with your previous works and declare that you will be pleased with your own works only when he, who, etc. Now judge for yourself: is it any wonder that your book has lowered you in the eyes of the public both as a writer and, still more, as a man?[3]

Gogol was indeed worried about misinterpretations of his earlier work. In a letter of July 25, 1845 to Smirnova—at which time he was deeply engaged in working on *Selected Passages*—he declared that the true meaning of *Dead Souls* was still a secret and that this secret would only be revealed in the succeeding volumes. The groundwork for the future battle between the author of *Selected Passages* and its critics was already being prepared, one and one half years before publication of the book.

By the end of July 1846, the first part of the book was ready for publication (it came out as a whole in late January 1847), and Gogol was more than ever convinced of its necessity—"for everyone." By the following October Gogol had sent P. A. Pletnyov, his publisher,[4] "the fifth and final notebook." The volume,

3. Translated by James P. Scanlan in *Russian Philosophy,* edited by James M. Edie, James P. Scanlan, Mary-Barbara Zeldin; with the collaboration of George L. Kline (Chicago: Quadrangle Books, 1965), I, 318.

4. P. A. Pletnyov (1792–1865), one of the foremost literary critics of the day, had been Pushkin's friend and took over the editorship of *The Contemporary,* the literary journal founded by Pushkin, after Pushkin's death in 1837. In 1846 Pletnyov sold *The Contemporary* to friends of Belinsky, who became its literary critic until his death in 1848. With the sale the

he said, "was necessary for the general good." "I am told this," Gogol went on, "by my heart and by God's mercy. . . . I acted firmly in the name of God when I was compiling my book; I took up my pen in praise of his Holy name. . . ."[5] Again, Gogol's desire was to help everyone, to perform a religious and moral service for mankind.

By December 1846, as the publication date was drawing closer, Gogol was becoming increasingly uneasy about the reception *Selected Passages* might obtain. As his letter of December 10, 1846, to A. O. Rosset, the brother of Smirnova, indicates, he was uncertain how the public would take his latest effort—because of what he had to say and the style in which he had chosen to say it.

In early January 1847, Pletnyov advised Gogol that the censors had objected to some of the letters.[6] Gogol replied,

I absolutely cannot see a reason why *it is better* not to print those letters, which, it seems to me, will make some civil servants examine themselves a little more severely—especially those who have beautiful souls and good intentions and sin through lack of knowledge. If only two or three people in all of Russia look more clearly at many things after my book, then it is already extremely good.[7]

The more he contemplated the reactions to his work, the more nervously did Gogol ask his friends for their comments and the more furiously did he inform them of his reasons for writing it. He told S. T. Aksakov[8] that everyone would attack, but the attacks would be necessary since they would give him much information, both about himself and about his readers. He told his mother that he was publishing his "Testament" in order to help

journal's orientation turned definitively liberal. Pletnyov was one of Gogol's closest friends and, at times, his patron.

5. Proffer, p. 163.

6. Nos. 19, 20, 21, 26, and 28.

7. Proffer, p. 167.

8. S. T. Aksakov (1791–1859) met Gogol as early as 1832 and remained friendly with him the rest of Gogol's life. The father of the Slavophiles K. S. and I. S. Aksakov, Aksakov is best known as the author of the realistic works *Years of Childhood* and *A Family Chronicle*. His *Recollections of Gogol* is an important source for all writers on Gogol.

others, because a real Christian must always remember death, and this remembrance will keep him from sin and thus earn him a good end—indeed, "the constant thought of death . . . lends strength for life and good deeds in life."[9] He told A. P. Tolstoy,[10] just after publication, that *Selected Passages* had been mangled by the censors. He informed Rosset that the practical point of the book had been ruined: "Almost everything that explains how to apply what is said to actual deeds was not passed—all the letters to people in government jobs, to civil servants in Russia in which I explain the possibility of doing truly Christian deeds in any position in our secular offices."[11]

Even though he was only beginning to receive opinions on *Selected Passages* in late January and early February 1847, Gogol was already aware of what at least the westernizers would say. His letter to Rosset of February 11, 1847, in part predicts what Belinsky would later write:

I did not compile this book to anger the Belinskys, Kraevskys, and Se(n)kowskis;[12] I was looking into the inside of Russia, not at literary society. Now the book consists of generalities, and instead of those peo-

9. Proffer, p. 169.

10. Gogol met A. P. Tolstoy (1801–1873), who had twice been a provincial governor, in Ostend during the summer of 1844. Tolstoy was in many ways a typical conservative administrator. His home was in Moscow, but he spent a good deal of time abroad. In the fall of 1848 and spring of 1849 Gogol lived at the Tolstoy house in Moscow. Gogol seems to have been impressed with Tolstoy's rank, although he also seems to have thought Tolstoy, who was of a rather mystical persuasion, needed much advice in order to make him a proper Russian administrator. Many of the letters in *Selected Passages* were addressed to Tolstoy.

11. Proffer, p. 171.

12. A. A. Kraevsky was coeditor, with Belinsky, of the journal *Notes of the Fatherland*. Kraevsky and Belinsky split in 1846 and Belinsky became literary critic of *The Contemporary*. Kraevsky was one of the bitterest critics of *Selected Passages*. O. I. Se(n)kowski was one of the editors of *Library for Reading*. He was also professor of Arabic, Turkish, and Persian at the University of St. Petersburg. He had been attacked some twelve years before the publication of *Selected Passages* in Gogol's article "On the Condition of Journalistic Literature in 1834 and 1835," printed in *The Contemporary* in 1835.

ple and subjects which should have stepped out before the readers, I alone stepped out on the stage, exactly as if I were publishing my book in order to display myself. . . .[13]

It was precisely this charge of pride that was shortly to be leveled against Gogol.

The responses to *Selected Passages* came quickly, and they were even worse than Gogol had expected. As he wrote to Zhukovsky[14] on March 6, 1847, "the publication of my book burst forth exactly like a slap in the face—a slap in the face of the public, a slap in the face of my friends, and, finally, a stouter slap in my face." While he felt that he might have made a fool of himself, still Gogol tried to explain: "the opponents as well as the defenders are more or less in an uneasy state, and many are simply nonplussed as to where to turn, being unable to make many apparently contradictory things harmonize—because of the sharpness with which they were expressed."[15] His sensitivity to criticism again overcame him, however, and he concluded his letter by suggesting that perhaps he had been guilty of those very sins that he had anathematized in his book.

At the same time, Gogol could not bring himself to agree with those who regarded him as a traitor to the cause of humanity and decency. Indeed, Belinsky was to call him a "proponent of the knout, apostle of ignorance, champion of obscurantism, panegyrist of Tatar ways. . . ."[16] Many (mostly extreme Slavophiles) saw *Selected Passages* as a definitive break with Gogol's past work and on this ground justified their own dislike of what Gogol had

13. Proffer, p. 171.
14. V. A. Zhukovsky (1783–1852) is best known as a translator, probably the finest that Russia has produced. Indeed, many Russians claim that his translations surpass the originals. He worked particularly with German and English poets of the eighteenth and early nineteenth centuries. He is very important for his work in shaping a Russian poetic language of feeling. He was considered, before Pushkin, the leader of the progressive literary movement in Russia.
15. Proffer, p. 173.
16. *Russian Philosophy,* I, 315.

previously written while praising his new effort. A few—Prince Vyazemsky among them[17]—thought *Selected Passages* was of a piece with Gogol's earlier writing, but the Prince also thought it went too far: Gogol must reach a middle way. Vyazemsky probably found it contradictory to accept Gogol as a great writer and to reject *any* of his works, so he took this way of getting around the problem. Only the article by Apollon Grigoryev[18] insisted that Gogol's opinions had not changed at all and that both Slavophiles and westernizers were wrong to think they had.

Most serious of all, however, was the series of attacks by Belinsky, climaxed by the open letter. It was Belinsky who carried the day. His opinion of *Selected Passages* has, indeed, prevailed from that time to this.[19]

Gogol's replies, in which he tried to explain his book and correct the impression it had created,[20] were of no avail. The only explanations for such a work as *Selected Passages*, so far as his critics were concerned, were either that Gogol had gone mad as a result of religious fanaticism (even a villain who had driven him to this madness was found—Father Matvey Alexandrovich Konstantinovsky, an Orthodox priest who was close to Gogol at this time[21]) or that he was attempting to ingratiate himself with the government so that he might receive financial support. It was perhaps the charge of having done a complete about-face that an-

17. Prince P. A. Vyazemsky (1792–1878), an intimate friend and appreciator of Pushkin, was also the foremost champion of romanticism in Russia in the 1820s.

18. A. A. Grigoryev (1822–1864), a poet and critic, became editor of *Moskvityanin* in 1850. As a critic, he operated on the theory of "organic criticism," according to which all art was an outgrowth of the national soil.

19. For details of the controversy surrounding the publication of *Selected Passages,* see Paul Debreczeny, *Nikolay Gogol and his Contemporary Critics* (Philadelphia: The American Philosophical Society, April 1966), pp. 50–63.

20. All Gogol's replies were in private letters, except for *An Author's Confession,* which was not published during his lifetime.

21. For an example of this attitude see David Magarshack, *Gogol* (London: Faber and Faber, 1957), pp. 261–262.

noyed Gogol the most, and he planned to republish some of his earlier essays, written some ten years before, along with another edition of *Selected Passages,* to prove that his ideas had been consistent.[22] Unfortunately, perhaps, he never did so.

Modern critics of *Selected Passages* are divided into two camps: those who follow Belinsky's opinions—by far the majority—and reject *Selected Passages* as a rather worthless work with a few flashes of intelligence here and there, and those of a religious persuasion who see the volume as a genuine expression of the ideals of Russian Orthodoxy. Almost none, however, follow Grigoryev's line and view *Selected Passages* as of a piece with Gogol's earlier opinions.[23] Indeed, there has long been a curious tendency amounting to a traditional prejudice on the part of Gogol critics to separate his fictional and nonfictional works, as well as to separate his writings before *Selected Passages* from the *Passages* themselves, as though Gogol were a schizophrenic (and not a very bright one at that). This means that very few have dealt seriously with the book, just as there has been little extended work on Gogol as a whole in the west. Most western readers have thus been forced to consider Gogol in a vacuum. There have so far been only six books entirely devoted to Gogol in English, three in German, eight in French, one in Spanish, and one in Italian.[24] Considering the enormous interest in Russian literature in recent years, and considering the great importance

22. Proffer, p. 230.

23. Carl Proffer is one of the few exceptions to this rule. For his opinion see footnote 1 to Gogol's letter of July 30, 1846, pp. 229–230 of his translation of Gogol's letters. I myself am strongly in agreement with Proffer.

24. English: Paul Debreczeny, *Nikolay Gogol and his Contemporary Critics* (Philadelphia: The American Philosophical Society, April, 1966); F. Driessen, *Gogol as a Short Story Writer: A Study of his Technique of Composition* (The Hague: Mouton, 1965), translated from the Dutch; Janko Lavrin, *Gogol (1809–1852), A Centenary Survey* (London, 1951); David Magarshack, *Gogol* (London, Faber and Faber, 1957); Vladimir V. Nabokov, *Nikolai Gogol* (New York: New Directions, 1961); Vsevelod Setchkarev, *Gogol—His Life and Works* (New York: New York University Press, 1965), translated from the German

German: W. Kasack, *Die Technique der Charakter-Darstellung bei Gogol*

of Gogol within that literature, these books are remarkably few. As for the literature in Russian, while there is a great deal of it, there has also been singular paucity of treatment of *Selected Passages*—most recently, indeed, almost no treatment of the book at all, as Soviet critics have concentrated either upon Gogol as a social critic of the old regime or upon Gogol's "literary" qualities. I have been unable to find even one contemporary article in any language entirely devoted to *Selected Passages*.

Of the works on Gogol published in the last three decades (and there are not many), only three make extended mention of *Selected Passages:* Konstantin Mochul'sky's *Gogol's Spiritual Journey* (published only in Russian), Paul Evdokimov's *Gogol and Dostoevsky: Descent to Hell* (published only in French), and Vsevelod Setchkarev's *Gogol: His Life and Works.* Of the three, only the first two, both written by men who are themselves concerned with religion, find *Selected Passages* of significance, in so far as they believe the volume expresses nineteenth-century Russian religiosity. Mochul'sky, for example, says that the basic idea of the book is the construction of a single Christian culture, a religious base for state and property, a complete church-world.[25] For Evdokimov, that *Selected Passages* "is the source of later religious thought is a demonstrated fact. All great Russian thinkers to the present day are in debt to his genius."[26] Nevertheless,

---

(Wiesbaden, 1957); Otto Kraus, *Der Fall Gogol* (Munich, 1912); F. Thiess, *Nikolaus W. Gogol und seine Bünenwerke* (Berlin, 1922).

French: Nina Gourfinkel, *Nicholas Gogol dramaturge* (Paris, 1956); Modeste Hormann, *Gogol, sa vie et son oeuvre* (Paris, 1946); Louis Leger, *Gogol* (Paris, 1914); D. S. Merejkovsky, *Gogol et le diable* (Paris, 1939), also published in Russian and German; N. A. Hilsson, *Gogol et Pétersbourg: Recherches sur les antécédents des contes pétersbourgeois* (Stockholm, 1954); B. F. Schloezer, *Gogol* (Paris, 1932 and 1946); A. Schick, *Nicolas Gogol—une vie de torments* (Sceaux, 1949); Raina Tyrneva, *Nicolas Gogol—Ecrivain et moraliste* (Aix, 1901)

Spanish: Claudio Giaconi, *Un Hombre en la trampa* (Santiago, 1960).

Italian: Enrico Pappacena, *Gogol* (Milan, 1930).

25. K. V. Mochul'sky, *Dukhovny put' Gogolya* (Paris, 1934), p. 101.

26. Paul Evdokimov, *Gogol et Dostoïevsky ou la Descente aux enfers* (Paris: Desclée de Brouwer, 1961), p. 131.

Mochul'sky still thinks of *Selected Passages* as somehow separated from Gogol's earlier work, while Evdokimov avoids a precise discussion of the problem.

Thus very few voices have been raised in opposition to what Belinsky decided more than one hundred and twenty years ago. One would have to search very far indeed to find a parallel situation in literature, or in any realm other than science, for that matter. The stumbling block has been precisely the one on which Vyazemsky stubbed his toe; that is, it is almost impossible to accept what appear to be reactionary, cruel—one might say stupid—opinions as the work of the same man who wrote *The Inspector General*, "The Nose," "The Overcoat," and *Dead Souls*, all of which most readers and critics consider to be violent satiric attacks on the social system of old Russia, in spite of what Gogol himself said on the subject. Since few wish to be identified with the practical suggestions offered by Gogol in *Selected Passages*, the possibility that the work is indeed "Gogolian" is rejected. At best, it is slighted on the ground that the man who produced such fictional monuments was simply not the same man who produced *Selected Passages*. The alternative, which only Evdokimov has faced, is to reinterpret Gogol's fiction, a formidable task indeed in the face of such overwhelming majority opinion.

At the risk of arousing further controversy, one might suggest, for example, that *Selected Passages* in reality constitutes a statement of the basic ideas which were to form the foundation of Part II of *Dead Souls*, if not also of Part III; that is, it points the way to a regeneration of the "dead souls" we find in Part I, in much the way Dante's *Purgatorio* shows the way of salvation for sinners—not a contradiction of *Inferno*, but a part of the same structure in which *Inferno*, *Purgatorio*, and *Paradiso* all have a definite place.[27] The first four chapters of Part II (all that

27. Even D. S. Mirsky, who rejects *Selected Passages* as largely of no value at all, believes that Gogol had something dantesque in mind when he wrote *Dead Souls* (*A History of Russian Literature* [New York: Vintage Books, 1958, pp. 154–155]).

were rescued from the fire when Gogol burned his manuscript just before he died) seem to bear out this point of view. If this suggestion has any validity, it certainly makes *Selected Passages* vital to an understanding of what Gogol was trying to do; it means that the same mind was responsible for both the fiction and the nonfiction, and that Gogol's claim of consistency was justified, Belinsky and his followers notwithstanding.

As Gogol pointed out in his letter to Rosset, *Selected Passages* as such, apart from its connections with his other work, was meant to be a practical book, almost, one might say, a conduct book, in much the same sense as Machiavelli's *The Prince* and Castiglione's *The Courtier* are conduct books. More important than a statement of the conduct recommended, however, since that could really be forceful only as exemplified in persons carrying out the conduct (Machiavelli gives us Cesare Borgia and Castiglione supplies examples of the courtier's conversation), is an understanding of the underlying orientation of the writer which makes that conduct comprehensible. What sense does Machiavelli make without his theories of history, of art, and of science? And what is Castiglione without Renaissance Platonism?

From this point of view, the most important essay in *Selected Passages* is the last one, "Easter Sunday," which by no means was so placed accidentally, any more than the famous troika passage accidentally ends the first part of *Dead Souls*. "Easter Sunday" is the summation of Gogol's attitude in so far as his objective is concerned and a final statement of the conviction that supports the rest of the book. Gogol makes it quite clear in this essay that he sees the essential fact of Christ (who should be the focal point of man's existence) as His gift of life through love, the love of brotherhood. As Mochul'sky remarks, "Gogolian religion is [a] sobornaya" religion.[28] As Gogol is also well aware,

28. *Op. cit.,* p. 92. The concept of *sobornost,* a word from which the adjective "sobornaya" is derived, is a complicated one. The words I should use to describe it are communion and union, the "I-we" relationship rather than the "I-you" relationship. It is basically an organic concept concerned

however, man has not yet attained that reality of salvation in this world that Christ offers him;[29] that is, the Garden of Eden

with A. S. Khomyakov's view of the character of the Church. Komyakov said in *The Church is One* (p. 3): "The unity of the Church follows of necessity from the unity of God: for the Church is not a multitude of persons in their separate individuality, but a unity of the grace of God, living in a multitude of rational creatures, submitting themselves willingly to grace." George Florovsky in his *Puti russkogo bogoslovia,* Paris, 1937, p. 277, puts it this way: "Sobornost for Khomyakov does not coincide with public opinion or corporateness. Sobornost for him, in its general meaning, is not the human but the divine character of the Church," which is unity. It is not a matter of historical reality but of spiritual reality. The religious tradition of *sobornost* is perhaps best expressed by Serge Bulgakov in his *The Orthodox Church* (translated by Donald Lowrie; Paris, 1935; pp. 74–75):

> The word is derived from the verb "sobirat," to reunite, to assemble. From this comes the word "sobor," which . . . means both "council" and "church." *Sobornost* is the state of being together. The Slavonic text of the Nicene Creed translates the epithet *katholiki,* when applied to the Church, as "sobornaya," an adjective which may be understood in two ways, each equally exact. To believe in a "sobornaya" church is to believe in a *Catholic* Church, in the original sense of the word, in a Church that assembles and unites; it is also to believe in a *conciliar* Church in the sense Orthodoxy gives to the term, that is, in a Church of the oecumenical councils, as opposed to a purely monarchical ecclesiology. To translate *"sobornost,"* I have ventured to use the French word "conciliarité," which must be used both in a restricted sense (the Church of the Councils) and in a larger sense (the Church Catholic, oecumenical). *Sobornost* may also be translated as "harmony," "unanimity." Orthodoxy, says Khomyakov, is opposed both to authoritarianism and to individualism, it is a unanimity, a synthesis of authority. It is the liberty in love which unites believers. The word *sobornost* expresses all that.

Bulgakov goes on to speak of this as a qualitative conception rather than a quantitative one. Since it is both qualitative and inward, I felt justified in using the word "communion" above. Furthermore, the idea involves, as Vladimir Solovyov has pointed out in his *Russia and the Universal Church* (translated by Herbert Rees; London: The Centenary Press, 1948), fidelity to a common tradition. It is doubtful that Gogol himself knew the term, although he was obviously aware of the tradition, since Khomyakov was known to him more as a poet than as a theologian. Indeed, the first complete edition of Khomyakov's writings was not published in Russia—because of censorship troubles—until 1860, shortly after Khomyakov's death and eight years after Gogol's death.

29. We find here a reference to that paradise on earth which forms the core of Father Zossima's teachings in *The Brothers Karamazov.*

is attainable only by a mankind purged of sins—in particular, the sin of pride. Over and over again, Gogol tells us that man, including himself, must become better. It is only his desire to become better that gives man hope (Gogol's conviction that this desire is innate in all men also informs *Selected Passages* with a constant optimism). If the Resurrection were to be celebrated as it ought to be celebrated, each man would embrace every other man as a brother. It is not abstract preachment of love that is meaningful, but concrete expression of love, a fulfillment of man's basic desire. Long before Dostoevsky had thought of Raskolnikov, Gogol was objecting to those who claim to love "Man," but cannot love men.

Gogol was not such a fool as to believe that this state of affairs had already come about; indeed, *Selected Passages* is no more sanguine about conditions in Russia than Gogol's earlier work had been—Gogol was castigating falsity, hypocrisy, and pettiness just as severely as he ever had. But "Easter Sunday" goes further than mere castigation to propose a solution to these evils, to point out the real possibility that is open to man. It was for this possibility that he was striving—for the attainment of this truth, not for the preservation of an obviously unsatisfactory status quo, as the outraged Belinsky thought.[30]

In accord with that Great-Russian nationalism peculiar to those born outside Great-Russia, Gogol was convinced that the true Christian possibility had been preserved only in Russia and in its religion, Orthodoxy.[31] Not only "Easter Sunday," but many other essays in *Selected Passages* oppose the "inner holiness" of Russia to "western falsity." The Orthodox Church, says Gogol in "A Few Words on our Church and our Clergy," is the Church

---

30. One can only wonder in this connection whether Belinsky really did read the whole of *Selected Passages,* despite his claim that he had read it through one hundred times.

31. The most violent passages in Belinsky's open letter are those which denounce Gogol's belief that religiosity is the prime characteristic of the Russian. What, one wonders, would Belinsky have said of Dostoevsky's *Diary of a Writer,* not to mention *Crime and Punishment, The Idiot,* and *The Brothers Karamazov?*

which, "like a chaste virgin, has uniquely preserved itself since apostolic times in the immaculate purity of its origins, this Church which is whole, whose profound dogmas and least external ceremonies are as though sent directly from Heaven for the Russian people" is the salvation of Russia and of the world. As Gogol also emphasizes, he is speaking only partially of the Church Visible. Even more important is the Church Invisible, for the Church lives in men's lives, not simply in formal relations.

In spite of—or because of—the great amount of time that Gogol spent abroad (he left Russia—because of the reaction to *The Inspector General*—in 1836 and did not return, except for sojourns during the winters of 1839–40 and 1841–42, until 1848), he was convinced that true morality resided in his homeland, if only its spiritual reality could be made manifest. Easter Sunday meant not only going to church but embracing one's brother like a brother. So far as Gogol was concerned, he had offered that embrace in *Selected Passages,* and he had been rejected, in spite of all the humanitarian and philanthropic aspirations voiced by Westerners and by Russian Westernizers. For Gogol, the West was already obviously a failure, from the point of view of the true God and true morality. He says in "Easter Sunday":

One would think the nineteenth century would joyously celebrate this day which is so much at the heart of its magnanimous and humanitarian movements! But on this day, as on a touchstone, you see how pale are all its Christian aspirations and how they are all only in dreams and thoughts, not in deeds. If on this day one should embrace his brother as a brother, he does not embrace him. He is ready to embrace all humanity as his brother, and he does not embrace his brother. He is so separated from this humanity, for which he prepares such a magnanimous embrace, that one man who has insulted him, the one whom Christ commands him immediately to forgive, he does not embrace. Having been separated from humanity, alone, clinging more conspicuously than others to the grievous sores of his spiritual unworthiness, more than all others demanding compassion for himself, he pushes him away and does not embrace him. He achieves an embrace only with those who have insulted him in nothing, with whom he has never come in conflict, whom he never knew and into whose eyes he never even looked. This is the kind of embrace a man of the present century gives to all mankind, and for that he thinks of himself as a real humanitarian and a perfect Christian! A Christian! They have driven Christ into the street, into the leper-houses and hospitals instead of summoning Him into their homes, under their roofs, and they think they are Christians!

It is a religious conviction, thus, which is at the base of Gogol's morality. It is a religiosity, further, which shows quite close connections with that of the Slavophile lay theologians of the time—such men as Khomyakov, Kireyevsky, and S. T. Aksakov,[32] for example, the last of whom Gogol knew well personally.[33]

Gogol's difficulty arose when he tried to apply the principles of "Easter Sunday," his religious principles, to practical affairs, that is, when he attempted to set down ethical precepts to guide the activity of individual human beings in the world, when he tried to spell out his superstructure, to use a Marxist expression.[34] The practical activity—the ethical code—he advocates, as the conclusion of his religious position, does appear to be reactionary and a betrayal of humanitarian principles. Some of it—for example the domestic advice he gives in "What a Wife Can Do for Her Husband in Simple Domestic Matters, as Things Now Are in Russia"—strikes the reader as downright silly. And what he recommends in such essays as "Woman in the World," "What the Wife of a Provincial Governor Is," "The Russian Landowner," "Rural Justice and Punishment," and "To One Who Occupies an Important Position" seems at best naïve, the

32. I. V. Kireyevsky (1806–1856) was one of the foremost of the Slavophile thinkers. His most important work was the article "On the Necessity and Possibility of New Principles in Philosophy," printed in the journal *Russian Colloquy (Russkaya Beseda)* in 1856.

33. What Dostoevsky's mature work owes both to Gogol and the Slavophile thinkers is incalculable, although still seriously underrated.

34. This is a difficulty Dostoevsky avoided—what was Alyosha meant to do in the world? We know no more than that he was to love actively. But Dostoevsky never tells us precisely, practically, what that activity is to be. As the writer of *Exodus* well knew, it is far easier, and more effective, to say what we should not do than it is to say what we should do. Indeed, Dostoevsky was to regard his great attempt to depict a positively good man in *The Idiot* a failure. One is also reminded of William Blake's remark that Milton was of the devil's party without knowing it.

work of a man who had so far withdrawn from the world that he no longer had the least idea of what it was like. Belinsky, indeed, accused Gogol of knowing nothing about Russia.

Gogol was giving his advice, however, not so that things might remain as they were, but so that they might be made different. The recommendations could be successful only if a change of heart first occurred, and if they were carried out in the spirit of that change. If we examine his recommendations, we discover that they are all concerned with the relations between men and predicated upon the attitudes of the persons involved. The moral activity we find in *Selected Passages* thus, while repugnant in a static world, becomes quite different if viewed in the light of Gogol's religious convictions. He thought of the moral activity as the practical result of realizing love for one's fellow man within oneself, on the one hand, and as conducive to the arousal of such love in those to whom the love was displayed, on the other. The moral activity is both born in the spirit and leads back to it. In Gogol's view, therefore, Belinsky's attack was un-justified, because Belinsky had understood neither Gogol's base nor his goal. Gogol was convinced, in other words, that he had been misinterpreted once again. In July-August 1847 he wrote to Belinsky (although he never sent the letter) :

Such a wrong view you have taken of the meaning of my works. My answer is in them. When I wrote them I held in reverence everything which man should hold in reverence. In my work there is no dislike and mockery of authority, nor of the basic laws of our country, but of per-version, of deviations, of incorrect interpretations, of bad application of them, of the scabs which have accumulated, of a life inappropriate to it. I have never mocked that which forms the basis of the Russian charac-ter and its great powers. There was mockery only of triviality unnatural to its character. . . . If we ignore the duties to people who are close to us and chase after society, then we will lose both the former and the latter in exactly the same way. Lately, I have met a great many fine people who are utterly confused. Some think that the world can be corrected by reorganizations and reforms, by turning in one or another direction: others think that by means of some special, rather mediocre kind of lit-erature (which you call *belles-lettres*), it is possible to have an effect on the education of society to a better condition. No constitutions can cor-rect discontent within. . . . Society forms and molds itself—of its own accord; society is made up of individuals. It is necessary for each individual to fulfill his duty. Man must remember that he is not at all a material brute, but an elevated citizen of an elevated heavenly community. Until he begins to live at least a little bit the life of a citizen of heaven, the earthly community will not come into order.[35]

How, Gogol must have wondered, could he have been accused of being a monstrous supporter of cruelty and oppression when he had intended just the opposite? Why had not his book been read fairly instead of, as he believed, angrily? How could anyone accuse him of doing an about-face? Gogol believed firmly that the attitude he had displayed in *Selected Passages* was precisely the same as the attitude that underlay his earlier comic works. It was because they had not proved useful that he had disowned them, not because of what they said; in other words, the failure lay in communication, not in content. After all, the corruptions portrayed in *The Inspector General* and *Dead Souls* had been portrayed just so that the spectators and readers would recognize these corruptions in themselves—would realize that they too were "dead souls" and would take steps to correct themselves, as he thought he was taking steps to correct himself, to become better, as he put it. *Selected Passages* represented, he thought, his own attempt to become better, and he hoped it would help others to do the same. It was, in this sense, an attempt to overcome the failure of his previous life and work. As he said in the "Preface": "I wanted . . . to atone for the uselessness of everything published by me up to now, since in my letters . . . there are more things needful to man than there are in my fictional works."

Selected Passages was, after all, a literary endeavor, and we find when we examine the literary essays in the book that Gogol's view of literature was part and parcel of his world view.[36] Far from having given up literature, as Belinsky claimed and as

35. Proffer, pp. 179, 184.
36. For a fuller discussion of Gogol's aesthetic theory, see my article in *Russian Review*. Most of the ideas expressed here were first expressed in that article

Setchkarev now claims, he considered it vital to his concerns.[37] Literature, like any other of man's activities in this world, has a purpose to serve (*Selected Passages* is imbued with the idea of service; everything a man does should be dedicated to the service of his fellow men and to the service of God; the opposite way, dedication to the ego, is the path of pride, evil, and damnation). Gogol saw the literary artist in much the way he had been seen in the great tradition stretching back to the ancient Greeks—as a prophet and seer who had been given his talent by the Divine so that he might reveal certain truths to man. He went further in that he believed that literature should contribute to the task of bringing about the brotherhood of mankind (this is a position, be it noted, which Leo Tolstoy was to reiterate almost half a century later in *What is Art?* although Tolstoy attempted to give his argument more logical structure than did Gogol). The Russian writer, rooted in his native land and in Orthodoxy, must serve a Christian end. Poetry must call man

to a battle, not for our temporal liberty, our rights and privileges, but for our soul. . . . Our poetry will be imbued with an angelic passion and, having struck every string there is in the Russian, it will move the most hardened soul with a holiness with which no power and no instrument in man can contend: it will evoke our Russia for us—our Russian Russia: not the one jingoist patriots coarsely show to us nor the one foreign Russians display to us from abroad, but the one that has its root in ourselves and will display us in such a way that everyone, without exception, however different their ideas might be, of whatever education and opinions, will say with one voice: "This is our Russia; it is a warm refuge for us, and now we are really at home in it, under our native roof and not in a foreign land."

Gogol's aesthetic theory was thus united with his religious,

37. It is hard to understand the charge that Gogol had lost his interest in literature when almost half the total number of pages in *Selected Passages* is concerned with literary topics. In addition, he continued work on *Dead Souls* until his death. That he burned his creative work just before he died is beside the point. We can hardly say that he had lost his creative powers without having read that work. It is quite possible that perfectionism (increased by the disappointing, to him, reception his earlier work had gained) rather than the loss of creative powers brought him to the destruction of what he had written.

moral, and national theories. Instead of giving up art for religion, he united them; rather, he showed how, in his view, art, like morality, depended on religion. Belinsky objected because he thought Gogol was no longer a member of his liberal camp; modern critics object because they think Gogol sold out art-for-art's-sake. But it is highly doubtful that Gogol himself ever took either position; certainly his writings indicate that he did not. He could hardly have betrayed what he did not believe in to begin with. The literary essays in *Selected Passages* (as well as the essays he wrote for *Arabesques* some twelve years earlier) tell us that art's excuse and reason lay within the larger context of spiritual purpose. Art, in other words, is a species of moral activity (a point of view also put forth by Schiller, whom Gogol greatly admired).

If *Selected Passages* is viewed in the way I have tried to suggest, then it becomes clear that the essays and letters form a united whole, in spite of their seeming disparity, not through the "position philosophy" which Setchkarev tries to ascribe to them, but through the religious, moral, national, and aesthetic views of Gogol, which are in fact one. It is entirely possible that *Selected Passages* in this sense constitutes a summation—in Gogol's eyes—of what he was trying to do, of what his work was at least intended to be all about.

Perhaps he took himself too seriously. Perhaps, in spite of the humor in his works and in spite of his personal penchant for practical jokes, one subject eluded Gogol's humor—himself. Perhaps, also, Gogol found discursive prose difficult, so that it often seems either flat (when he tries too hard to be clear) or incoherent (when he tries too hard to be poetic). This is true of many another creative writer—Dostoevsky comes to mind—who tries to explain what he is after. It is not that he is wrong—it is rather that the mode of expression fails, just as Gogol believed (on quite good evidence) that the mode of expression in his fictional work had failed. I venture to say that Gogol's difficulty lay in an inability to communicate his thought because he did not have the form to fit it. He was trying to set literature on another path. "No," he said, "neither Pushkin, nor anyone else, ought now to be our model: other times have come."

In other words, Gogol's difficulty in *Selected Passages* lay in his originality so far as Russian literature was concerned. When one form, his fiction, which was largely new in Russia, had proved inadequate, he tried another. The historical record is clear: the second form could not manage it either.

It is surely no sufficient answer, however, to say that Gogol did not know what he was talking about when he wrote discursive prose, any more than it is an answer to say that his fiction was the result of the unconscious impulse of genius, that *The Inspector General* and *Dead Souls* were written by an angel or demon who somehow managed to bypass the conscious mind of Nikolai Gogol. He did undergo a "descent to hell," as Evdokimov puts it, but he certainly seems to have thought that was only the first act of a larger drama that concludes with "Easter Sunday."

It is, I think, a distinct failure of the critical attitude that Gogol has only sporadically been listened to when he tried to speak for himself, as he did in *Selected Passages*. This has occurred, it seems to me, simply because he said things about himself and his work that most critics preferred—and prefer—not to believe. But surely, what the author thinks he is saying is more to the point than what we choose him to say, T. S. Eliot notwithstanding. The reactions to *Selected Passages* in Gogol's day and since indicate which path critical opinion has chosen to take. In short, before we decide what Gogol's works signify, it behooves us to consider what Gogol thought they signified. *Selected Passages* at least gives us the opportunity to do so.

Gogol cast *Selected Passages from Correspondence with Friends* in the form of familiar letters to individuals whom he knew well. Some of the letters—probably those headed by such designations as "To Zh———y" (I have supplied the names in place of the initials whenever I could be reasonably sure of whom the initials indicated) may well have been actually addressed to individuals. Others he wrote especially for the volume. Some were dated, some not. In any event, the informality of the letters bears stressing, since Gogol seems to have thought he could accomplish his purpose better by an avoidance of art rather than by a concentration upon it. It was straightforward communication he desired, the communication of one soul, as he might have put it, with another rather than literary artistry, the desperate attempt of a man who felt lonely and misunderstood to make his ideas and feelings clear. In this sense, *Selected Passages* constitutes an intensely personal record, as Gogol was himself aware. In his letter to Belinsky of about June 20, 1847, commenting upon Belinsky's article which had appeared in *The Contemporary*, Gogol said that this was "a book in which the personal spiritual history of a man is involved, a man who is not like others and, in addition, a secretive man who has long lived within himself and suffered from the inability to express himself."[38]

Yet, with all his attempts to say precisely what he meant, Gogol did a lot of stumbling and stuttering through *Selected Passages*. He had never been stylistically an easy writer, and *Selected Passages* seems to have increased his stylistic difficulties instead of lessening them. He often appears to have felt frustrated by a language that did its best to keep him from saying clearly things that demanded clarity. The work is full of repetitions, involutions, awkward phrasings, long and involved sentences, blunt, almost crude expressions, so that the reader sometimes feels that Gogol is engaged in a battle both with himself and with the reader. It is as though he was trying too hard and the effort clogged his pen.

All this has presented the translator with some difficulties, since this translation is meant to serve two purposes: to give the reader of English a chance to find out what Gogol himself thought without being befogged by the often prejudiced remarks of com-

38. Proffer, p. 177.

mentators and to allow the reader of English to see the image of himself personally that Gogol wished to project. These purposes are, I believe, in accordance with Gogol's own when he wrote *Selected Passages*. The difficulties consisted in deciding how far Gogol should be clarified—by smoothing out his often awkward phrasing, by rewording his repetitions, by changing the sequence of his word order, by softening the emotional stress so evident in the original. I have tried to avoid doing any of these things so far as I could, since my aim has been to let Gogol speak for himself without interposing my own prejudices and tastes. *Selected Passages,* in short, is Gogol's personal record and should stand as such. I wanted the translation to be accurate, but not slavish, grammatically clear, but not free. This has been a narrow line to walk, and it may be that I have occasionally slipped. For any such slips I can only apologize and beg the reader to remember that both Shakespeare and Browning occasionally split an infinitive or dangled a participle.

One further note: it may be that a reader well acquainted with the literature on Gogol will find some resemblance between my ideas on the subject and those of Merezhkovsky, Mochul'sky, and Evdokimov. I am indeed indebted to the work done by these men, although an introduction seemed an inappropriate place to enlarge greatly on that indebtedness.

This is the place, however, for me to express my deep gratitude to Professor Serge A. Zenkovsky of Vanderbilt University for his enormous help in checking the manuscript and suggesting changes. His knowledge and kindness saved me from many a false step, although I am, of course, responsible for any faux pas that may remain.   J. Z.

SELECTED
PASSAGES
FROM
CORRESPONDENCE
WITH
FRIENDS

PREFACE

I was grievously ill; death was near. Summoning up what strength remained to me and taking immediate advantage of my mind's clarity, I wrote a will in which, among other things, I charge my friends with the duty of publishing some of my letters after my death. By this act I wanted at least to atone for the uselessness of everything published by me up to now, since in my letters, in the opinion of those to whom they were written, there are more things needful to man than there are in my fictional works. The divine grace of God has turned the hand of death away from me. I have almost recovered; I feel better now. Nevertheless, sensing a debility in my strength which constantly warns me that my life hangs by a thread and preparing myself for a long voyage to the Holy Land,[1] indispensable to my soul and during which anything can happen, I wanted to leave something of myself by way of farewell to my compatriots. Out of my recent letters that I have managed to recover, I myself selected everything pertaining to the questions occupying present society, removed all passages that can make sense only after my death, and excluded all those that can be meaningful only to a few. I add two or three literary articles and I adjoin my will itself, with the proviso that in case of my death, if it should take me

1. Gogol first conceived the idea of going to the Holy Land around 1843. He did not set out on his journey, however, until January 1848, about one and one half years after writing this "Preface." He landed in Odessa, after the journey, in May 1848, the first time in almost six years that he had set foot in Russia. He did not leave it again.

unawares during my travels, it will instantly have the force of law, as having been certified by all my readers.

My heart tells me that my book is necessary and that it can be useful. I think so, not because I have a high opinion of myself or because I am relying on my skill to be useful, but because I have never before felt such a powerful desire to be useful. Sometimes it is enough for us to hold out a hand to receive help; it is not we who help, God helps, granting His power to the powerless word. Therefore, as unimportant and insignificant as my book may be, still I allow myself to have it published and I ask my compatriots to read it through several times; at the same time, I ask those among them who have the means to buy several copies of it and distribute them among those who cannot buy it, informing them as they do so that all the money above the expenses of my prospective voyage will be used, on the one hand, for the support of those who, like me, feel an inner need at the approach of Lent to set off for the Holy Land and have no possibility of accomplishing it by their own means; on the other hand, it will be for the relief of those whom I meet on the way already going there. All of them will pray before the Holy Sepulchre for my readers, their benefactors.

I would like to accomplish my voyage as a good Christian. That is why I here ask pardon of all my compatriots for everything of which I have been guilty towards them. I know that by my ill-considered and immature works I have brought distress to many, and that I have even provoked others to attack me openly and in general have produced displeasure in many. For my justification, I can only say that my intentions were good and that I did not want to distress anyone or to provoke anyone to attack me openly; it was only because of my foolishness, my haste and precipitation, that my works were presented in such an imperfect way and led almost everyone into error concerning their real significance. For everything in them that seems deliberately offensive, I ask to be pardoned with that magnanimity with which only a Russian soul is capable of pardoning. I also ask pardon of all those who, for a long time or short, have happened to meet me on the road of life. I know that it has been my lot to cause unpleasantness to many people and even to some, perhaps, deliberately. In general, my attitude toward people has always been quite unpleasant and repellent. In part, this is a result of my avoidance of meetings and acquaintances, owing to my feeling that I could not utter intelligent and needful words to men (I did not want to utter empty and useless words); at the same time I was convinced that, because of my innumerable shortcomings, it was indispensable for me to re-educate myself apart from people. And in part it is the result of a trivial vanity, peculiar to those among us who have made our own way from the gutter into society and esteem that they have the right to regard others arrogantly. However that may be, I ask pardon for all personal offenses I have happened to inflict on anyone whatsoever, from the time of my childhood to the present moment. I also ask pardon of my fellow men of letters for everything disdainful or disrespectful on my part towards them, manifested either intentionally or unintentionally: anyone among them for whom it is difficult to pardon me, I will remind that he is a Christian. As one preparing himself for the sacrament of the confession which he is ready to make to God asks pardon of his brother, so I ask pardon of him; and just as no one at that moment dares not to pardon his brother, so he may not dare not to pardon me. Finally, I ask pardon of my readers for anything in the present book which may be displeasing and offensive to any one of them. I beg them not to nourish any concealed anger against me, but rather nobly to bring forward all the faults they are able to discover in this book —the faults of the writer as well as the faults of the man: my foolishness, thoughtlessness, presumption, my unjustified self-confidence; in short, everything there is in all men, although they do not see it themselves, and is probably in greater measure in me.

In conclusion, I ask everyone in Russia to pray for me, beginning with the bishops, whose whole life is a single prayer.

I ask prayers also of those who humbly do not believe in the efficacy of their prayers, as well as of those who do not believe in prayer at all and even consider it useless; but, however powerless and unprofitable their prayers, I ask them to pray for me with their powerless and unprofitable prayers. Before the Tomb of Our Lord will I pray for all my compatriots, not excepting one among them; my prayer also will be powerless and unprofitable if His Holy Heavenly Mercy does not convert it into what our prayer ought to be.

July 1846

I

TESTAMENT

Finding myself in full possession of my memory and of sound mind, I here set forth my last wish:

I. I do not bequeath my body to the grave until such time as clear signs of decomposition have appeared. I mention this because already in the course of this illness they have found moments of numbness in my vital organs, my heart and my pulse have ceased to beat. . . . Because in the course of my life I have been a witness of numerous sorrowful events resulting from our unwise haste in all matters, even in interment, I announce this here, at the beginning of my testament, in the hope that perhaps my posthumous voice will be a general reminder of caution. Let my body be delivered to the earth without attention to the place where it lies; nothing should be associated with my dusty remains; shame on him who draws any attention to a rotted flesh that is already no longer mine: he is worshipping the worms nibbling it; I ask rather that my soul be prayed for fervently, and that, instead of all these funeral honors, in my name a simple meal be offered to those who miss their daily bread.

II. I bequeath that no monument be raised to me, that such trifles not be thought of, for they are unworthy of a Christian. Let the one of my friends to whom I have really been dear erect a different monument to me: let him erect it in his inner conscience by his steadfastness in the vicissitudes of life, by the courage and freshness he gives to everyone around him. Whoever, after my death, achieves a loftier soul than the one he had during my lifetime will show that he really loved me and was my friend; only in this way will he erect a monument to me. For I too, although I was weak and insignificant, always encouraged my friends: not one who has become intimate with me in these last years, not one in his hours of pain and grief saw me despondent, although I too have passed through difficult moments and have not suffered less than others—let each of them remember this after my death, pondering everything that I have said to him and rereading all the letters written to him a year before.

III. I bequeath in general that no one weep for me. Sin would be conceived in the soul of anyone who sees my death as a significant or universal loss. Had it been given to me to do something useful and had I begun to fulfill my duties really as was fitting and death had carried me off at the beginning of my work (intended not for the satisfaction of a few but for the need of all)—even then no one should abandon himself to sterile distress. Even if, instead of me, there had died in Russia a man who was really necessary to it in its present circumstances, still no living person ought to be despondent, he should realize that if people useful to everyone are prematurely taken, it is a sign of divine wrath removing the instruments and means that would help some of us draw nearer the goal assigned to us. We must not abandon ourselves to distress at every sudden loss, rather should we look at ourselves sternly, thinking not of blackness to others, and not of blackness to the entire world, but of blackness to ourselves. Terrible is the soul's blackness, and it is only perceived when inexorable death is already before our eyes!

IV. I bequeath to all my compatriots (for the sole reason that every writer ought to leave behind some good thought as a legacy to his readers), I bequeath to them the best of everything that my pen has produced, I bequeath the work entitled "A

Farewell Tale." As they will see, it is concerned with them. For a long time I have carried it in my heart as my most precious treasure, as a mark of the divine grace of God to me. It was a source of tears, unperceived by anyone since my childhood. To them I leave it as a legacy. But I beg that none of my compatriots be insulted if he should discern something like preaching in it. I am a writer, and the duty of a writer is not only to furnish pleasant pursuits for the mind and taste; he will be held accountable if things useful to the soul are not disseminated by his works and if nothing remains after him as a precept for mankind. Rather, let my compatriots remember that each of our brothers, author or not, has the right when abandoning this world to leave us something like a brotherly precept; in this connection, we should not care about the littleness of his rank, nor his lack of talent, nor even his lack of wisdom: it is only necessary to remember that a man lying on his deathbed sees differently from and better than those who are still in the world. Nevertheless, in spite of all my rights, I would never have dared to speak of what they will discern in my "Farewell Tale"; for it is not up to me, the worst of all in soul, suffering from the grave illness of my own imperfection, to utter such speech. But another major motive impels me: Compatriots! It is fearful! My soul is frozen with terror simply at having heard of the magnificence of the life beyond the grave and of those spiritual sublimities of the creations of God, next to which the magnificence of all His creations which we behold in astonishment here below is dust. All my mortal frame groans, sensing the gigantic growth of the fruits whose seed we have sown in this life, without seeing clearly and without perceiving what horrors will arise from them. . . . Perhaps my "Farewell Tale" will operate in certain measure on those who until now have considered life a game, and their hearts will perceive, be it only in part, its austere mystery and the innermost divine music of this mystery. Compatriots!—I have no idea what I should call you at this time. Away with empty propriety! Compatriots! I have loved you;

I have loved you with that inexpressible love that God has given me, for which I thank Him as for His best boon, because that love has been my joy and my consolation in the midst of my most lacerating sufferings. In the name of that love, I ask you to listen to my "Farewell Tale" with your heart. I swear, I neither composed it nor imagined it: it arose of itself out of a soul which God himself educated by ordeal and grief, and its sounds were taken from the innermost powers of that Russian nature which is common to us all, by which I am related to you all.[1]

V. I bequeath that at my death no one hurry either to praise or censure my work in public newspapers and reviews: all that would be as prejudiced as it was during my lifetime. In my work there is much more to be condemned than to be accorded praise. All the attacks on it were, at bottom, more or less just. No one has been guilty towards me; whoever would reproach anyone for anything would be ungrateful and unjust to me. I also declare publicly that no work of mine exists beyond what has been published up to this time: everything there was in manuscript has been burned by me because it was feeble and lifeless, written in a state of sickness and tension. And therefore, if anyone should publish anything under my name, I ask you to consider it a contemptible forgery. Rather, I impose upon my friends the responsibility of collecting all my letters, written to no matter whom, beginning with the end of 1844, and, after having made a strict choice of only those which may be of some benefit to the soul and having rejected all others which served for empty amusement, to publish them in a separate volume. There were in these letters some things which might have been of benefit to those to whom they were written. God is merciful: perhaps they will be of benefit to others, and this would strike

---

1. Gogol's note: " 'A Farewell Tale' will not appear during my lifetime: what derives its meaning from death makes no sense so long as we are still alive." The story has been lost, if it was ever written at all.

from my soul a part of its heavy responsibility for the uselessness of what I had written earlier.

VI.[2] When I am dead, none of my household will have the right to be free; they ought rather put themselves at the disposition of the afflicted, the suffering, and all those who have felt sorrow in life. Let their abode, their country house, have more the air of a hospital, an asylum, than that of a landowner's property; let he who presents himself be received by them as a parent and a friend of the heart, let them question him gently and be concerned about his means of livelihood, in order to know if he does not need someone to come to his aid, or at least to know how to comfort him and solace him, in order that no one may leave his village without having been helped. If it is a question of someone habitually on the road, used to a wretched life and rather embarrassed at being lodged in a bourgeois house, then let him be led to the house of the most comfortable and best lodged peasant of the village, who besides would have the most exemplary morals and could aid him by his good counsel. He will also question his guest gently on the conditions of his way of life, will comfort him, and will furnish him with a reasonable amount of provisions for the road; nor will he forget to inform his master of how he has acted in accordance with his counsels or his aid, so well that no one would ever again leave these places without having been consoled.

VII. I bequeath—but I remind myself that I cannot dispose of some things. Because of my imprudence, my proprietary rights have been stolen from me: against my will and without my permission my portrait has been published abroad. For many reasons that I need not declare, I did not want this; I have

2. The edition used for this translation (N. V. Gogol, *Polnoe sobranie sochinenii*, Moskva, Izdatelstvo Akademii Nauk SSSR, 1952, v. 8) has the following footnote at this point: "This article contains instructions in domestic matters. It probably was not Gogol's intention to include the VIth item in the text of the book. . . ." I have translated this section from the French translation of Jean Chuzeville, entitled *Nicolas Gogol: Lettres spirituelles et familières* (Paris: Grasset, 1947), pp. 15–16.

not sold anyone the right to publish it and I have refused all the bookstores that have assailed me with their offers. I would contemplate permitting it only in the case that God would help me to accomplish that labor with which my thought has been occupied all my life, and besides, accomplish it so that all my compatriots would say with one voice that I have honestly fulfilled my task and would even wish to learn the lineaments of the man who worked in silence for a long time and did not want to profit from undeserved fame. Another circumstance is joined to this one: my portrait could be sold immediately in a great number of copies, which would bring considerable profit to the artist who had engraved it. There is an artist who has labored in Rome for some years engraving the immortal picture of Raphael, "The Transfiguration of the Lord." He has sacrificed everything for his labor—a labor destroying, devouring years and health, and he has accomplished it with a perfection (it is now approaching the end) that no other engraver has attained. But by reason of his high price and the small number of experts, this print cannot be distributed in sufficient quantities to pay him back for everything. My portrait would help him. Now my plans are wrecked: once the image of anyone is published abroad, it is anyone's property, taken up by the publishers of engravings and lithographs. But if it should happen that my posthumously published letters are of some general benefit (even if it be only by their sincere effort to furnish it), and if my compatriots should also want to see my portrait, then I ask all those publishers generously to renounce their rights; those of my readers who, by a vain fancy for things that have enjoyed a certain fame, will have acquired some portrait of me, I ask to destroy it forthwith upon reading these lines, especially since it was badly done and bears no resemblance to me, and to buy only the one on which will appear "Engraved by Yordanov."[3] This at least will be a just act. And it will be still more just if

3. F. I. Yordanov, or, more correctly, Yordan (1800–1883), a noted Russian painter and engraver, was a good friend of Gogol's.

those persons who have the means buy, instead of my portrait, the engraving of "The Transfiguration of the Lord," which, even in the opinion of foreigners, is the crown of the engraver's art and constitutes a Russian glory.

My testament must be published immediately after my death in all the newspapers and reviews, so that no one may in ignorance be innocently guilty towards me and bring reproaches down upon his soul.

1845

II

WOMAN IN THE WORLD

You believe that you cannot have any influence on society;
I believe the opposite. The influence of a woman can be very
great, especially now, in the present order or disorder of society,
in which there is a kind of spiritual chill, a kind of moral fatigue,
demanding reanimation. In order to produce this reanimation,
the co-operation of woman is indispensable. This truth, in the
form of a dim presentiment, is being carried through all the
world, and everyone is now awaiting something from woman.

Leaving all others aside, let us look at our Russia, and in
particular at that which among us is so often before our
eyes—the multitude of abuses of all kinds. It is obvious that
the major part of the bribes, of the injustices in the service, and
other similar things, of which both our functionaries and non-
functionaries of all classes are accused, proceeded either from
the extravagance of wives who are avid to shine in both high
and low society, and for that demand money from their husbands, or from the emptiness of their domestic lives, which they
have devoted to some ideal dream rather than to the substance
of their duties, which are more beautiful and elevated than all
their dreams. Husbands would not allow themselves one tenth
of the disturbances they bring about if their wives had accomplished even a bit of their duty. For a man the soul of a woman
is a preserving talisman, guarding him from moral infections;
it is a power holding him to the straight path, a guide leading

him back from the crooked to the straight; on the other hand, the soul of a woman can be his evil and ruin him forever. You have felt this yourself and expressed it better than any woman's lines have expressed it up to now.

But you say that all other women have vocations in prospect and you have none. You see them at work everywhere, either reforming and correcting what is already tainted, or re-establishing what is necessary, in short, helping in all ways. You alone see nothing and sorrowfully repeat, "Why am I not in their place?" Know that this is an expression of a general blindness. It now seems to everyone that he could do much good in the place and position of someone else, and that he cannot do it only because of his present position. This is the source of all our evils. All of us must now consider how we can do good just where we are. Believe me, it is not for nothing that God directed everyone to be in the place in which he now is. You need only take a good look around yourself. You ask why you are not the mother of a family, obliged to fulfill the duties of a mother, which now appear to you so clearly; why your estate is not in disorder, so that you would be compelled to live in the country and be busy about the house; why your husband is not busy with some difficult work of public interest, so that at least you could help him and be his strength, his refresher; and why, instead of all this, you have only these empty sallies into the world and empty worldly society which now seems to you more deserted than the most desert place.

But that world is not uninhabited; there are people in it who are the same as they are anywhere. They too are sick, and struggle, and are in need, and wordlessly call for help— alas! they do not even know how to ask for it. Which needy person should be helped first: the one who can still go out into the street or the one who has not even the strength to hold out his hand? You say that you do not know and that you cannot even imagine how you could be useful to anyone in the world; that one must have an arsenal of arms, that one must be a woman of intelligence and universal knowledge, and that your mind turns only to the thought of all this. And if it is only necessary to be what you already are? If you now have those necessary arms? Everything you say about yourself is absolutely true: you are, in fact, too young; you have acquired neither a knowledge of people nor a knowledge of life, in short, nothing of all that which is indispensable for rendering sincere aid to others; perhaps you will never acquire it, but you have other arms, with which everything is possible for you. First, you already have beauty; second, a spotless name, above scandal; third, the power of a pure soul. The beauty of woman is still a mystery. Not for nothing did God decree that some women be beautiful; not for nothing was it determined that beauty should startle us all equally—even those who are insensitive to everything and incapable of anything. If the thoughtless caprice of a beautiful woman was the cause of the overturn of the world and reduced the most intelligent people to folly, what then would happen if this caprice were sensible and directed to the good? How much good could a beautiful woman bring about in comparison with other women! Thus, this is a powerful arm.

But you have a still more sublime beauty, the pure fascination of a special innocence which belongs to you alone, which I do not know how to define in words but in which your tender soul shines forth to everyone. Do you know that the most dissolute of our youth have admitted to me that in your presence they not only do not dare to utter one of the double-entendres with which they regale others, but not even a simple word, feeling that everything next to you is gross and implies something insolent and indecent? This is your influence, accomplished without your even being present! No one dares to permit himself a foolish thought of which he would be ashamed in front of you; and even if the conversion is only momentary, it is nonetheless a man's first step towards becoming better. In this way also your arm is powerful. In addition, you already have in you, established by God in your very soul, an aspiration or, as you might call it, a thirst, for the good. Do you rather think that it is for nothing that you are inspired by this thirst which does not leave you tranquil for a moment? Hardly have you taken in marriage a man of nobility, of intelligence, one who has all the qualities to make a wife happy, than, instead of immersing yourself in your domestic happiness, you torment yourself with the idea that you are unworthy of such happiness, that you do not have the right to enjoy it when all around you there is so much suffering, when at every moment you hear news of all kinds of disasters: famine, fire, insupportable spiritual trials and tribulations, and fearful mental sicknesses, with which our generation is infected. Believe me, it is not for nothing. Whoever has in his soul such celestial unease in regard to people, such angelic depression about them even in the midst of his amusing diversions, can do much, really much, for them; his career is everywhere, because people are everywhere. Do not flee the world, in the midst of which you are destined to be, do not quarrel with Providence! In you lives that supernatural power which the world now needs: your very voice, because of the constant aspiration of your thought to fly to men's aid, has acquired certain sounds familiar to everyone, so that if you speak, accompanying your speech with your pure gaze and with that smile which never leaves your lips, which is yours alone, it seems to everyone that a heavenly sister has spoken to them. Your voice has become all-powerful; you can command and be a despot as no one of us can be. Command without words, by your presence alone; command by your very weakness, at which you are so indignant; command by your feminine fascination which, alas! the women of the current world have lost. With your timid inexperience you can do much more than a woman of intelligence who tries everything in her prideful presumption: her most solid convictions, with which she might have wanted to put the contemporary world on the right road, will be strewn upon her head as evil epigrams; but no one will dare to move his lips in epigrams when you with one silent look, wordlessly, ask some one among us to become better.

Why are you so frightened of talk of worldly debauchery? Certainly it exists, and in even greater measure than you think, but you may know about it. Is it for you to fear the pitiable temptations of the world? Fly to the world boldly, with the radiance of your smile. Enter into the world as into a hospital filled with sufferers, but not as a doctor who bears stern prescriptions and bitter medicines; it is not for you to examine who is sick with what sickness. You are not capable of diagnosing and of curing sicknesses, and I will not give you the advice which it would be fitting for me to give to another woman capable of it. Your duty is only to bring your smile to a sufferer, and that voice in which a man hears his sister flying to him from Heaven, and nothing more. Do not stay too long among some, hasten to others, because you are needed everywhere. Alas! in all corners of the earth they are waiting, and they are waiting for nothing other than those familiar sounds, that very voice which is yours. Do not go in for social chitchat; compel society to speak about the things about which you speak. God guard you from all pedantry and from those conversations which rise from the lips of our contemporary lionesses. Carry into the world the most open-hearted stories which find expression in you so eloquently when you are in a circle of friends at home, when each of the simple words of your speech shines and it seems to the souls of those listening to you that they are joyously talking with angels about the heavenly childhood of man. These are precisely the words for you to introduce into the world.

1846

III

THE MEANING OF SICKNESS

From a letter to Count A. P. Tolstoy

Count A. P. Tolstoy is identified in
note 10 to the "Introduction."

. . . My powers decline constantly, but not my spirit. Never
before have my physical ailments been so exhausting. Often
suffering becomes too severe, such a frightful weariness is felt
in all the frame of your body, that you are glad, and God knows
why, finally to end the day and go to bed. Often, in spiritual
weakness, you cry: "God, when will I reach the shore?" But
then, when you examine yourself and look deep within, your
soul may do nothing but break out in tears and thanks.

Ah! how necessary these ailments are to us! From among
the many benefits which I have extracted from them I will
cite only one to you: whatever I may be now, at least I am
better than I was before; were it not for these ailments I
would have thought that I was already as I ought to be. I am
not speaking of that good health which incessantly urges Russians to cut capers and to the desire to show themselves off to
others, and would have pushed me too to commit a thousand
indecencies. Now, during those cool moments which Divine
Grace has accorded me in the midst of my sufferings, there
sometimes occur to me thoughts which are incomparably better
than my former ones, and I see that now everything which

issues from my pen will be more meaningful than heretofore. Without the sufferings of my grave ailments, where would I not have been led? What an important person I would have imagined myself to be! But, having constantly perceived that my life hangs by a thread, that my infirmities could abruptly halt all my labor, on which all my significance is based, and that the benefit which my soul so desires to bring will only remain in the state of powerless desire without passing into fulfillment, that I will not give any interest on the talents given to me by God and will be judged like the last of criminals . . . having perceived all that, I constantly humble myself, and I cannot find words to thank Divine Providence for my sickness. So do you too submissively accept your ailment, believing henceforth that it is necessary. Only pray to God that its wonderful meaning and all the profundity of its sublime import may be revealed to you.

1846

IV

A QUESTION OF WORDS

Pushkin, when he read the following lines from an ode of Derzhavin's[1] dedicated to Khrapovitsky[2]

> *The satirist may gnaw me for my words,*
> *But should praise me for my deeds,*

declared, "Derzhavin is completely incorrect: the words a poet uses are the essence of his trade." And Pushkin was right. The poet, in so far as his profession of words is concerned, ought to be as irreproachable as anyone else in his profession. If the writer should justify himself by circumstances—that they are the cause of his insincerity, of his lack of reflection, or of the precipitancy of his words—then any corrupt judge could justify his taking bribes and his trading in justice by blaming his fault

1. G. R. Derzhavin (1743–1816) was one of the foremost pre-Pushkin poets of Russia. D. S. Mirsky says of him: "He combines in a curious way a high moral sentiment of justice and duty with the resolute and conscious decision to enjoy life to the full. He loved the sublime in all its forms: the metaphysical majesty of a deistic God, the physical grandness of a waterfall, the political greatness of the Empire, of its builders and warriors. Gogol was right when he called Derzhavin 'the poet of greatness.'" *A History of Russian Literature* (New York: Vintage Books, 1958), p. 51. It would perhaps be fairest to say that Derzhavin was more a predecessor of greatness than a first-rate poet in his own right.

2. A. V. Khrapovitsky (1749–1801) was a minor writer who was a good friend of Derzhavin's. The two had been colleagues in the imperial service. Derzhavin wrote two poems to Khrapovitsky, the one Gogol quotes in 1797 and an earlier one in 1793.

on his difficult circumstances, on his wife, on his large family; in short, on anything it is possible for him to allege. Difficult circumstances appear among men suddenly. It does not matter to posterity whose is the fault that the writer said something foolish or absurd, or generally expressed himself irreflectively and immaturely. It will not try to make out who jogged his hand: whether it be a myopic friend pushing him to early delivery of his work or a journalist interested only in the profit of his journal. Posterity has no respect either for favoritism or for journalists, nor for his embarrassing position. She gives him the reproof, not they, saying, "Why did you not stand your ground? You were sensible of the honor of your rank; it was your idea to prefer it to other more profitable vocations, and you did so not out of some fantasy, but because you heard the divine call within yourself; in addition, you received an intelligence which saw things somewhat further, more largely and more profoundly than those who urged you on. Why were you a child and not a man, since you received everything necessary to be a man?" In short, any ordinary writer could justify himself by circumstances, but not a Derzhavin. He hurt himself a great deal by not burning at least half his odes. That unburned half is indeed striking: nobody up to now has made such a fool of himself, of the holiness of his own most religious feelings, as has Derzhavin in this unfortunate half of his odes. To be precise, it is as though he here tried to paint a caricature of himself: everything which elsewhere in him is so beautiful, so free, so inwardly penetrated with the strength of his spiritual flame, is here cold, soulless and constrained; and what is worst of all is that here he repeats the same locutions, the same expressions, and even whole phrases which are so eagle-like in his animated odes and which are here simply ridiculous, like a dwarf who puts on the armor of a giant, and, furthermore, puts it on backwards. How many people have now pronounced judgment on Derzhavin on the basis of his banal odes! How many have doubted the sincerity of his feelings only because in many passages they found them feebly and soullessly expressed; what ambiguous rumors have been formed on his character, on his spiritual nobility, and even on the incorruptible judgment which he stood for. And all that because he did not burn what he should have given to the flame.

Our friend P———[3] has the habit of publishing any lines of a well-known writer he may get hold of, without considering whether they are to the writer's honor or dishonor. He authorizes it by that well-known stipulation of the journalists: "We hope that our readers and posterity will be grateful to us for the communication of these precious lines; everything of a great man's is worthy of interest, etc., etc." That is all nonsense. A lesser writer would be grateful; but posterity will spit on these precious lines, if it already knows what is soullessly repeated in them, if it does not hear in them the holiness of what should be holy. The higher truths are, the more cautious one must be with them; otherwise they are converted into common things, and common things are not believed. Atheists have not produced so much evil as hypocrites have produced, or even simply those who preached God without being prepared for Him, daring to pronounce His name with unsanctified lips. The word must be treated honestly. It is the highest gift of God to man. It is unfortunate that the writer sometimes pronounces it when he is under the influence of passion, of vexation, of wrath, or of some personal dislike, in short, at moments when his soul has still not achieved harmony: a language

3. M. P. Pogodin (1800–1875) was a Moscow journalist (he was editor of *Moskvityanin* from 1841 to 1856) and later Professor of Russian History at the University of Moscow. Gogol met him in 1832, and it was through Pogodin that Gogol became friends with the Slavophile Aksakov family. Gogol was to remain friendly with Pogodin, in spite of Pogodin's severe analysis of *Selected Passages,* for the rest of his life. Pogodin was to lend Gogol money many times and to put Gogol up at his home. While not a particularly original author himself, Pogodin did recognize Gogol's genius. In 1846–1847 Gogol was irritated with Pogodin because Pogodin published Gogol's portrait without having secured Gogol's permission to do so.

loathsome to everyone results. And thus out of the highest
desire for good evil may be produced. Our friend P——— is a
guarantee of this: all his life he has been in a hurry, hastening
to share everything with his readers, to report to them everything he has collected without analyzing whether the thought
has matured in his own brain so that it could be made closer
and more accessible to all—in short, he has displayed himself
to his readers in all his sloppiness. And then what? Have his
readers noticed the noble and fine transports which often glitter
so in him? Have they accepted of him what he wanted to share
with them? No. They have noticed in him only sloppiness and
untidiness, what a man notices first of all, and they have
accepted nothing from him. This man worked for thirty years,
busy as an ant, hurrying all his life more quickly to put in
the hands of everyone everything that he had found useful
for the enlightenment and education of Russians. . . . And not
one man said thank you to him; I have not met one grateful
youth whom I would say is obliged to him for some new
light or a fine aspiration to the good which his words might
have inspired. On the contrary, I even had to argue and stand
up for the honesty of his intentions, for the sincerity of his
words, before the very people who, it seems, should have been
able to understand them. It was even difficult for me to convince some, because he so succeeded in masking himself that
there is definitely no possibility of showing him as he really
is. Let him speak of patriotism—he speaks about it so that his
patriotism seems suborned; his love for the Tsar, which he
sincerely and sacredly nourishes in his soul, he expresses so that
it resembles servility and a kind of mercenary flattery. His
sincere, unfeigned annoyance with all tendencies injurious to
Russia is expressed in him as though he were sending forth a
denunciation of persons known to him alone. In short, at
every step he is his own calumniator.

It is dangerous for a writer to play with words. May a
corrupt word never issue from your lips! If this ought to be

applied to each of us, without exception, then a hundred times more should it be applied to those whose profession is the word, who are appointed to speak of the beautiful and the sublime. It is bad if on the subject of sacred and sublime things corrupt words begin to be heard; rather let corrupt words be heard on corrupt subjects. All great educators imposed a long silence precisely on those people who were verbal masters to no good purpose, precisely when they wanted above all to make a show of their words and their souls were dying to say something of much use to people. They knew how one may dishonor what he is trying to exalt, and how at every step our language is our betrayer. "Make doors and bars to thy mouth," says Jesus the Son of Sirach. "Melt down thy gold and silver, and make a balance for thy words, and a just bridle for thy mouth."[4]

4. *Ecclesiasticus,* 28: 28, 29 (D.V.).

1844

V

ON PUBLIC READINGS
OF RUSSIAN POETS

A letter to L

"L" is probably V. Leshkov, who was
Professor of Law at Moscow University
and censor for the journal *Moscovite*.

I am glad that we have finally begun to have public readings
of our writers' works. I have already been written to from
Moscow about this: various contemporary literary productions
have been read there and my tales were among the number.
I have always thought that public reading is indispensable to
us. Somehow we are rather made to act in common, even if
only in reading; individually, we are all slothful, so that if
we do not see others move, we do not move ourselves. We
must create artist-readers: we have few orators to cut a figure
in Palace or Parliament, but there are many people capable
of empathizing with one. To communicate, to share an impression with others has turned into a passion that becomes
stronger and stronger as one begins to realize more keenly that
he does not know how to express himself orally (a mark of the
aesthetic nature). The education of readers is assisted by our
language, which is as though created for artistic readings, containing in itself as it does all the nuances of sound and the
boldest transitions from the sublime to the simple in one and

the same speech. I even think that in time public readings will replace spectacles among us.

But I do wish that our current readers would choose something really worthy of public reading, and that the reader would take pains beforehand. There is nothing in our contemporary literature worth while; indeed, there is no need to read the contemporary. But the public reads it nevertheless, thanks to its passion for novelties. All these new tales (among their number, mine) are not sufficiently important for a public reading to be made of them. We must appeal to our poets, to those great compositions in verse which have been long considered and mentally cultivated and on which the reader must also work a long time. Until now our poets have been almost unknown to the public. They have been much spoken of in the journals, they have been discussed most verbosely, but the critics were talking more about themselves than about the poets under discussion. The reviews have succeeded only in bewildering and confusing the public's understanding of our poets, so that in its eyes the personality of each poet is now split in two, and no one can definitely know which of the two is real and which is his own creation. Only skillful reading can establish a clear understanding of them. But of course the reading must be done by the kind of reader who is capable of reproducing all the subtle features of what he is reading. For that we do not need an ardent young man who is rashly prepared, without taking a breath, to read in the course of one evening a tragedy, a comedy, an ode, and anything else that may strike his fancy. Proper reading of a lyric work is no bagatelle; long study is needed for it. One must sincerely share with the poet those lofty sensations with which the poet's soul is filled; one must feel all his words in soul and heart—and only then bring the reading before the public. This reading will not be in the least flashy, feverish, or heated. On the contrary, it can even be very calm, but an unknown force will be heard in the voice of the reader, the witness of a really moved internal state. This force will be communicated to every-one, and it will work a miracle: even those whom the sounds of poetry have never shaken will be touched. The reading of our poets can bring much public good. There is much beauty in them that has not only been entirely forgotten but has even been defamed, slandered, presented to the public with some base meaning of which our noble-hearted poets did not dream.

I do not know whose was the idea of turning these public readings into benefits for the poor, but the idea is a fine one. It is especially to the point now, when there are so many in Russia suffering from hunger, conflagrations, diseases, all kinds of misfortunes. Perhaps the souls of the poets who have left us will be consoled by such a use of their works.

1843

VI

HELP THE POOR

From a letter to Mme. A. O. Smirnova

Mme. A. O. Smirnova is identified in
note 1 to the "Introduction."

. . . I turn to your assaults on the folly of Petersburg youth,
who have offered golden garlands and toasted goblets to
foreign singers and actresses when whole provinces in Russia
are starving. This is not a result, however, of folly, nor of
hardness of heart, nor even of frivolity of thought. It is a
result of normal human heedlessness. The miseries and horrors
produced by hunger are far from us; they are happening in the
interior of the provinces, they are not before our eyes—that is
the solution to and the explanation of everything! The same
person who payed a hundred rubles for a theater seat in order
to enjoy Rubini's[1] singing would have sold his last possessions
had he been a witness to one of those frightful pictures of
starvation in comparison with which all the terrors and
horrors represented in our melodramas are nothing. It is not
a matter of our making donations; we are all ready to do-
nate. But donations really for the benefit of the poor are
not now made very willingly among us, in part because we are
not all confident that they will reach their destination as they

1. Giovanni Rubini (1795–1854), an Italian, was one of the best known
tenors of the day.

ought and fall into the hands into which they ought to fall. It usually happens that the aid, like water carried in the hand, trickles away on the road before it is delivered, and the needy person must be content with looking at a dry hand containing nothing. It is fitting to reflect on this theme before collecting donations. We will talk a little about this later, because the question is of no little importance and deserves to be talked about sensibly. But now let us speak of where help is most quickly needed.

First of all, it is necessary to help him to whom sudden misfortune has come, a misfortune which suddenly, in a moment, robs him of everything: maybe it is a fire that has consumed everything from bottom to top, or a cattle disease that has annihilated all his cattle, or death stealing his only support—in short, any sudden loss which brusquely presents a man with a poverty to which he has not yet succeeded in accustoming himself. Bring your help there. But this help must be given in a really Christian way; if it consists only of the distribution of money, it will mean exactly nothing and will not be converted into good. If you have not first pondered the entire situation of the man whom you wish to help, and if you have not brought with you instructions for him to follow henceforth in leading his life, he will not receive great good from your help. The value of the aid accorded rarely equals the value of the loss; in general, it hardly consists of half of what a man has lost, often only a quarter, and sometimes even less. A Russian is capable of every extreme: seeing that he cannot lead the same life as he used to with the small amount of money he has received, out of grief he may rapidly squander what has been given him for his long-term needs. Therefore, teach him how he should recover with the aid you have given him: explain the true meaning of misfortune to him, so that he may see that it has been sent to him so that he may change his former way of life, so that henceforth he may not be as he was formerly but become like another man, materially and morally. You will be able to say it wisely if you only go deeply into his nature and his circumstances. He will understand you: misfortune softens a man; his nature then becomes more sensitive and more accessible to the understanding of subjects beyond the conception of a man in his habitual, daily situation; he is then as though turned into warm wax from which you can fashion what you will. Nevertheless, it would be better if the help be produced by expert hands and sensible priests. Only they are in a position to interpret to this man the holy and profound purport of misfortune, which, under whatever form and under whatever aspect it be shown to man on earth, whether he inhabits a thatched hut or a palace, is always the same heavenly appeal crying to man to change all his former life.

1844

VII

THE ODYSSEY IN ZHUKOVSKY'S TRANSLATION

A letter to N. M. Yazykov

N. M. Yazykov (1803–46) was one of the most
important poets of the time and is still
widely anthologized. His gift ran more to verbal
pyrotechnics, however, than to content. Gogol
thought very highly of his skill with language.
He wrote to him often.

The publication of *The Odyssey* will mark the beginning of a
new era. *The Odyssey* is without doubt the most perfect work
of all the centuries. Its breadth is enormous; *The Iliad* is an
episode next to it. *The Odyssey* takes in the entire ancient
world, both public and domestic life, all the vocations of the
people of that time, their trades, their knowledge, their beliefs
. . . in short, it is difficult to say what *The Odyssey* does not
take in or what is left out of it. For many centuries it served
as an inexhaustible well for ancient, and afterwards for all,
poets. Subjects for innumerable tragedies and comedies have
been drawn from it. All that was spread throughout the world,
became a common heritage, and *The Odyssey* itself was forgotten.

The fate of *The Odyssey* was strange: in Europe they did
not value it; the fault is partly the lack of a translation that
would artistically reproduce the splendor of the ancient work,
and partly the lack of a language rich enough and full enough

to reflect its innumerable elusive beauties as they are in Homer and in Hellenic literature in general; it is, finally, partly the lack of a people sufficiently gifted with a pure virginal taste, which is necessary for Homer to be appreciated.

Now this translation of the foremost poetic creation has been done in the fullest and richest of all European languages.

It is as though the whole literary life of Zhukovsky was a preparation for this task. He had to work out his lines with the help of works and translations of poets of all nations and languages; in order to make himself capable of rendering the eternal lines of Homer, he listened to all lyres, so that he might become sufficiently sensitive to the nuances of Hellenic sound; it was not only necessary for him to fall in love with Homer, but also to conceive a passionate desire to compel every one of his compatriots to fall in love with Homer, for the aesthetic profit of the soul of each one of them; it was necessary for the translator to undergo many experiences which would lead his soul to that harmony and calm indispensable for the reproduction of a work planned with such harmony and calm; finally, it was necessary for him to become a more profound Christian, in order to acquire that enlightened, profound attitude towards life which none but a Christian (who automatically comprehends the meaning of life) may have. Such are the conditions which had to be fulfilled so that the translation of *The Odyssey* might not appear as a servile reproduction and so that *the living word* might be heard in it and all Russia might accept Homer as its own!

Thus a kind of miracle resulted. This is not a translation, but rather a re-creation, a restoration, a resurrection of Homer. The translation somehow introduces us into the life of antiquity better than the original. The translator imperceptibly became the interpreter of Homer, became a kind of optic nerve, a clarifying lens for the reader through which all Homer's numberless treasures are displayed with more definiteness and distinctness.

In my opinion, all conditions, as though by chance, are now present to make the appearance of *The Odyssey* almost indispensable to our time; in literature, as elsewhere, there is a chill. As we are weary of enchantment, so are we weary of disenchantment. Even the convulsive, sick productions of this century, with their mixture of undigested ideas introduced by political and other ferments, have begun to decline considerably: only belated readers accustomed to line up behind the leaders of the press still read a little here and there, without realizing, in their simple-mindedness, that the sawhorses leading them have long been uncertain, not knowing themselves where to lead their lost flock. In short, it is now vital for a work harmonious in all its parts to appear, one which represents life with astonishing distinctness and at the same time conveys a calm and almost child-like simplicity.

Among us, *The Odyssey* produces an influence both *generally on all* and *separately on each*. Greek polytheism will not tempt our people. Our people is sensible: without racking its brain it will comprehend what the intellectuals do not understand. Here it will see the proof of how difficult it is for a man without prophets and without a revelation from on high to come to know God in his true aspect, and in what absurd aspects His image has been presented by the division of His unity and unified powers into numerous forms and powers. He will not even laugh at the pagans of that time, knowing that they were in no way at fault: the prophets did not speak to them, Christ was not born then, there were no Apostles. No, our people will rather scratch the backs of their necks, sensing that even he who knows God in his true aspect, who has his written law in his hands, who even has commentators on the law in the spiritual Fathers, prays more slothfully and accomplishes his task less well than a pagan of antiquity. The people will realize why the supreme power aided a pagan because of his good life and zealous prayer, although in his ignorance he appealed to Him in the form of Poseidon, Chronos, Hephaistos, Helios, Aphrodite, and others of that kind who fill the imagination. In short, he will drop the polytheism and will extract from *The Odyssey* what he ought to extract from it, what is palpable in it for everyone, what constitutes the spirit of its content and why *The Odyssey* itself was written, that is, to teach that everywhere, in every vocation, much trouble comes to man and he must struggle against it—and it is for this that life has been given to man; that in any case he should not lose heart, as Ulysses did not lose heart when in all his difficult and grave moments he called out in his heart, without doubting that by this interior call within himself he was creating an interior prayer to God, which in moments of distress every man accomplishes, even he who has no understanding of God. That is the *general,* the spirit of its content by which the impression of *The Odyssey* is produced on everyone, even before some are carried away by its poetic qualities, the fidelity of its pictures, and the vigor of its descriptions; even before others are struck by the exposure of the treasures of antiquity in a detail which neither sculpture, nor painting, nor, in general, any of the ancient monuments has retained; even before a third group stands dumbfounded at the extraordinary knowledge of all the coils of the human soul, all of which were recorded by the all-seeing blind man; even before a fourth group is struck by the profundity of the views on government, by the knowledge of the difficult science of ruling people and wielding power over them which the divine old man possessed, the legislator of his and future generations; in short, before anyone is seduced by any passage of *The Odyssey* whatsoever about his trade, his occupations, his inclinations, and his personal peculiarities. And all because the spirit of the content is tangibly perceived, it is its inner essence, which no other work has displayed so powerfully through externals, penetrating everything and dominating everything, especially when we consider how vivid each episode is, how each might have eclipsed the principle.

Why is it felt so powerfully? Because it resided in the depths of the old poet's soul. You see how at every step he wished to clothe what he wanted to affirm for all time among men in all the bewitching beauty of poetry, how he tried to strengthen whatever may be commendable in popular customs, to remind man that there is something better and holier in him, which he is always liable to forget, to leave to every person an example of his profession in each of his characters, and to leave to all in general an example in his tireless Ulysses of the profession of man in general.

The stern respect for customs, the reverential esteem for power and superiors, notwithstanding the organized limits of power, the virginal modesty of his young people, the benevolence and good humor of the old people, the cordial hospitality, the respect, almost reverence, for man, in so far as he shows forth the image of God, the belief that not one happy thought can be conceived in his brain without the supreme will of a Being infinitely higher than us, and that he can do nothing by his own means—in short, everything, every least detail in *The Odyssey* speaks of the inmost desire of the poet of poets to leave to the men of antiquity a living and complete book infused by law at a time when there was still neither law nor founders of order, when there were still no civil and written enactments determining the relations between people, when the people had not yet seen much and did not even have a presentiment, when only this divine old man saw everything, heard, imagined, had a presentiment—a blind man, deprived of the sight normal to all people and armed with that inner eye that other people do not possess!

And how skillfully was all this labor, so long considered, hidden under the most naïve fiction. It is like a grandfather who, having brought all his kin together in one family and having seated himself among his grandchildren, is ready to behave like a child with them; he tells his good-natured tales and is careful only to bore no one, not to intimidate by an unbecoming length of instructions but to disseminate and spread them through the tale so that they may all collect them as though playing with them (although they are not given to man for him to play with), and so that everyone may imperceptibly absorb what he knew and saw better than anyone of his age and time. Anything spontaneously expressed may be admired, if an attentive examination later discloses a marvelous structure both in its entirety and in each separate song. How stupid are those German savants who imagine that Homer is a myth and all his creation popular songs and rhapsodies!

But let us examine the influence that *The Odyssey* can produce *on each of us separately*. First, it will work upon our writing brothers, on our authors. It will restore many to the light, leading them like an artistic pilot through the bustle and the shadows piled up by unsettled, unorganized writers. It will remind all of us anew with what ingenuous simplicity we must imitate nature, how to render each of our thoughts with an almost tactile plainness, with what balanced tranquillity our speech should be expressed. It will make all our writers feel anew that old truth, which we should always remember and which we always forget, namely, never to take up the pen until everything is established in our brains in such clarity and order that even a child's powers would understand everything and keep it in memory. Still more than on the writers themselves, *The Odyssey* will work on those preparing themselves to be writers in secondary schools and universities, who see their future career dimly and vaguely. From the beginning, it can lead them in the right road while saving them useless vacillations in the face of the tortuous ins and outs which their predecessors ran into.

In the second place, *The Odyssey* will work on taste and on the development of the aesthetic sensibility. It will rejuvenate criticism. Criticism is worn out; it is entangled in the analysis of mysterious literary works of the latest fashion; it is woefully beside the point and, deviating from questions of literature, it rushes into nonsense. On the ground of *The Odyssey* much really sensible criticism could appear, the more so as there is scarcely one work in the world which could be looked at from so many sides as *The Odyssey*. I am certain that the talk, analyses, judgments, annotations, and thoughts excited by it will resound in our press for many years. Readers will lose nothing from this: the criticisms will not be worthless. They will reread much, look at it anew, experience and rethink; besides, a hollow, superficial man will not be able to say anything about *The Odyssey*.

In the third place, *The Odyssey,* in the Russian dress with which Zhukovsky has clothed it, can operate meaningfully for the purification of the language. Never yet in any one of our writers—not only in Zhukovsky in everything that he has written up to now, but even in Pushkin and Krylov, who are incomparably more exact than he in terms and expressions—has the use of the Russian language attained such fullness. There are all the resources and locutions in all their variations. Infinitely immense periods, which in any one else would be sluggish and obscure, and concise, short periods which in another would be stale and abrupt, which would make the speech bitter, are in him so well united with one another; all the passages and transitions are accomplished with such harmony, everything is so well merged into a unity where the cumbersomeness vanishes into thin air, that it would seem that all the style and quality of speech flows on of itself; there is no trace of contrivance, as there is none of the translator himself. In its place, we have before our eyes, in all his majesty, the old man Homer, and one hears those stately eternal speeches which are not on the lips of any other man but whose fate it is to be heard eternally throughout the world. It is here that we writers see with what wise attention one must make use of words and expressions, how each simple word may be restored to its lofty dignity when we know how to put it in its proper place, and how much it means for a work meant for general use, a work of genius, this highest work of all, to have a proper outward form: the least little mote is noticed and springs to our eyes. Zhukovsky justly compares these motes to trash dragged into a splendidly appointed room where everything shines like a polished mirror, from ceiling to floor; what the visitor first sees is this trash, for the same reason that he would not have noticed it at all in a disordered, dirty room.

Fourthly, *The Odyssey* will work upon all curious dispositions, as well of those occupied with scholarship as of those who have not been instructed in learning, by disseminating a living knowledge of the ancient world. You will not read in any history what you will find in it: all the past breathes from it; antique man is there as though living before your eyes, as though you had met him and spoken with him. You see him in all his actions, at every hour of the day: as he reverently prepares a sacrifice, as he chats decorously with his guest at table, as he dresses, as he strolls in a public square, as he listens to an old man, as he instructs a young one; his house, his chariot, his bedroom, the least bit of furniture in his house, from his movable tables to the bands and bolts on his doors—everything is before your eyes, with more freshness than in the excavations at Pompeii.

Finally, I even think that the appearance of *The Odyssey* will make an impression on our contemporary society. Precisely at the present time, when, by a mysterious decree of Providence, everywhere is heard an unhealthy murmur of dissatisfaction, the voice of human displeasure with everything that exists in the world: against the order of things, against the time, against oneself. When one finally begins to become suspicious of the perfection to which the latest constitution and public education have led us; when one perceives in everyone a kind of uncontrollable thirst to be something other than what he is, perhaps even proceeding from a fine source—to be better; when through the absurd clamor and the thoughtless propagation of new but dimly perceived ideas one perceives a kind of general attempt to be closer to a mean, to find the real law of our actions, as well those of the mass as of persons taken separately—in short, it is precisely at this time that *The Odyssey* strikes with the majesty of the patriarchal, ancient mode of life, with the simplicity of uncomplicated social lines, with the freshness of life, with the clarity of man's childhood. In *The Odyssey,* our nineteenth century will hear a strong reproach, and the reproaches will go on the more it is scrutinized and carefully read.

It is possible, for example, that the reproach which expands in your soul will be stronger when you discern how ancient man, with his poor means, with all the imperfections of his religion, which even permit him to cheat, to avenge, to resort to perfidy for the extermination of his enemy, with his recalcitrance, cruelty, absence of obedient character, with his worthless laws, nevertheless knew, by the simple fulfillment of old customs and rites which were not senselessly established by the ancient sages and were preserved to be transmitted from father to son as something holy—by the simple fulfillment of these usages and customs he succeeded in acquiring a harmony and even beauty of conduct, so well that in him everyone becomes majestic from head to foot, from speech to least gesture, even to his well-made clothes, and it seems that you really perceive in him a man of God-like descent. And we, with our enormous means and instruments for perfecting ourselves, with all our centuries of experience, with our supple imitative nature, with our religion, given to us precisely to make us saints and inhabitants of Heaven—with all our instruments, we have come to such a sloppiness and disorder, both externally and internally, that we have succeeded in making ourselves into scraps, into petty creatures, from head to very clothes, and in addition to all that, we so loathe one another that no one respects anyone, not even excepting those who speak of the respect due to all.

In short, *The Odyssey* will operate on those who suffer and are ill because of their so-called European "perfection." It will remind them of the beauty of their youth now, alas! lost, but which humanity must recover as its legitimate legacy. Many will meditate over many things in it. And, among others, many things about the patriarchal era, with which Russian nature has so much affinity, will invisibly be spread abroad over the face of the Russian land. By the fragrant lips of poetry there will be wafted into the soul something that implies neither law nor power!

VIII

A FEW WORDS ON OUR CHURCH
AND OUR CLERGY

From a letter to Count A. P. Tolstoy

There is no reason for you to be disturbed by the attacks on our Church that are now being heard in Europe. To accuse our clergy of indifference is also unjust. Why do you want our clergy, which up to now has been notable for a majestic tranquillity (so proper to it), to take part in these European brawls and begin, like them, to print precipitate brochures? Our Church has acted wisely. In order to defend it, one must first know it. And for the most part we know our Church badly. Our clergy is not inactive. I know very well that in the depths of the monasteries and in the silence of the cells irrefutable works in defense of our Church are being prepared. But they know their business better than we: they are not in a hurry, and, knowing what the subject requires, they accomplish their task in profound calm, praying, training themselves, expelling from their souls all inappropriate passions, all mad fevers, raising their souls to the height of that celestial impassivity in which one must abide in order to have the strength to speak of these things.

But these defenses will not serve fully to convince western Catholics. Our Church should be sanctified in us and not in our words. We should be our Church, and it is by us that its truth should be proclaimed. They say that our Church is life-less. They have spoken a lie, because our Church is life; but they have logically deduced their lie, their conclusion is valid. We, not our Church, are the corpses, and it is because of us that they have called our Church a corpse. How will we defend our Church and what answer can we give them if they pose the following questions to us: "Has your Church made you better? Has each of you fulfilled his duty as he ought?" What will we answer them, being suddenly aware in our souls and consciences that for a long time we have walked past our Church and scarcely know it now? We possess a priceless treasure and not only do not trouble to care for it, but we do not even know where we have put it. The master is asked to display the best thing in his house, and the master himself does not know where it is. The Church which, like a chaste virgin, has uniquely preserved itself since apostolic times in the immaculate purity of its origins, this Church which is whole, whose profound dogmas and least external ceremonies are as though sent directly from Heaven for the Russian people, which alone has the power to decide all our tangled perplexities and questions, which can, in the face of all Europe, produce the unheard-of miracle of having forced to their legal limits all estates, ranks, and positions among us, and, without having changed anything in the State, gives Russia the strength to amaze all the world by the concordant harmony of that same organism by which up to now it has frightened it—this Church is unknown to us! And we have not introduced this Church created for life into our lives!

No, God keep us from now defending our Church! That would mean harming it. For us there is only one possible propaganda—our life. It is by our lives that we should defend our Church, which is all *life;* by the fragrance of our souls should its truth be raised. Let the missionaries of western Catholicism beat their breasts, brandish their arms and with eloquence and oratory extort tears quickly dried. The preacher of Catholicism in the East should come before the people in such a way that by his humble aspect alone, by his calm eyes and quietly impressive voice issuing from a soul in which all desire for the world is dead, everyone will be moved before he has even explained one thing; and with one voice they will say to him, "Do not utter a word: we hear the holy truth of your Church without that!"

IX

ON THE SAME SUBJECT

From a letter to Count A. P. Tolstoy

The observation that the power of the Church has been weakened among us, that our clergy lacks luster and skill in its relations with society is no less absurd than the contention that our clergy is entirely removed from all contact with life by the rules of our Church and bound in its actions by the government. Our clergy has stated laws and precise limits to its relations with the world and with people. Believe that if it should meet with us more often and take part in our daily gatherings and strolls or enter into family matters, it would be unfortunate. There are many temptations before the clergy, more even than before us: it is then that it would be embroiled in those intrigues of which the Roman Catholic priests are accused. Roman Catholic priests have become bad precisely because they have become too worldly. Our clergy has two legitimate realms in which it may meet us: confession and preaching. In these two realms—of which the first only occurs one or two times a year and the second can take place every Sunday—it is possible to do a great deal. If only the priest, seeing much evil in the people, knows how to keep silent about it for a time and ponder for a long time on what he is going to say, so that each word will go straight to the heart, he will speak about it more powerfully in confession and in his sermon than he would ever say it in daily conversation with us. He must speak to the man who is in the world from such a height that it is not his presence which the man experiences but the presence of God himself, hearkening to both of them equally, and both would feel fear of His invisible presence. No, it is rather good that our clergy finds itself somewhat apart from us. It is good that even their clothes, which are not subject to the changes and whims of our silly fashions, separate them from us. Their clothes are beautiful and majestic. They are neither a senseless survival of eighteenth century rococo, nor the shabby clothes of the Roman Catholic priests which explain nothing. They have a meaning: they are modeled on and like unto those clothes our Savior himself wore.[1] In these clothes they must wear the eternal memory of Him Whose image they must present to us, so that they do not for one instant forget and lose themselves in the paltry needs of the world; for a thousand times more is exacted of them than of any one of us; let them hear incessantly that they are, so to speak, other, higher men. No, so long as the priest is still young and life is unknown to him, he should not even meet with people otherwise than in confession and sermon. If he enters into conversation, let it be only with the wisest and most experienced, who may acquaint him with the soul and heart of man, show him life in its true aspect and light, not as it appears to an inexperienced man. Also, a priest must have time for himself; he should work at himself. He ought to take an example from the Saviour, who lived for a long time in the desert and not until after preparation by forty days of fasting came to people to teach them. Certain wits today imagine that one must meddle in the world in order to learn about it. This is simply rubbish. The refutation of such an opinion is all those worldly people

1. Gogol probably had the robes of the ordinary clergy in mind, the loose, long robes which might well be reminiscent of the dress of the ancient Greeks or Jews in their simplicity. The robes of the higher clergy are modeled on those of the Byzantine court.

who eternally meddle in the world and, for all that, are the most frivolous of all. Let them be instructed for the world not in the midst of the world, but far from it, in profound internal contemplation, in searching their souls, for there are the laws of everything and for everything: only first find the key to your own soul; when you have found it, then it is with that very key that you may open all souls.

X

ON THE LYRICISM OF OUR POETS

A letter to V. A. Zhukovsky

Zhukovsky is identified in note
14 to the "Introduction."

Let us speak a little of the article on which a sentence of death has been pronounced, that is, the article entitled "On the Lyricism of our Poets."[1] First of all, my thanks for this sentence of death! This is the second time that I have been saved by you, oh, my true mentor and teacher! Last year it was your hand that stopped me when I wanted to send my remarks on Russian poetry to Pletnyov for *The Contemporary;*[2] now you also deliver to destruction this new fruit of my folly. You are the only one still to restrain me, while all the others—I don't know why—urge me on. How many follies would I already have committed if I had listened only to my other friends! Thus, it is to you, first of all, that my song of thanks goes!

Now let us turn to the article itself. I am ashamed to think of how stupid I have been up to now, how I barely know how to talk about anything intelligent. My thoughts on and understanding of literature are the most absurd of all. Everything

1. Evidently Gogol had sent Zhukovsky an earlier version of this article which Zhukovsky had criticized severely.
2. See note 4 to "Introduction."

that I have written on this subject is singularly obscure and unintelligible. I have not the strength even to deliver my thought, which I not only see in my mind but have in my heart. The soul perceives many things, and I can neither repeat nor transcribe them. The bases of my article are correct; nevertheless, I explain myself in such a way that all my expressions give rise to contradiction. I reiterate: in the lyricism of our poets there is something which is not in the poets of other nations, namely, a kind of biblicism, that highest mode of lyricism which is alien to the flux of passion and is firmly based on the light of reason. It is the supreme triumph of spiritual solidity. Leaving aside Lomonosov and Derzhavin, even in Pushkin we perceive that stern lyricism as soon as he touches lofty subjects. Only recall his poem to a pastor of the Church, *The Prophet* (posthumously published) with that mysterious flight from the city at the end. Take Yazykov's lines and you will see that he constantly strains to hold himself immeasurably above passions and above himself when he begins to touch upon something lofty. I will cite one of his youthful poems, entitled *The Genius;* it is not long:

> *When, thundering and blazing,*
> *The Prophet had flown to Heaven,*
> *A mighty fire penetrated*
> *The living soul of Elijah.*
> *Filled with holy feeling, his soul*
> *Took heart, was strengthened, rose*
> *And, illumined by inspiration,*
> *Perceived God.*
>
> *So does a genius tremble with joy,*
> *Experience sublimity,*
> *When before him another genius*
> *Thunders, blazes, and flies.*
> *His resurrected power*

>*Instantly perceives a miracle,*
>*And a new world glitters—*
>*The Heaven of the Elect.*

What splendor and what stern majesty!

I explained this by saying that our poets saw every lofty object in its legitimate contact with the supreme source of lyricism, God, some consciously, others unconsciously, because the Russian soul, owing to its Russian nature, already somehow perceives this of itself, without knowing why. I said that in our poets two subjects evoke this almost biblical lyricism. The first of them is *Russia*. In this name alone there is something which suddenly clarifies the gaze of our poet; his horizon is extended, everything is broader in him, he himself is clothed in a kind of majesty and is placed above ordinary men. This is something more than ordinary love for the fatherland. Love of the fatherland would echo mealy-mouthed boasting. The proof of it is our well-known jingoists: after their praises, although they are somewhat sincere, they spit on Russia. But when Derzhavin speaks of Russia, you sense a supernatural power in him; it is as though you are breathing the grandeur of Russia. Simple love of the fatherland would not have given the strength not only not to Derzhavin but even to Yazykov to express themselves so loftily and solemnly every time they touch on Russia. For example, the verses in which Derzhavin describes how Batory advanced upon Russia:

>*. . . imperious Stephen*
>*In a mighty camp*
>*Had gathered his dense battalions,*
>*That he might defeat the citizens of Pskov,*
>*Then annihilate Russia!*
>*But you, love of fatherland,*
>*You of whom our ancestors boasted,*
>*You took up arms. Blood for blood—*
>*And it was not he who celebrated the victory!*

This sober, heroic power, which at times is united to an involuntary need to prophesy about Russia, is born of an involuntary contact of thought with that supreme Providence which is so manifestly perceived in the fate of our fatherland. Besides love, a secret awe is also involved at the sight of the events which God has caused to be accomplished in the land appointed to us for a fatherland, a glimpse of a beautiful new edifice which for the moment is not clearly revealed to everyone, and which can only be heard by the all-hearing ear of the poet or by a religious spirit which can discern *the fruit in the seed.* Now others are beginning to perceive this little by little, but they express themselves so unclearly that their words seem insane. You are wrong to think that the young people of today, raving about Slavic origins and prophesying the future of Russia, are following a kind of modish fad. They do not know how to ripen their thoughts in their heads, they hasten to announce them to the world, without being aware that their thoughts are still silly—childish, that is all.

Among the Hebrew people, four hundred prophets suddenly began to prophesy; only one among them was chosen by God, he whose phrases were entered in the holy book of the Hebrew people; all the others probably spoke superfluously, but he did not perceive less vaguely and obscurely the same things that the elect knew how to say sensibly and clearly; otherwise the people would have beaten them with stones. Why are neither France nor England or Germany infected by this fad, why do they not prophesy about themselves, why is Russia the only one to prophesy? Because more strongly than the others does it feel the hand of God in all which has been visited upon her and it scents the approach of a new kingdom. That is why the accent of our poets is biblical. And this is what there cannot be in the poets of other nations, as strongly as they may love their motherlands and as ardently as they may know how to express that love. And do not argue with me about this, my fine friend!

But let us pass on to another subject, concerning which we hear the same lofty lyricism in our poets we have been talking about, that is, *love for the Tsar*. Because of the great number of hymns and odes to the Tsar, our poetry, from the time of Lomonosov and Derzhavin, has been invested with a kind of royal grandeur of expression. The sentiments are sincere—there is no question of that. Only a jester would be capable of thinking for a moment that he sees flattery and the desire to get something in them, and such a supposition would be founded on some insignificant and bad odes of the same poets. But he who has more wit, he who is wiser, will stop before those odes of Derzhavin in which he outlines a vast realm of beneficent activity for the sovereign, in which he himself, with tears in his eyes, speaks to him of other tears which are ready to flow from the eyes not only of Russians, but even of the brute savages living on the borders of his Empire, simply through contact with that mercy and that love which only an all-powerful authority can show to the people. So much is powerfully said that if there should ever be a sovereign who for one moment forgets his duty, he would recall it anew in reading these lines and would be moved by the holiness of his rank. Only icy hearts will reproach Derzhavin for his exaggerated praises to Catherine; but whoever has not a heart of stone will not read without tender emotion those remarkable strophes where he says that if a marble statue passes him on to posterity, it will only be because:

> *I have sung the Tsarina of the Russians,*
> *Of whom another like we will not find,*
> *Neither here nor ever in all the vast world.*
> *Be proud of it, be proud of it, my lyre!*

Not without real spiritual agitation will he read the verses Derzhavin wrote just before his death:

> *Age has chilled my spirit, the voice of my lyre has flown:*
> *The Muse of Catherine sleeps.*
> *. . . Sing*

I cannot. I leave my antique strings
To other singers to pluck.
May they once again elicit from them
Those pure, fiery flames
With which I sang three Tsars.

An old man does not lie on the threshold of the grave. All his life he carried this love as something holy and he bore it into his grave as something holy. But this is not the point. Whence comes this love?—that is the question. That all the people in some way feel this sentiment and therefore the poet, as the purest reflection of the people, should be sensitive to it to the highest degree—this explains only half the matter. A really complete poet does not devote himself to anything he cannot account for without verifying it by the light of his reason. Born with an ear to hear, aspiring to recreate in its plenitude the object that others see fragmentarily, from one or two sides and not from all four, he cannot but see clearly the whole course of the reign. How intelligently did Pushkin define the meaning of an all-powerful monarchy, and how generally intelligent he was in everything that he said in the last days of his life! "Why is it necessary," he said, "that one of us be above all and even above the law? Because the law is unbending; a man feels in the law something cruel and unbrotherly. You do not get very far with only the literal fulfillment of the law; certainly none of us should transgress or violate it; for that a superior mercy is needed, to soften the law, a mercy which can be manifested among the people only by an all-powerful sovereign. A state without an all-powerful monarch is an automaton: it is already much if it achieves what the United States has achieved. And what is the United States? Carrion. A dead body. A man there is so empty spiritually that he is not worth an egg. A state without an absolute monarch is an orchestra without a conductor: all the musicians could be excellent, but if there is no one to control them with his baton, the concert will not take place. It seems that he does nothing himself, he plays no instrument, only gently waves his baton and looks at the musicians; but one look from him is sufficient to soften, in this or that place, a rough sound emitted by a fool of a drum or a clumsy trombone. Thanks to him, the first violin will not dare to break loose at the expense of the others; he will be concerned with the whole composition, he, the animator of the whole, the supreme head of this supreme harmony!" How aptly Pushkin expressed it! How he understood the meaning of these great truths!

This inner essence—the power of the autocratic monarch—he has also partially expressed in one of his poems which you published in the posthumous collection of his works, you even corrected a line in it, without glimpsing its purport. I now reveal its secret. I am speaking of the ode to Emperor Nicholas, which appeared in print under the modest title, "To N———" Its origin is the following. It was one evening at the Annichkov Palace, one of those evenings to which only the select of our society are invited. Pushkin also was there among them. Everyone was already assembled in the salon; but the Emperor still had not come. Apart from the others, in another wing of the palace, profiting from this moment of relaxation from current affairs, the Emperor opened *The Iliad*, and without realizing it himself he was carried away by reading it—while for a long time music had been sounding in the salon and the dance was in full swing. He came late to the ball, still wearing on his face a trace of the impressions he had just felt. The contrast between the two was not noticed by anyone, but it left a strong impression on Pushkin's soul. Its fruit was the following magnificent ode, all of which I repeat here (it is all in one strophe):

For long did you talk alone with Homer,
For long did we await you.

And you were radiant when you came from those mysterious
    heights
Bearing your Tables to us.
But what? You found us in a tent in the desert,
In the madness of a festal feast,
Singing wild songs and leaping about
The idol we had forged.
We were afraid and shunned your rays.
In a fit of wrath and grief
You cursed us, your mad children,
And you smashed your Tables of the Law.
Cursed us? Oh, no! You love to descend
From the heights into the shadows of the vales,
You love the thunder of Heaven and you heed
The murmur of bees among the crimson roses.[3]

Let us leave aside the personality of the Emperor Nicholas
and investigate the monarch in general, as the anointed of the
Lord, obliged to speed the people who have been entrusted to
him to that light where God lives: in truth, was Pushkin right
to compare him to the ancient seer Moses? He of all men
upon whom falls the fate of millions of his fellows, who because of his terrible responsibility for them is freed before God
from all responsibility before men, who aches with the terror
of that responsibility and when no one sees perhaps lets tears
flow and suffers from pains of which no man placed below him
has any idea, who in the midst of his diversions hears the
incessant call of God resounding in his ears, incessantly crying

3. The reference is to a poem Pushkin wrote in 1832 to his fellow poet
N. I. Gnedich (1784–1833), a poet of the high classical style. Gogol omits
the last eight lines of the poem, even though he says he is quoting it in
full. Those omitted eight lines make it clear that Pushkin is talking about
the difference between the lofty style of the ancients, the style of Gnedich,
and the lowness of the moderns. The Emperor Nicholas is not involved
in the poem at all, in spite of Gogol's implication that Pushkin was, if
not dedicating it to the Tsar, at least glorifying him. Nothing was further
from Pushkin's mind.

to him—he could well be compared to the ancient seer, like him he could break the Tables of the Law, cursing the frivolous dancing of a tribe which, instead of aspiring to Him to whom everything on earth ought to aspire, leaps about idols forged by itself. But Pushkin was checked by a still higher meaning of that power which the helpless weakness of humanity implored of Heaven, implored not by an appeal to celestial justice, which not a man of earth may escape, but by an appeal to the celestial love of God, which is prepared to forgive us every-thing—forgetfulness of our duty and our grumblings themselves —everything that man on earth does not forgive, so that one alone might gather all power unto himself, be apart from us all and be above all, that by this he may be closer to all, that he may from on high condescend to everything, from the thunder of Heaven to the lyre of the poet and down to our least conspicuous diversions.

It seems that in this poem Pushkin, posing to himself the question of what this power is, lowered himself into the dust before the grandeur of the response which appeared in his soul. We cannot overemphasize that this was the same poet who was so proud of the independence of his opinions and of his personal merit. No one has spoken of himself as he has:

> *I have raised a monument not hand made,*
> *The people's path to it will never be forgotten;*
> *Its bold top will rise*
> *Above the column of Napoleon.*

Even if the one responsible for that "column of Napoleon" is you, still we may suppose that even had the line remained in its original form it would serve all the same as evidence that Pushkin, while feeling his pre-eminence as a man com-pared with many crowned heads, at the same time compre-hended the triviality of his rank next to the rank of the crowned head and knew how to bow reverently before the sovereigns who showed the majesty of their rank.[4]

Our poets have begun to see the higher meaning of the monarch clearly, perceiving that he must at the end inevitably be made all *love,* and in this way it will become evident to everyone that the sovereign is the image of God, as our entire land knows. The importance of the sovereign in Europe is inevitably approaching this expression. Everything leads to it, so that the sovereigns' sublime, divine love for their peoples may be evoked. We have already heard the wails of the suffering caused by the mental disease with which almost every European is now infected, floundering about without himself knowing how and from whom help may come: the least touch only aggravates his wounds; any instrument, any aid devised by the mind is too coarse for him and brings no cure. These cries will finally be so intensified that the most insensitive hearts will burst with pity, and a wave of unprecedented compassion will evoke another wave of unprecedented love. Man will burn with a love for all humanity with which he has never before burned. No one of us individually can conceive such a love; it remains in ideas and thoughts, but not in actions; only those can be completely penetrated by it on whom was imposed the inevitable law of loving everyone as one man. Loving every person in his empire, each man of every class and rank, and making them all, so to speak, a part of his own body, all his soul empathizing with all, grieving, sobbing, and praying day and night for his suffering people, a sovereign acquires that omnipotent voice of love which alone can be intelligible to a sick humanity and whose touch will not be cruel to its wounds, which alone can reconcile all classes and turn the nation into an harmonious orchestra. The people can only be completely cured where the monarch attains his highest meaning: to be

4. Gogol is referring to the first four lines of Pushkin's poem "Exegi monumentum," written in 1836. In the original the "column" is Alexander's, not Napoleon's.

on earth the image of Him Who is Himself love. In Europe it has not occurred to anyone to explain this sublime meaning of the monarch. The politicians, the legislators, and the lawyers have seen him from one side only, namely, as the highest functionary of the state, put in his position by men; and they do not know how to behave with this power, how to show it its own limitations since, because of constantly changing circumstances, it is sometimes necessary to enlarge his prerogatives, sometimes to restrict them. The sovereign and his people are therefore in a strange situation in regard to each other over there: they regard each other almost as though they were antagonists, each desiring to seize power at the expense of the other. Among us, the poets and not the legislators have clearly seen the lofty meaning of the monarchy, in trembling have they heard the will of God to establish it in Russia in its legitimate form; that is why their sounds always become biblical the moment the word "Tsar" escapes their lips. Even those of us who are not poets perceive this, because the pages of our history speak most manifestly of the will of Providence: it is in Russia that this power will achieve its complete and perfect form. Every event in our fatherland, beginning with the Tatar enslavement, is visibly aimed at the assemblage of power in the hands of one person, in order that he may have the strength to carry out that famous conversion of the whole into an empire, to shock everyone, and, after having awakened everyone, to arm each of us with that critical insight into himself without which it is impossible for a man to analyze himself, to judge himself, and to raise in himself the same struggle against ignorance and darkness that the Tsar had raised throughout the empire; so that later, when every man burns for that holy struggle, and all are conscious of their strength, there will be one above all who, torch in hand, will direct all his people like one soul towards that supreme light to which Russia cries out.

Consider by what a marvelous means, even before the full

meaning of this power had been explained either to the sovereign or to his subjects, the seeds of a mutual love were sown in their hearts! No royal house began so extraordinarily as the house of the Romanovs began. Its beginnings were already a feat of love. The last and humblest subject of the empire yielded up his life to give us a Tsar, and the purity of his sacrifice has inseparably bound the sovereign to his subjects ever since. Love has entered into our blood; it has bound us in a blood relationship with the Tsar. And the sovereign is so established, so become one with his subjects, that we all now see what universal misfortune would arise should the sovereign forget his subjects and withdraw from them, or should the subjects forget their sovereign and withdraw from him. How manifestly the will of God is shown in the choice of the family of the Romanovs and not of another! How incomprehensible is this elevation to the throne of an adolescent unknown to all! There were in the ranks the most ancient families and, besides, valourous men who had just saved their fatherland: Pojarsky, Troubetskoy,[5] and princes descended in a direct line from Ruric. The vote left them aside, without one dissenting voice: not one dared to claim his rights. And this happened at the Time of Troubles, when everyone could squabble and dispute and gather gangs of adherents! And who was chosen? One allied through the feminine line to a Tsar[6] whose reputation for cruelty had but lately run through all the land, to such a point that not only the boyars oppressed and tormented by him, but the people themselves, whom he had barely persecuted at all, for a long time repeated the saying: "Fine was his head, but now, thanks to God, the earth is his bed." Nevertheless, all unanimously, from the boyars down to the last poor landless peasant, decreed with a single voice that he should be on the throne! These are the things that happen in our nation! How could you expect,

5. Pojarsky and Troubetskoy were commanders of the armies which in 1612, the Time of Troubles, retook Moscow from the Poles.

6. The reference is to Ivan IV, "The Terrible," who was married to Anastasia Romanov. Thus the Romanov claim to the throne was through the female line rather than through the male.

after that, that the lyricism of our poets, who perceived the attributes of a Tsar in the books of the Old Testament, and at the same time saw so closely the will of God in all the events in our fatherland—how could you expect the lyricism of our poets not to be full of biblical echoes? I repeat, simple love would not have clung to such severe, sober sounds; for this the full and firm conviction of reason is also necessary, not the uncontrolled feeling of love alone. Otherwise, their sounds would have been soft, like yours in your youthful works, when you abandoned yourself to the sentiments of your loving soul. No, there is something strong, really strong, in our poets, which is not in the poets of other nations. Your not seeing it does not prove that it is not there. Remember that you do not contain all the facets of Russian nature; on the contrary, some of them have attained such a degree of development in you that they have left no room for others, and consequently you have become an exception to the general Russian character. All the most gentle and tender strings of our Slavic nature are in you; but the broadest and strongest of its strings, those which make a mysterious chill of fright run through all the human frame, are not so well-known to you. But they are the source of the lyricism of which we are speaking. This lyricism in any case cannot but rise to God as to its unique supreme source. It is austere, it is timid, it detests verbosity, everything which clings to earth appears sickly to it, since it does not see the imprint of divinity on it. He who possesses but one grain of this lyricism, in spite of all his insufficiencies and faults, contains in himself an austere and lofty spiritual nobility before which he shivers himself and which forces him to flee everything resembling human gratitude. The best he has done suddenly disgusts him, if some recompense to himself followed upon it: he is too well aware that everything lofty should be loftier than recompense.

Only after the death of Pushkin was his real attitude to the sovereign and the secret of two of his best works discovered. During his lifetime he spoke to no one of the feelings suffusing him, and he acted wisely. Owing to the greasy exclamations of the hostile gazettes, and owing to all the angry, sleazy, vehement tricks played by both jingoistic and nonjingoistic patriots, we in Rus ceased to believe in the sincerity of printed effusions, so that it was dangerous for Pushkin to be published: he would certainly have been treated as a corrupt and anxious man. But now that his works have appeared posthumously, in all Russia you would not find one person who would dare to call Pushkin a flatterer or a fawner. Consequently, the sacredness of his lofty sentiment has been preserved. And anyone who has not the power to comprehend the matter with his own mind makes it an article of faith, saying, "If Pushkin himself thought so, then it is the real truth." The Tsarist hymns of our poets have astonished foreigners by their majestic composition and style. Recently, Mickiewicz spoke of this in his lectures in Paris, and he said it at a time when he was himself annoyed with us and when everyone in Paris was indignant with us. Nevertheless, in spite of that, he solemnly declared that there is nothing servile or low in the odes and hymns of our poets, but, on the contrary, something free and majestic; and therefore, although it did not please his fellow-countrymen, he rendered homage to the nobility of character of our writers. Mickiewicz was right. Our writers truly possess the features of a somewhat superior nature. In their moments of creation they have left their psychological portraits, which would be like boasting if their lives did not confirm them. Here is what Pushkin says while thinking about his future destiny:

For long will I be dear to my nation,
For I roused their finest feelings with my lyre,
For I aided them by the charm of my vivid lines,
And summoned mercy for the fallen.[7]

7. These lines form the fourth stanza of Pushkin's "Exegi monumentum." In *The Poems, Prose and Plays of Alexander Pushkin,* selected and edited, with an Introduction by, Avrahm Yarmolinsky, New York, The

It is enough to recall Pushkin to see how correct this portrait is. How he brightened and blazed when it was a matter of lightening the fate of an exile or of giving a hand to someone fallen! How he awaited the first sign of the Tsar's favor in order to mention to him, not himself, but someone else unfortunate and fallen! This is a typical Russian trait. Only recall that touching spectacle when people in a body meet convicts departing for Siberia and everyone brings something from his home—one food, one money, one a word of Christian consolation. There is no hatred for the criminal, no quixotic passion to make a hero of him, to collect portraits of him, or to look at him as a curiousity, as they do in enlightened Europe. There is something more here: it is neither the desire to justify him nor to snatch him from the hands of justice; rather it is the desire to raise his fallen soul, to console him, as brother consoles brother, as Christ himself has commanded us to console one another. Pushkin valued to the highest this aspiration to raise the fallen. That is why his heart proudly palpitated when he heard of a trip of the Emperor to Moscow at the time of the cholera horrors—a thing hardly any other crowned head has done and which evoked these remarkable verses:

> *I swear: whoever risks his life*
> *To the darkness of disease*
> *To hearten dimming eyes—*
> *I swear he will be otherwise judged*
> *In Heaven than he was*
> *On this blind earth.*

Modern Library, 1936, p. 88, Babette Deutsch translates the lines as follows:

> *I shall be loved, and long the people will remember*
> *The kindly thoughts I stirred—my music's brightest crown,*
> *How in this cruel age I celebrated freedom,*
> *And begged for ruth toward those cast down.*

Gogol gives the third line as I have quoted it in the text. Deutsch follows an alternative reading, the same as that given in A. S. Pushkin, *Sobranie sochinenii* (Gosudarstvennoe izdatelstvo, khudozhestvennoi literatury, Moskva, 1959), p. 460.

He also knew how to value another trait in the life of another crowned head, Peter. Recall the poem entitled "Banquet on the Neva," in which he asks in amazement about the reason for an extraordinary celebration in the imperial palace; the clamor along the Neva, which is shaken by cannonades, has been heard all over Petersburg. He goes through all incidents joyous to the Tsar which could be the reason for such a revel: the birth of an heir to the throne, the name's day of his wife, a triumph over an invincible enemy achieved by the fleet (which was the sovereign's prime passion), and here is his response:

> *No, he is reconciled with his subjects.*
> *Forgetting the faults*
> *Of the guilty, he makes merry*
> *As the cup foams.*
> *Therefore is the celebration merry,*
> *The speeches of the guests tipsy, noisy.*
> *And the Neva by a violent cannonade*
> *Is shaken afar.*

Only a Pushkin could feel the beauty in such an action. To know not only how to pardon his subjects, but to celebrate this pardon like a victory over the enemy—this is a truly divine trait. Only in Heaven do they know how to act so. Only there is there more joy at the conversion of a sinner than at a just man, and all the assembly of invisible powers takes part in this celestial banquet of God. Pushkin was an expert appraiser of everything truly great in man. How could it be otherwise, if spiritual nobility is already the portion of almost all our writers? It is noteworthy that in all other lands the writer is disrespected by society in so far as his personal character is concerned. It is the opposite among us. Among us, a simple scribbler, who is not a writer and not only has no beauty of soul but is even at times a scoundrel, in the depths of Russia will by no means be taken as such. On the contrary, among everyone in general, even among those who hardly ever hear anything about writers, there is the conviction that a writer is something superior, that he certainly should be someone noble, that even though he is often improper, he should not permit himself what is forgiven to others. In one of our provinces, at the time of the gentry elections, a gentleman who was also a man of letters was going to raise his voice in favor of a man whose conscience was somewhat tarnished—all the gentry forthwith addressed him and reproached him, saying, "And he still calls himself a writer!"

1846

XI

CONTROVERSIES

From a letter to L

Controversies over our European and Slavic origins, which are already, as you say, elbowing their way into the salons, indicate only that we are beginning to awaken, but that we are still not completely awakened. There is therefore nothing astonishing if a lot of nonsense is recorded on both sides. All these Slavists and Europeanizers—or old believers and new believers, or orientalists and westernizers, I don't know what to say they are in reality, since at the moment they all appear to me to be caricatures of what they would like to be—all are speaking of two different sides of one and the same object, without suspecting that there is neither controversy nor contradiction between them. One comes too close to the building, so that he sees only a part of it; the other goes too far away, so that while he sees the whole facade he does not see the parts. It stands to reason that the truth is more on the side of the Slavists and orientalists, because they see the whole facade and therefore speak of the principal thing and not the parts. But there is also truth on the side of the Europeanists and westernizers, because they speak in a quite detailed and distinct manner of the wall which stands in front of their eyes; their mistake is only that, because of the eaves crowning this wall, they do not see the summit of the entire building, I mean the cupola and everything above.

Some advice may be given to both—to the one to endeavor to come closer, be it for an instant, to the other to retreat a few steps. But to this they will not agree, because the spirit of pride has seized them both. Each is persuaded that he is right once and for all and that the other is a liar once and for all. There is more conceit on the side of the Slavists: they are boasters; each imagines that he has discovered America and inflates his little seed into a turnip. It goes without saying that with their obstinate bragging they arm the Europeanists still more against them— Europeanists who have long been ready to retreat, because they are beginning to perceive many things unperceived before, but they are stubborn, not wanting to concede to one with too many trumps. All these controversies would still be nothing if they stopped with salons and journals. But the difficulty is that the two opposed opinions, both of which are still so immature and vague, have already entered the heads of many civil servants. I have been told that it happens (especially in those activities where function and power are in two separate hands) that, while one works completely in the European spirit, the other resolutely endeavors to follow the old Russian way, consolidating all the former procedures, contrary to what his colleague contemplates. In such a way, affairs, like the subordinate officials themselves, come to grief, for they no longer know whom to heed. Further, since the two opinions, in spite of their sharpness, are not exactly defined, it is only the fisher in troubled waters who profits, as they say. A swindler may now find the opportunity, under the mask of a Slavist or Europeanist, depending on what his superior wants, to get an advantageous post and promote his swindles, either as a champion of the old or as a champion of the new. In general, controversies are the kinds of things to which intelligent people of a certain age ought never meanwhile to pay any attention. Let youth get out of it by itself; that's its affair. Believe me, it is normal and necessary that these progressive bawlers scream to their hearts' content so that the reasonable people may meanwhile reflect to their hearts' content. Lend your ear to controversies, but do not meddle in them. The thought of the work with which you desire to occupy yourself is full of good sense, and I even trust that you will accomplish it better than any other man of letters. I ask but one thing of you: work at it, so far as possible, cooly and calmly. May God preserve you from temper and fever in the least of your expressions. Wrath is out of place above all in a matter of law, because it obscures and troubles it. Remember that you are a man who is not only not young but even advanced in years. Let a young man be angry; at least in the eyes of some people he will be a picturesque spectacle. But when an old man begins to get heated he simply becomes disgusting; youth will bare its teeth and ridicule him. Be careful that they do not say of you: "Hey! That dirty old man! All his life he's done nothing but sit on his behind and how he's blaming others for not having done the same!" From the lips of an old man there ought to issue words of good will and not of shouting controversy. A spirit of the purest gentleness and meekness ought to imbue the noble speeches of an old man, so that youth will find nothing to say to him in objection, feeling that its words would be unseemly and that gray hairs are already holy.

1844

XII

THE CHRISTIAN GOES FORWARD

A letter to Shch

"Shch" is probably M. S. Shchepkin (1788–1863),
an actor of the time who is usually credited
with introducing the realistic style into comic acting
in Russia, displacing the vaudeville style. Gogol
thought highly of his talents. On the other hand, some
commentators believe that this letter was
originally addressed to the publicist and professor
of literature S. P. Shevyrev (1806–64).

My friend, do not consider yourself otherwise than as a school-boy and pupil. Do not think that you are too old to study, that your powers have attained their genuine maturity and that your character and your soul have received their final form and cannot become better. For a Christian there is no graduation: he is eternally a pupil, a pupil until the grave. Custom tells us that in the natural course a man attains the full development of his intelligence at thirty years. From thirty to forty his powers may still go somewhat forward; after forty nothing progresses in him, and everything that he produces will not only not be better than before, but will be even weaker and colder than before. But it is not so for the Christian; where for others the limit of perfection has been reached, for him it is only a beginning. The most capable and gifted people, when they have passed forty years of age, grow stupid, weary, and feeble. Look through all the philosophers and the most universal geniuses: their best season was only the time of their full maturity; then little by little they became dotards, and in age even fell into infantilism. Remember Kant, who in his last years completely lost his memory and died in second childhood. But consider the lives of all the saints: you will see that they increased in wisdom and in spiritual power in just the degree that they approached decrepitude and death. And even those among them who did not receive any shining gifts from nature and who all their lives were considered simple, foolish people, later amazed everyone by the wisdom of their speech.

What does this mean? That among them there has always resided that power of aspiration which customarily exists in a man only during the years of his youth, when he sees the deeds whose recompense is universal applause ahead of him, when he is dreaming of that distant rainbow which has so much attraction for youth. The deeds die out in the distance—the power of aspiration dies also. But the distance shines eternally before the Christian, and new deeds are disclosed. Like a young man, he craves the struggle for life; he knows with whom to make war and where to act, because his gaze, directed upon himself, since it constantly becomes brighter, discloses new faults in himself with which he must fight anew. Thus all his power cannot only not fall asleep within him nor be enfeebled but must be sharpened incessantly; the desire to become better and to earn the applause of Heaven gives him such incentives as the most insatiable ambition cannot give to the most insatiably ambitious man. That is why the Christian progresses when others retrogress, and why the further he goes the more intelligent he becomes.

Intelligence is not our highest faculty. Its function is no more than that of a policeman: it can only bring order and arrange in proper place things which are in us already. It does not act so long as all the other faculties in us from which it draws its wisdom do not act. You will force it forward very little by abstract readings and incessant scientific studies; sometimes it is even suppressed and hindered in its development. It depends incom-

parably more on the spiritual state; as soon as passion begins to
rage, it works blindly and foolishly; if the soul is calm and no
passion seethes, then the intelligence is clear and works sensibly.
Reason is an incomparably higher faculty, but it is obtained in
no other way than by a victory over the passions. The only ones
who have it are people who have not neglected their inner education. But reason itself does not give a man the whole possibility
of aspiring further.

There is a still higher faculty: its name is wisdom and Christ
alone can give it to us. It does not belong to any of us from birth,
it is not in any of us by nature, but it is a matter of the loftiest
divine grace. He who already has intelligence and reason cannot
receive wisdom otherwise than by praying for it day and night,
asking God for it day and night, raising his soul to the mildness
of the dove and gathering into his very inner self all possible
purity in order to admit that celestial guest who shies away from
dwellings to which a moral order and an absolute harmony in all
things has not come. If it does enter his house, then a celestial
life begins for a man, and he comprehends all the marvelous
sweetness of being a pupil. Everyone becomes a teacher for him;
all the world is his teacher: the most insignificant person can be
his teacher. From the simplest counsels he extracts the wisdom of
the one counsel; the most foolish object shows him its wise side,
and all the universe becomes a book of instruction for him: more
than others will he draw treasures from it, for more than others
will he perceive that he is a pupil. But if for one instant he imagines that his study is finished and that he is no longer a pupil,
if he is outraged by anybody's lesson or instruction, then wisdom
is quickly taken away from him and he remains in the dark, like
King Solomon in his last days.

1846

XIII

KARAMZIN

From a letter to N. M. Yazykov

N. M. Karamzin (1766–1826), whose early career was
devoted to literary work and to reform of the
language, introduced numerous Gallicisms into Russian
while campaigning against the use of Old Slavonic
and Latin syntax. It might almost be said that his
efforts in this direction founded a literary school.
His later career was devoted to historical labors which
produced his most famous work, the monumental
History of the Russian State in twelve volumes.
Karamzin did much in this work to give Russians a
sense of the unity of Russian history.

It is with great pleasure that I read Pogodin's eulogy of Karamzin. It is Pogodin's best work so far as decorum is concerned,
both inwardly and outwardly: there are none of the gross, clumsy
habits of a coarse, slovenly style which have done him great
harm in it. Here, on the contrary, everything is harmonious, re-
flective, arranged in the finest order. All the passages of *Karamzin* have been chosen so intelligently that it is as though Karamzin himself had designed them, and, having weighed his words
and appraised himself properly, placed them vividly before the
eyes of the reader. Karamzin really is an extraordinary phenomenon. He is one writer of whom we can say, he fulfilled his duty
well, buried nothing in the ground, and for the five talents given

him truly returned another five. Karamzin is the first to have shown that among us a writer can be independent and honored by all equally as the most notable citizen of the empire. He is the first to have solemnly made the point that censorship cannot hinder a writer, and that if a writer has been filled by the purest desire for the good, to such a degree that this desire, occupying all his soul, has become his meat and drink, then no censorship is severe for him, and there is ample room for him everywhere. He said it and proved it. No one but Karamzin has spoken so boldly and nobly, without hiding any of his opinions and thoughts, even though they have not always conformed to the rule of the time, and you cannot help feeling that he alone was right. What a lesson for our brother writers! And, after that, how ridiculous are those who maintain that in Russia one cannot speak the full truth and that among us its eyes are put out. He who expresses himself so absurdly and foolishly rather puts out the eyes of truth himself by the arrogant words with which he speaks his truth, displaying the slovenliness of his own tattered soul, and then is astonished and indignant because no one accepts and listens to the truth from him! No. Have a soul as pure, as well organized as Karamzin had, and then proclaim your truth: everyone will listen to you, from the Tsar to the last beggar in the realm. And they will listen with a love not accorded in other lands to a parliamentary champion of the right or to the best preacher of our time who assembles the leaders of fashionable society around himself, a love with which only our marvelous Russia can listen—a Russia which rumor has it does not love the truth at all.

1846

XIV

ON THE THEATER, ON THE ONE-SIDED VIEW TOWARDS THE THEATER, AND ON ONE-SIDEDNESS IN GENERAL

A letter to Count A. P. Tolstoy

Gogol's reference is perhaps to the Hegelian notion of *Einseitigkeit*.

You are very one-sided, and it is not long since that you became one-sided; and you became one-sided because it would be impossible, given your spiritual state as it now is, for any man not to become one-sided. You are thinking only of your spiritual salvation, and, not having found the road by which you were destined to attain it, you see everything in the world as temptation and hindrance to your salvation. Monks are less severe than you. Your attacks on the theater are one-sided and unjust. You reinforce yourself by what some well-known ecclesiastics bring up against the theater. But they are right and you are wrong. Rather, bethink yourself whether they are really bringing up things against the theater or only against the way the theater is now presented to us. The Church began to rise up against the theater in the first centuries of the universal establishment of Christianity, when the theaters alone were the refuge for a paganism everywhere proscribed as a den of scandalous baccanalia. That is why Saint John Chrysostom thundered against it so strongly. But times have changed. The earth was cleansed

by the generations of European unspoiled peoples whose education was based on Christianity, and then the saints themselves
were the first to begin to introduce the theater: theaters were
established in ecclesiastical academies. Our Dmitri of Rostov,[1]
justly placed among the holy Fathers of our Church, composed
plays meant for staging.

Thus the theater is not at fault. Anything can be perverted and
can be given a perverse meaning; man is clever at this. But the
matter must be considered more profoundly, as it should be, not
judged by the caricature which has been made of it. The theater
is by no means a trifle, nor a petty thing, if you take in consideration that it can accommodate a crowd of five or six thousand
persons all at once, and that this multitude, whose members
taken singly have nothing in common, can suddenly be shaken
by the same shock, sob with the same tears, and laugh with the
same general laughter. It is a kind of pulpit from which much
good can be spoken to the world. Only separate the properly
named higher theater from those capering ballets, vaudevilles,
melodramas, and tawdry-splendrous spectacles which pander to
depraved tastes or depraved hearts, and then you will see the
theater. The theater in which high tragedy and comedy are presented must be entirely independent of all that. It is most odd to
juxtapose Shakespeare with ballet dancers or with dancers in
skin-tight pants. What connection is there between them? Let
feet be with feet and head with head. This is understood in some
parts of Europe where the theater of high dramatic presentation
is separated from the others and is the only one to enjoy the
support of the government, but they have understood it only as
an external kind of relationship. It was proper to think seriously
about supplying the best works of dramatic authors with the
kind of setting that would attract the public and would open up
to it that morally beneficial influence which is in all great writers.

1. Dmitri Tuptalo (1651–1709), Bishop of Rostov, was an important ecclesiastical writer of the end of the seventeenth and early eighteenth centuries.

Shakespeare, Sheridan, Molière, Goethe, Schiller, Beaumarchais, even Lessing, Regnard, and many other secondary writers of the last century produced nothing that would divert respect from great subjects; in them there is not even an echo of what seethed and boiled in the fanatic writers of that time, who were occupied with political questions and spread disrespect for holy things. Now they mock hypocrisy, now blasphemy, now twisted interpretations of the law, but never what constitutes the root of human valor; on the contrary, the feeling for the good is strictly observed, even when epigrams grumble. An oft-repeated dramatic composition, that is, one of those truly classic plays in which our attention is focused upon the nature and soul of man, necessarily begins to solidify the principles of society, insensibly compels our dispositions to stability, while all those plays flooded with emptiness and lightness, beginning with vaudevilles and un-thought-out dramas and ending with glittering ballets and even operas, only dissipates them, scatters them, makes society light and frivolous. Distracted by the millions of sparkling objects scattering thought in every direction, the world no longer has the strength to meet Christ directly. The divine truths of Christianity are far from it. It will be afraid of them, as of a gloomy monastery, if you do not by invisible degrees prepare it for Christianity, if you do not raise it to some lofty place from which it may better see all the boundless horizon of Christianity and may better understand the very thing which before was inaccessible to it. There are many things on earth which serve by invisible degrees as an approach to Christianity for those who are separated from Christianity. The theater can be of this number if it addresses itself to this purpose. We must put on stage in all their magnificence all the finest dramatic compositions of all centuries and all nations. They must be given more often, as often as possible, repeating the same play over and over again. This can be done. All the plays can be made fresh, new, interesting for everyone, from little to great, if only you succeed in staging them as they ought to be staged. It is nonsense to think that they have aged and that the public has lost its taste for them. The public is not capricious; it goes where it is led. If the authors themselves had not regaled it with their rotten melodramas, it would not have felt a taste for them and would not have demanded them. Take the most playable plays and stage them properly, and the public will come in a mob. Molière will be a novelty to them; Shakespeare will appear more interesting than the most modern vandevillian.

But the staging of the works must be really and fully artistic, the business must not be entrusted to anyone but the first and best of the actor-artists that may be found in the troupe. And there must be no hindrance by any official. Let the actor-artist alone be in charge of it all. Particular care must be taken that all responsibility be his alone, that he alone be the one to decide to act before the eyes of the public, in sequence, one after the other, all the secondary roles, so that he may leave living models to the secondary actors, who ordinarily learn their roles from lifeless models inherited from some obscure tradition, who were formed by bookish teaching and do not of themselves see any living interest in their roles. Only the performance of secondary roles by a first-class actor can attract the public to see the same play twenty times running. Who would not be anxious to see how Shchepkin or Karatygin[2] would play roles they have never played before? Then, when this actor, having played all these roles, returns to his earlier one, he will have a surer grasp of his own role as well as of the play as a whole; and the play will have a still stronger interest for the spectators because of this completeness of execution—a thing until then unheard of! There is no greater impression than that which is produced in a man by a perfect, harmonious accord of all the parts, which he has formerly been able to hear only in a musical orchestra, which may be the reason that a dramatic work can be given more times running than the most beloved opera. Say what you will, still the

2. For Shchepkin, see note 1 to "The Christian Goes Forward." Karatygin was also a well-known actor of the time.

sounds of the soul and heart, expressed in words, are much more varied than musical sounds. But I repeat, all this is possible only if the thing is really done as it ought to be done, and the full responsibility for the whole, down to every part of the repertory, is entrusted to a first-class actor, that is, if tragedy is managed by the first tragic actor and comedy by the first comic actor, and these alone are the *exclusive* rulers. I say *exclusive* because I know how many among us are willing to sneak in on every business surreptitiously. Immediately that some post with money to be gained appears, in a flash a secretary fastens himself on to it. Whence he comes, God knows: it is just as though he emerged from a swamp; then and there he will prove that he is clearly indispensable, as clearly as 2 times 2 equals 4; at first he will be occupied only with scribbling financial particulars down on paper, then, little by little, he will begin to mix into everything, and affairs will pass out of your hands. These secretaries are like invisible moths gnawing away at every job; they confound and confuse relations of subordinates with superiors and, conversely, of superiors with subordinates. Not long ago, you and I discussed all the positions that exist in our state. Examining each one in its legal limits, we found that they are exactly what they ought to be: all are united in that they are as though created from on high to answer to all the needs of state-life, and not so that everyone in rivalry might strive either to enlarge his own limited position or, indeed, run beyond its limits. Each, as honest and intelligent as he might be, strove to be the highest in his post, even if only by an inch, thinking that in this way he would improve both himself and his job. At that time we looked over all the bureaucracy, from high to low, but we forgot the secretaries, and it is precisely they who strive most of all to overrun the limits of their positions. When a secretary is hired only in the capacity of a copyist, he will want to play the role of an intermediary between his superiors and their subordinates. When he is really designated as a necessary intermediary between his superiors and their subordinates, then he begins to ride a high horse: before the subordinates he poses in the role of his superior, he sets himself up in an outer office, he compels people to wait for hours—in short, instead of facilitating the access of the subordinate to his superior, he only impedes him. Sometimes this is done with no other thought than to ennoble his secretarial position. I have even known some by no means stupid, sensible people who, before my very eyes, acted towards the subordinates of their superior in such a manner that I blushed for them. My Khlestakov was nothing next to them. All that, of course, would still be nothing if too many regrettable consequences did not result from it. Many useful and even indispensable people have given up their employment solely because of the brute behavior of a secretary demanding for himself the same respect which they were obliged to pay to the superior alone, one who avenged himself for their recalcitrance by slandering them with suggestions that their opinions were stupid—in short, by all those abominations of which only a dishonorable man is capable. Of course, in the management of a craft, of an art, and of similar things, either a committee or an immediate superior rules and there is no place for a secretary-intermediary: he is used solely to write down the decisions of others or to conduct the financial business; but sometimes it happens that, because of the laziness of some persons or because something is not working, he, little by little insinuating himself, becomes the intermediary and even the ruler in artistic matters. And then the devil knows what will ensue: a pastry cook will be set to shoemaking, and the shoemaker will play the pastry cook. Instructions for the artist in no way written by an artist will ensue; orders will appear and it will be impossible to understand why anything has been ordered. Often one will be astonished that a person still capable of being intelligent could put out such a foolish document without inwardly feeling guilty about it: the document issued from a corner which no one could suspect; as the proverb says: "A little scribbler, a lapdog, wrote it."

In business, it is necessary, whatever the craft may be, that the entire production should rest on the chief craftsman in that craft, by no means on someone who is a hanger-on who should be used only for financial calculations or correspondence. Only the chief craftsman can teach his art, being fully aware of its necessities, and no one else. Only a first-class actor-artist can make a good choice of plays and select them properly; only he knows the secret of how to carry out rehearsals, only he understands how important are frequent readings and well-prepared rehearsals of the plays. He will not even allow an actor to learn his role at home but will make sure that they all study together and that each one have his role by heart for the rehearsals, so that they all, thus surrounded by the atmosphere of the situation, because of this contact will involuntarily hear the true tone of their roles. Then even a stupid actor can insensibly learn what is good, while it is possible for actors who have not yet learned their roles by heart to imitate much from a better actor. Thus each one, without quite knowing how, will acquire truth and naturalism both in his diction and in his gestures. Pose a pompous question, and you will receive a pompous response; pose a simple question, and simple will be the response you receive. Every really simple man is capable of answering with tact. But if the actor has only studied his role at home, he will give a pompous and studied response, and this response will remain with him forever; there will be no way for him to break out of it; then he will not borrow one word from a better actor; he will become remote from all surrounding circumstances and characters, so that he will become remote and a stranger to the whole play and like a dead man he will move among dead men. Only a true actor-artist can perceive the life contained in the play and make that life manifest and vivid to the other actors; he alone can know the proper limits of rehearsals—know when to carry them out, when to stop them, how many are enough before the play may be presented to the public in its best form. Only succeed in inducing the actor-artist to take this business up, as a business that belongs to him alone, show him that it is his duty and that the honor of his art demands it of him—and he will do it, he will carry it out, because he loves his art. He will go even further, taking care that the least of his actors plays well, seeing just as much to the strict fulfillment of the whole as to his own role. He will not allow on stage any trite and insignificant play, such as some bureaucrat would allow, worrying as he does only about augmenting the cash-box collection, because the actor-artist allows nothing which offends his inner aesthetic sensibilities. Indeed, it would be impossible for him, even if he should think of bringing some pressuring action or relatively pressing annoyances to bear (as subordinates do): his own reputation does not allow him. Any sort of subordinate-secretary will boldly trot out his dirty tricks in the conviction that, whatever those dirty tricks may be, no one will know about them, because he himself is an unknown pawn. But let a Shchepkin or a Karatygin do something unjust and the whole city will soon be babbling about it. That is why it is especially important that the principal responsibility in all matters should fall on a man already known to everyone. Finally, the artist-actor, living entirely for his art, which is the supreme thing in his life, whose purity he regards as sacred, will never allow the theater to become a preacher of depravity.

So the theater is not to blame. First, clean out its rubbish, its trash, then analyze it and judge what the theater is. I spoke here of the theater not because I strictly wanted to speak of it, but because what I said about the theater can be adapted to almost everything. There are many subjects which suffer because their sense has been distorted; just as there are many people in the world who act in a fit of temper; as our proverb says, "When you are angry with the lice, you throw your fur coat into the stove," which is as much as to say that much which still has a useful purpose is destroyed.

One-sided people, who are also fanatics, are the ulcer of society; unhappy the land and the state where any authority is found in the hands of such people. They have neither Christian humility nor self-doubt; they are convinced that the whole world lies and they alone speak the truth. My friend! look at yourself more humbly. It is precisely now that you find yourself in this dangerous situation. It is a good thing that for the present you have no position and that you are not in control of anything; otherwise, you, whom I know as one capable of dispatching the most difficult and most complicated functions, would be capable of causing more harm than the most incapable of the incapable. Be very careful in all your judgments! Do not be like those hypocrites who would like to wipe out everything in the world at once, seeing only the diabolic in everything. Their lot is to fall into the same crude errors. Something analogous happened not long ago in literature. Some began to say, in print, that Pushkin was a Deist, not a Christian, just as though they had been on a visit to Pushkin's soul, just as though it was incumbent upon Pushkin in his verse to speak of the prime Christian dogmas, which a holy man of the Church itself presumes to do only with great fear and after having prepared himself for it by the profound holiness of his life. According to them, everything supreme in Christianity ought to be invested with rhyme and made into a kind of poetic plaything. Pushkin acted very wisely in not daring to transfer into poetry what his soul had not been thoroughly imbued with; he preferred rather to remain an imperceptible means of approach to the Most High for all those who are too distant from Christ than to alienate them from Christianity by such soulless poems as are written today by those who pose as Christians. Indeed, I cannot understand how a critic, in print, in the sight of everyone, could seriously raise such an accusation against Pushkin: that his works serve for the corruption of the world, when the censorship is directed, in case the meaning of some work should not be completely clear, to interpret it frankly in the author's favor, not distorted and harmful to him. If this is directed by law for the censor, who is silent and dumb, who cannot even make reservations for himself before the public, then how much more so must it be directed by the law of criticism, which can explain and make reservations for the least of its acts?

To represent publicly a man as a non-Christian and even as an enemy of Christ on the basis of a few imperfections of his soul and because he has been carried away from this world, as each of us will be carried away from it—is this really the Christian way? Who among us is a Christian? I can charge such a critic himself with non-Christianity. I can say that the Christian does not conceive such certitude in his mind that he may resolve this dark matter, which is known only to God, knowing that our mind will be fully enlightened and able to embrace its object from all sides only through the holiness of our life, while his life is perhaps not so holy. A Christian, before accusing anyone of such a criminal offense as the nonrecognition of God, bearing in mind that the Son of God himself commanded that he be recognized upon his descent to earth, will meditate, for this is a terrible thing. He will say this: in poetry there are still many secrets, indeed, all poetry is a secret; it is difficult to pronounce judgment on an ordinary man; only he can pronounce final and full judgment on a poet who contains the poetic essence within himself and is himself almost already the equal of the poet—anyone can judge a little in any ordinary trade, but only the master of a specific trade can fully judge that one. In short, the Christian will show his humility before everyone, it is the first sign by which he may be recognized as a Christian. The Christian, instead of speaking of those passages in the work of Pushkin whose sense is still obscure and which can be interpreted in two ways, will speak of what is clear, of what was produced by him in the years of his intelligent manhood and not in his mad youth. He will quote his sublime stanzas to a pastor of the Church, where Pushkin says that even in those years when he was carried away by the vanities and charms of the world the sight alone of a servant of Christ struck him:

> *And even then the sly strings' sound*
> *I instantly broke,*
> *When your sublime voice*
> *Suddenly staggered me.*

A torrent of tears unexpectedly ran,
And the pure balm
Of your fragrant words
Consoled the wound of my shame.

And now from the spiritual heights
You stretch your hand to me.
And with gentle, loving strength
You humble my turbulent dreams.

My soul, scorched with your fire,
Rejected the ashes of earthly vanity,
And the poet thrills to the harp
Of Serafim in sacred terror.[3]

Such is the poetry of Pushkin which the Christian critic will
point to! Then his criticism will make sense and will do good: it
will strengthen the matter by showing how that man who contained in himself all the heterogeneous beliefs and questions of
his time which are so confusing, he who took us so far away from
Christ, how that very man, in the best and brightest moments of
his poetic vision, most loftily drew Christian sublimity out of
everything. But what is now the sense of criticism? I ask. What
use is there in troubling people by engendering doubt and suspicion of Pushkin? It is foolish to propose the most intelligent man
of his time as a nonacknowledger of Christianity! That man
upon whom the intellectual generation looks as a leader and a
progressive by comparison with other people! It is a good thing
that the critic was untalented and could not start a similar lie
going, and that Pushkin himself left a refutation of him in his
verses; but had it been otherwise, what other than unbelief in the
place of belief would he have propagated? That is what may
happen if you are one sided!

3. Gogol is quoting Pushkin's poem "When out of sport or idle boredom," written in 1830. Gogol omits the first stanza. How much the poem
has to do with "a pastor of the Church" is questionable.

My friend, God keep you from one-sidedness: with it a man causes harm everywhere: in literature, in the service, in the family, in the world—every place! The one-sided man is self-confident; the one-sided man is insolent; the one-sided man raises everybody against himself; the one-sided man cannot anywhere find the golden mean. The one-sided man cannot be a true Christian: he can be only a fanatic. One-sidedness in thoughts shows only that a man is still on the road to Christianity but has not attained it, because Christianity confers a many-sided mind. In short, God keep you from one-sidedness! Judiciously examine everything and remember that in each case there can be two absolutely opposed sides, of which one has so far not been exposed to you.

There is theater of divers kinds, just as the enthusiasm of the public is of two sorts: one is the enthusiasm generated when some ballet dancer raises her leg a little higher, and another is the enthusiasm generated when a powerful character raises by a stupendous speech the lofty feelings in a man a little higher. One thing is tears because a passing singer caresses a man's ear—tears which, I hear, are now shed in Petersburg even by anti-musicians; another thing again is tears when the spectator is thoroughly renewed by a living representation of the noblest deed of man and, upon leaving the theater, with new strength sets about his duty, seeing its execution as an heroic deed. My friend, we are summoned into this world, not in order to annihilate and destroy, but, like unto God Himself, to direct everything towards the good—even what man has already corrupted and turned to evil. There is no instrument in the world that should not be destined to the service of God. Even the trumpets, the tympani, the lyres and cymbals with which the pagans celebrated their idols, by the victories King David gained over them were turned to praising the true God, and still more did all Israel rejoice at hearing His praise upon those very instruments on which it had never before resounded.

1845

XV

SUBJECTS FOR THE LYRIC POETS OF THE PRESENT TIME

Two letters to N. M. Yazykov

1

Your poem "Earthquake" enraptured me. Zhukovsky is also en- thusiastic about it. In his opinion, it is the best not only of yours but of all Russian poems. To take an event of the past and to change it into the present—what a clever and rich idea! And the application to the poet concludes the ode in a way that fits each one of us, whatever his vocation may be, so that we may apply it to ourselves in these hard times of universal earthquake where everything has grown insecure through fear of the future! My friend, a living spring is opened before you. In your words to the poet,

> *And bring to trembling men*
> *The lofty prayer!*

there are contained words addressed to you. The secret of your muse is revealed to you. The present time is precisely the field for the lyric poet. By satire you will produce nothing; with a sim- ple picture of reality examined by the eye of a contemporary worldly man you will awaken no one: our century is gloriously asleep. No, look for an event in the past which resembles the present, force it to appear vividly and throw it in everyone's face, as it was in its time thrown by the Heavenly wrath; flay our present by the past, and your word will be clothed with twice its power: the past will appear more alive, and the present will raise its cry. Leaf through the Old Testament: there you will find each of our present events, you will see more clearly than day how the present has sinned before God, and the terrible judgment of God upon it so manifestly presented that the present will shake with trembling. You have instruments and ways: in your verse is a power which reproaches as it elevates. Just now both are necessary. It is necessary to encourage some and to reproach others: to encourage those who are confused by the fears and the callousness surrounding them; to reproach those who, at the holy moment of Divine wrath and sufferings everywhere, dare to abandon themselves to the turbulence of their passions and shameful pleasures. Your verses must be in the eyes of everyone like those letters traced in the air which appeared at the feast of Balthazar, which terrified everyone even before they could penetrate their meaning. And if you want to be still better understood by everyone, then, after having acquired the spirit of the Bible, descend with it, as with a torch, into the depths of the Russian past, and with that past strike the shame of the present, and at the same time deepen further in us that before which our shame becomes still more shameful. Your verse will not be dull, believe me; the past will lend you its colors and of itself will inspire you! It is so alive and so stirring in our chronicles.

Recently, a book has fallen into my hands, *An Imperial Progress*. One would think it dull, but it has words and names of imperial decorations, of rich fabrics and precious stones—a real treasure for a poet; each word should be enshrined in your verse. You will marvel at the jewels in our language: its sonority is already a gift; everything is grained and hard as pearls, and, really, the name is still more jewel-like than the thing itself. Yes, if you only ornament your verse with words of this kind you will lead the reader wholly into the past. As for me, after having read three pages of this book, it was as though I saw everywhere

a Tsar of olden times reverently going to evening services in all his antique imperial attire.
1844

2

I write to you under the influence of that same poem of yours, "Earthquake." For God's sake, do not abandon a work begun! Rereading the Bible attentively, acquire a knowledge of the Russian past and look at the present in its light. Many, many subjects will be offered to you, and it is a sin for you not to see them. Not for nothing did Zhukovsky call your poetry an ecstasy without any definite direction. It is a shame to waste your lyric power in the form of blank shots in the air when it was given to you to explode rocks and move cliffs. Look around you: today everything is a subject for the lyric poet; each man demands that he be appealed to lyrically; on whatever side you turn, you see that it is necessary either to reproach or to refresh someone.

Above all, reproach—with powerful, lyrical reproaches—intelligent but discouraged people. You will persuade them, if you show them the question in its true light, that is, that the man who gives in to discouragement is trash, for discouragement is cursed by God. The true Russian you will lead to inveigh against discouragement, you will raise him above the terrors and shakings of earth, as you raised the poet in your "Earthquake."

In powerful lyrical form appeal to the man who is splendid but asleep. Throw him a plank from the shore and cry to him with all your strength so that he may save his poor soul; he is already far from shore, carried by the paltriness of worldly life, carried by dinners, by dancers' legs, by daily sleep-producing drunkenness; insensibly shaped by flesh, he becomes flesh, with almost no soul. Shout aloud and show him the witch of age advancing upon him, made of an iron next to which iron itself is merciful, which neither gives nor returns a crumb of feeling. O, if you could read to him what my Plyushkin will say, if I attain to the third volume of *Dead Souls*.

In an angry dithyramb, heap ignominy upon the new usurer of modern times—his cursed luxury and his abominable wife, who ruins herself and her husband with her fashions and her finery, the despicable threshold of their rich house, the foul air breathed there—so that all the world may flee them like the plague, run away and never return.

In a triumphal hymn, exalt the unknown toiler who, to the honor of the lofty Russian race, although among grafters, still does not accept bribes, even when all the world accepts them. Exalt him and his family, his noble wife who would rather wear her old, unfashionable cap and be the object of others' laughter than permit her husband to be unjust and mean. Put forward their fine poverty, so that, like a holy thing, it may strike everyone's eyes and so that each of us may wish to be poor himself.

In your hymn, celebrate the giant who could issue only from the Russian land, who, suddenly awakened from his shameful sleep, becomes something other than what he was: in the sight of all spitting on his abominations and infamous vices, he will become the foremost champion of the good. Show how this heroic enterprise is accomplished in a really Russian soul; but show it so that the Russian nature in each cannot help vibrating and so that everyone, even those of the lowest and roughest estate, cries out, "Ah, what a stalwart!" feeling that he would be capable of a like deed himself.

Many, many are the subjects for a lyric poet—it is impossible to put them into a book, much less into a letter. The true Russian sentiment is dying out and there is no one to arouse it! Our boldness sleeps, our decisiveness and courage sleep, our firmness and power sleep, our intelligence sleeps amid the sluggishness and mollycoddling of the worldly life which has introduced us, under the name of enlightenment, to empty, petty innovations. Shake the sleep from your eyes and abolish sleep from others' eyes. Go on your knees before God and beg his wrath and his love! Wrath against what ruins man, love for the poor soul of the man who has been ruined and who ruins himself. You will find the words, the expressions will be found; fire, not words, will fly from your lips, as they did from the lips of the ancient prophets, if only, like them, you make it a matter of your own heart and blood, if only, like them, you bestrew your head with ashes and tear your clothes and sobbing supplicate God for the power and consecrate yourself to the salvation of your land, as they consecrated themselves to the salvation of their chosen people.

1844

XVI

COUNSELS

A letter to Shch

In instructing others, one instructs oneself. In the midst of my unhappy and difficult times, to which were added spiritual sufferings, I have had to carry on a far more active correspondence than I have ever had to do in the past. As though on purpose, it has happened that almost all those close to my soul have been shaken by internal events. All, as though by instinct, have turned to me, demanding my aid and counsel. Only since that time could I see the close relationship among these human souls. It is sufficient for one to have suffered himself for him to understand other sufferers and for him almost to know what must be said to them. Better yet—the intelligence itself is clarified: the formerly hidden attitudes and situations of people become known to one and their needs are made apparent.

Lately I have also happened to receive letters from people almost completely unknown to me, and I have given them answers which I would not have been able to give formerly. I am, however, no more intelligent than anyone else. I know people who are more intelligent and educated than I who could give much more useful advice than mine; but they do not do it, and they do not even know how to start doing it. Great is the God who makes us wise. And how does He make us wise? By that very grief which we flee and from which we seek to hide ourselves. It is by suffering and grief that we are destined to procure some grains of a wisdom impossible to acquire from books. But whoever has acquired one of these crumbs has not the right to conceal it from others. It is not yours but the property of God. God produced it in you; all the gifts of God are given to us so that we may serve our fellows: He commanded us to teach one another constantly. Consequently, do not halt, teach and give counsel! But if at the same time you want it to be useful to yourself, do it in the way that I think and as I am determined henceforth always to do it. All counsels and all admonitions that you have the opportunity to give to anyone, be it to a man on the lowest level of education with whom you can have nothing in common, address them to yourself at the same time, and what you counsel another, counsel yourself; the very reproach that you make against another make also against yourself. Believe me, it all reverts to you, and I do not know that there is one reproach with which you could not reproach yourself, if only you observe yourself intently. Act with a two-edged weapon! If you happen to become angry with someone, be angry at the same time with yourself, be it only for having been able to be angry with another. And do this without fail! In no circumstances take your eyes off yourself. Always have yourself as an object before others. Be an egoist in this connection! Egoism is not a bad characteristic; some people choose to give it a bad interpretation, but real truth is at the bottom of egoism. First look after yourself, and then after others; purify your own soul first, and then attempt to make others more pure.

1846

XVII

ENLIGHTENMENT

A letter to V. A. Zhukovsky

Once more I write to you en route. Brother, I thank you for everything! At the Tomb of Our Lord I will ask him to help me to return to you, although it be only in part, that mental good which you have dispensed to me. Have faith, and let not your heart be troubled! Your arrival in Moscow will be like a return to your own family. She will offer you your desired refuge, and there will be more tranquillity for you there than here. Neither the vain hubbub of the bustling world nor the thunder of carriages will disturb you: they will be careful to avoid the street where you live. If someone should come to visit you, whether he be an old friend or a man hitherto unknown to you, he will first ask you not to return his visit, fearing lest you lose a minute of your time. We know, and know well, how to honor those who are wholly devoted to the accomplishment of their task. Whoever has irreproachably and honestly used all his gifts, without allowing any of his faculties to doze off, without being idle for one moment in his life, whoever has kept his old age as green as his youth, while everyone around him was wasting it in frivolous temptations and young people were being transformed into puny old men—whoever does this has a right to courteous respect. In Moscow you will be like a patriarch, and all the young people will accept your old man's words as worth their weight in gold.

Your *Odyssey* will contribute much to the common good, I predict it to you. It will refresh contemporary man, weary of the disorder of his life and thought; in his eyes it will renew many things abandoned by him as obsolete and useless for his existence; it will return him to simplicity. But no less good, if not, indeed, even more, will be brought by those works to which you were inspired by God Himself and which you are sensibly keeping back. In them a common need is touched upon. Do not be embarrassed, but firmly look ahead! And do not be frightened by any disagreement you may meet. There is a conciliator in our land which is not yet visible to everyone—our Church. Already it is preparing to lay claim to its full rights and beginning to shine throughout the land. In it is everything necessary for a truly Russian life, in all respects, from the sovereign to the simple family: it is the framework for everything, the direction for everything, the legitimate and right way for everything. In my opinion, it is folly to introduce any innovation into Russia outside our Church without obtaining its blessing. It would be even absurd to inoculate our thought with any kind of European ideas, so long as it has not baptized them with the light of Christ. You will see how all that will suddenly be recognized by you and by everyone in Russia, by believers as well as by nonbelievers, since our Church reconciles them all.

It was the inscrutable will of Providence that an incomprehensible blindness should fall on many eyes. When I intently investigate the course of worldly events, I see all the wisdom of God in allowing the temporal division of the churches, commanding that one stand immutable, as though afar from men, while the other undergoes the same agitations as men; let the one not take into itself any innovation except those introduced by the Saints of the great epochs of Christianity and by the original Fathers of the Church, and let the other, changing and conforming to all the circumstances of time, to the soul and habits of people, introduce innovations, even those made by depraved, unholy bishops; let the one, for a time, die in a way to the world, and let the other, for a time, in a way take possession of the world; let the one, like the modest Mary, putting aside worldly cares, take its place at the feet of the Lord himself, in order the better to hear his words before adapting and transmitting them to men, and let the other, like the careful housekeeper Martha, hospitably fuss about with people, transmitting to them the word of the Lord unsupported by reason. The one has chosen the good part because she has for so long lent her ear to the word of the Lord, while bearing the reproaches of her short-sighted sister, who has dared to call her a *dead* cadaver, even lost and an apostate of the Lord. It is not easy to apply the word of Christ to men; it was indeed necessary that the Church herself had first to be profoundly penetrated by it.

In return, everything necessary for the present awakening of society is preserved in our Church. In its hands are the helm and rudder for the coming new order of things, and the more I enter into its heart, its mind, and its thought, the more I am astonished at its admirable ability to reconcile all contradictions that the Church of the West no longer has the power to reconcile. The western Church was sufficient for an early uncomplicated order; it could govern the world well enough and reconcile it with Christ in the name of the one-sided and incomplete development of humanity. But now that humanity has attained a more complete development of all its powers, of all its faculties, the good as well as the bad, it only alienates it from Christ: the more anxious it is for reconciliation, the more discord it brings, since its narrow beam of light has not the power to clarify all present-day subjects in all their facets. All the world realizes that, by its introduction of numberless human institutions, made by bishops who had still not attained a full and many-sided Christian wisdom through the holiness of their lives, it narrowed its view of life and the world and could not encompass them. The full and total view of life remained in the eastern Church, manifestly kept in reserve for the later and more complete education of man. She has room not only for the soul and heart of man, but also for his reason, in all its supreme powers; in her is the way and the road by which everything in man will turn into an harmonious hymn to the Supreme Being.

My friend, do not let anything trouble you! If present circumstances should be seventy-seven times more confused, our Church would still balance and unravel them. Already, in some mysterious way, even secular people who have sprung up among us begin to feel that there is some kind of treasure from which salvation comes—a treasure which is among us and which we do not see. Let the treasure sparkle, its luster will shine over everything. And the time is already not far off. Without thinking, we now repeat the word "enlightenment." And we have never even reflected on whence this word came and on what it means. This word does not exist in any other language; it is only in ours. "To enlighten" does not mean to teach, or to edify, or to educate, or even to illuminate, but to illuminate a man through and through in all his faculties and not in his intelligence alone, to take all his nature through a purifying fire. This word is borrowed from our Church, which has pronounced it for almost a thousand years, in spite of all the darkness and ignorant gloom surrounding it on every side, and it knows why it pronounces it. It is not for nothing that the bishop, in the celebration of the service, raising with one hand the three-branched candelabrum, which signifies the Holy Trinity, and with the other the two-branched candelabrum, which signifies the descent to earth of the Word in its double nature, divine and human, by them clarifies everything, pronouncing, "May the light of Christ enlighten all!" It is not for nothing either that at another moment of the service there loudly thunders forth, as though from Heaven, the words: "Lord of enlightenment!" and nothing more is added.

1846

XVIII

FOUR LETTERS TO DIVERS
PERSONS APROPOS *DEAD SOULS*

1

You are wrong to be indignant at the intemperate tone of some of the attacks on *Dead Souls*. There is a good side to it. Sometimes it is necessary to have embittered people against oneself. He who is captivated by the beauty of things does not see the faults in them and forgives everything; but he who is embittered does his utmost to unearth all the rottenness in us and bring it into the open so glaringly that you see it in spite of yourself. It so rarely befalls us to hear the Truth that for one grain of it we can forgive all the abusive voices by which it was pronounced. There is much justice in the criticisms of Bulgarin, Se(n)kowski, and Polevoi,[1] beginning with the advice given to me first to learn how to read and write in Russian and only then to write. It is true, if I had not been in a hurry to publish the manuscript and had kept it for a year, I would then have seen myself that it should not appear in the world in such a slovenly condition. Indeed, the very epigrams and the ridicules aimed at me were necessary to me, even though at first they cut me to the quick. Oh, how we need these continual nips and this abusive tone, and these sarcastic jibes which pierce us through! So much pettiness is hidden in the depths of our soul,

---

1. T. V. Bulgarin (1789–1859) and X. A. Polevoy (1801–1867), both writers and literary critics, had long been antagonists of Gogol's. For Se(n)kowski, see note 12 to "Introduction."

so much paltry self-love, so much touchy, nasty vanity, that at every moment we ought to be pricked, struck, beaten by all possible arms, and we must every moment thank the hand striking us.

I would have wished, however, for a little more criticism, not on the part of men of letters, but on the part of people of busy lives, on the part of practical people; as ill luck would have it, except for the men of letters nobody answered.

Meanwhile, *Dead Souls* made a great deal of noise, aroused much grumbling, cut many to the quick by its jibes, by its truth and justice, and by its caricature; it discussed an order of things which we all daily have before our eyes; it is full of blunders, anachronisms, and obvious ignorance of many subjects; indeed, cutting and offensive things were designedly placed in it: perhaps some one will rate me properly and in swearing and wrath tell me the truth of what I have attained.

If one soul had raised his voice! Anyone could have. And sensibly! The working bureaucrat could have clearly proven to me, in the sight of everyone, the improbability of the events I had depicted, by adducing two or three facts which have really occurred, thus refuting me better than in words, or he could have done it so as to support and justify the fairness of my account. The adducing of facts that have occurred is a better proof than mere words and literary verbiage. The businessman and the landowner could have done the same—in short, any literate person, whether he does not stir from his place or roams far and wide across all the face of the Russian land. Besides his personal point of view, every man, whatever be his place and rank in society, has an opportunity to see things from an angle from which no one but he can see them. On the occasion of *Dead Souls*, another incomparably more interesting book than *Dead Souls* could have been written by a mass of readers, and it could have taught not only me but the readers themselves, because—nothing may conceal this sin—we all know Russia very badly.

And if but one soul had begun to speak out in public! It was exactly as though everything had died out, as though Russia in fact was inhabited not by living but by *Dead Souls*. And they reproach me for knowing Russia badly! As though, by the strength of the Holy Spirit, I ought unfailingly to know everything that is done in all its corners—to learn it without having been taught! But by what means could I learn, I, a writer, already condemned by the vocation of a writer to a sedentary, secluded life, I, who am sick besides, and therefore compelled to live far from Russia, by what means could I learn? I could not learn from men of letters and journalists who are themselves secluded desk people. For a writer there is only one teacher—his readers. But the readers refused to teach me. I know that I will have a terrible account to render to God for not having performed my work as I should have, but I also know that others will render an account for me. And I do not speak in vain. God sees that I do not speak in vain!

1843

2

I had a presentiment that all the lyrical digressions in the poem would be taken in a false sense. They are so vague, they are so little in accord with the objects passing before the eyes of the reader, so irrelevant to the form and manner of the work as a whole, that they led both adversaries and defenders astray. All the passages in which I vaguely mentioned a writer were laid to my account; I even blushed at explanations of them in my favor. It serves me right! In no case should I have published a work which, even though not badly made, was sewn with white threads, like a dress a dressmaker has only brought for a fitting. I only marveled that I was so little reproached in regard to my art and creative knowledge. The angry temper of my critics was disturbed by this, unaccustomed as they are to close examination of how a work is built. One would have to show them how the monstrously long parts are connected with the others where the writer betrayed himself by not sustaining the tone he had adopted as his very own. No one even noticed that the last half of the book is less worked over than the first, that there are great gaps in it, that capital and important events have been condensed and abbreviated, unimportant and tangential ones spread out, and instead of the inner spirit of the whole work appearing, the mixed character of the parts and its scrappiness strike the eye. In short, it would have been possible to raise incomparably more efficient attacks, to rebuke me much more than I am now rebuked, and to rebuke to the point. But there was no talk of that. The talk was of the lyrical digressions, which the journalists in particular have attacked, seeing in them signs of presumption, of a boasting and a pride until now unheard of in any writer. I mean that passage in the last chapter where, having described the departure of Chichikov from the town, the writer, for a time abandoning his hero in the middle of the high road, puts himself in his place and, struck by the tedious monotony of the landscape, by our uninhabited, shelterless spaces and the sorrowful songs arising from every feature of the Russian land from sea to sea, in a lyrical appeal addresses himself to Russia herself, asking her for an explanation of this incomprehensible feeling with which he is filled, that is: wherefore and why does it seem to him as though everything in her, from inanimate things to animate, fixes its eyes on him and expects something from him? These words were taken for a pride and boasting unheard of till now, while they are neither the one nor the other. They are simply an awkward expression of a real feeling. It seems the same to me now. I have never been able to bear the doleful, lacerating sounds of our songs which rush across all of boundless Russian space. These sounds eat into my heart, and I marvel that everyone is not aware of the same thing. Whoever at the sight of these uninhabited, empty spaces unrelieved by village or home does not feel depressed, whoever in the doleful sounds of our songs does not hear painful rebukes to himself— indeed, to himself—either has fulfilled his duty as he should, or is not a Russian in his soul. Things must be seen as they are. Al-

most 150 years have elapsed since our sovereign Peter I cleared
our eyes by the purgatory of European enlightenment; he put in
our hands all the means and instruments of action, and still our
spaces remain just as empty, sorrowful, and unpeopled, just as
homeless and unfriendly all around us; just as though we still
have no home, no roof of our own but somewhere homeless pause
on a public road and breathe from Russia not the hearty natal
air which welcomes brothers but a kind of cold chill at a post
station where only a guard indifferent to everything is seen,
stalely responding: "No horses!"

What then? Who is to blame? We or the government? But the
government all this time acted ceaselessly. In witness whereof
there are whole tomes of enactments, statutes, and institutions, a
great number of houses built, a great number of books published,
a great number of institutions of all kinds instituted—educa-
tional, philanthropic, religious, and, in short, such as the government of no other state has set up. It is from on high that the demands resound, the responses from below. Sometimes demands
resound from on high that testify to the chivalric and magnanimous operations of many sovereigns acting even to the detriment
of their own interests. But how was all this responded to from below? It is a matter, you see, of adapting and applying whatever
idea it may be in such a way that it is accepted by and lodged
within us. An edict, as well-considered and precise as it may be, is
no more than a formal statement, if there is no sincere desire below to put it into practice in the proper way, as it must and
should be and as only he who has an enlightened understanding
of divine rather than human justice will be able to see clearly.
Otherwise, everything is turned into evil. The proof of it is all our
subtle swindlers and grafters who know how to bypass all decrees,
for whom a new decree is only a new source of profit, a new way
to encumber the exercise of business with greater complications, a
new way to trip people up. In short, wherever I turn, I see that
expediency is at fault, that is, our colleagues: either the fault is
that they are in a hurry, desiring too soon to become famous and

to grab a decoration; or the fault is that they rush forward too heatedly, desiring, in the Russian way, to give proof of their self-sacrifice; without any appeal to reason, without any reflection, in the heat of the affair they take over as though they are experts, and then suddenly, still in the Russian way, they grow cold witnessing their defeat. Or the fault, finally, is that, because of a slight insult to their vanity, they throw up their place, which they had once pursued so nobly, cede it to the first rogue who comes along—let him rob the people. In short, rare is he among us whose love of the good is sufficient for him to resolve to sacrifice his ambition and vanity to it, together with all the easily irritated details of his egoism, and lay down for himself one definite rule—to serve his country and not himself, every moment remembering that he accepted his place for the happiness of others and not for his own. On the contrary, these latter days, as though on purpose, Russians have attempted openly to exhibit all the shabby details of their irritated vanity. I do not know whether there are many among us who have done all that they ought to have done, who could openly say before the whole world that Russia has nothing to reproach them with, that not one soulless object in its empty spaces gazes at them reproachfully, that all are contented with them and nothing is expected of them. I only know that I have heard this reproach. And I hear it now. And that in my career as a writer, modest as it may be, it may be possible to do something more useful and more durable. What has resulted because the desire for the good has always dwelt in my heart and I took up the pen uniquely because of it? Have I fulfilled it? This my work which has just appeared under the title *Dead Souls*—has it produced the impression that it would have produced if it had been written as it should have been? My personal thoughts, simple, unpuzzling thoughts, I did not know how to transmit, and I myself gave grounds for these misinterpretations, and on the harmful rather than the useful side. Whose fault? Can I really say that the petitions of my friends urged me on, or the impatient desires of elegant amateurs charmed by empty, transitory sounds? Can I really say that circumstances squeezed me and, desiring to procure the money necessary for my subsistance, I had to hasten to a premature issue of my book? No, no circumstances can shake one who has resolved to fulfill his task honestly; he will stretch out his hand and ask for alms if it comes to that, but he will ignore passing censures as well as the vain social niceties of the world. He who corrupts a task necessary to his country for the vain social niceties of the world does not love his country. I recognized the contemptible weakness of my character, my mean cowardice, the impotence of my love, and that is why I heard the painful reproach addressed to me by all those things missing in Russia. But a higher power raised me: it was not irreparable faults, not even the empty spaces which had inflicted melancholy on my soul, ravishing me by the great scope of their space, by their wide field of action. From my soul this appeal was uttered to Russia: "How could one not be your hero when there is a place for him to display himself?" This was not said for the sake of the picture or as a boast: I really felt it; I feel it now.

In Russia, now, it is possible to make oneself a hero at every step. Every rank and place demands heroism. Each of us has so disgraced the holiness of his rank and position (all positions are holy) that heroic powers are necessary to lift them to their legitimate height. I perceive that great vocation which is not now possible for any other people, which is possible for the Russians alone, because before them alone is there such scope and their soul alone is acquainted with heroism—that is why that exclamation was wrenched out of me, and it was taken for vainglory and presumption!

1843

3

You, you who are such an expert and knowledgeable man, you are inclined to set me the same empty questions which others know how to set. Half of them are concerned with things that are still in the future. What is the use of a curiousity like this? One question alone is wise and worthy of you, and I wish that others had set it to me, although I do not know whether I can answer it wisely. Here is the question: Why are the heroes of my last works, and especially those of *Dead Souls*, although far from being portraits of real persons, although their characteristics are so unattractive, close to the soul, without anyone's knowing why, just as though some sort of spiritual circumstance had participated in their composition? A year ago it would have been awkward for me to answer on this point, even to you. Now I say everything directly: my heroes are close to the soul because they come from the soul; all my last works are the story of my own soul. In order to explain all this better, I will define myself to you as a writer.

I have been much interpreted, most of my facets discussed, but no one has defined my principal essence. Only Pushkin perceived it. He always told me that no other writer has the gift of representing the banality of life so clearly, of knowing how to depict the banality of a banal man with such force that all the *petty details* which escape the eyes *gleam large* in the eyes. That is my principal virtue, belonging to me alone, precisely that which is in no other writer. Only afterwards was it deepened in me by its union with some spiritual circumstance. But I was in no condition to reveal it then, even to Pushkin.

This characteristic appeared with greater strength in *Dead Souls*. *Dead Souls* did not frighten Russia and make such a noise in it because it laid bare some of its wounds or its internal sicknesses, nor even because it presented a shocking picture of evil triumphant and innocence conquered. Not at all. My heroes are not at all villains; if I had only added one good feature to any one of them the reader would have been reconciled with them all. But the banality of all of them frightened my readers. What frightened them is that my heroes follow one after the other, one more banal than the other, that there is not one consoling scene, that there is nowhere for the poor reader to rest and take a breath, and, after having read the whole book, it seems exactly as though he were emerging from some stifling cellar into God's light. I would sooner have been forgiven if I had presented pictures of monsters: but banality I was not forgiven. The Russian is more frightened of his insignificance than of all his vices and short-comings. A splendid event! A capital fear! Whoever is strongly disgusted at his insignificance probably has everything opposite to insignificance. Thus, this is my principal virtue; but this vir-tue, I say again, would not have developed in me with such strength if my own spiritual circumstance and my own spiritual history had not been united with it. None of my readers knew that while laughing at my heroes, he was laughing at me.

There was not one overpowering vice in me which appeared more visibly than all my other vices, just as there was not one picturesque virtue which could have given me a picturesque ap-pearance: but rather, instead of that, in me was a collection of all possible abominations, a little of each, and besides, in such num-bers as I have thus far not encountered in any individual. God has given me a many-sided nature. He has also inspired in me, since my birth, some good characteristics; but best of them all, for which I do not know how to thank Him, was *the desire to be better.* I have never loved my bad qualities, and if God's divine love had not commanded that they be revealed to me gradually, a little at a time, instead of being revealed suddenly and immedi-ately before my eyes, at a time when I still had no understanding of His infinite mercy, I would have hanged myself. In proportion to the rate at which they were revealed, the desire to be delivered of them was strengthened in me by a wonderful impulse from on high; by an extraordinary spiritual event, I was driven to transfer them to my heroes. What the nature of that event was you may not know: if I had seen any use in it for anyone, I would already have announced it. From that moment on, I began to provide my heroes with my own rottenness in addition to their abomina-tions. This is how it was done: taking one of my bad qualities, I pursued it under another name and in another field, I tried to represent it as a mortal enemy who had inflicted the worst outrage on me, I pursued it in anger, with sarcasm and anything else that fell to my hand. If anyone had seen the monsters which first issued from my pen, he would promptly have shuddered for me. It is enough for me to tell you that when I began to read the first chapters of *Dead Souls* to Pushkin, in the form in which they formerly were, Pushkin, who always laughed at my readings (he loved laughter), slowly became gloomier and gloomier, and finally he was completely somber. When the reading was finished, he uttered in an anguished voice: "God, how sad is our Russia!" This amazed me. Pushkin, who knew Russia so well, had not noticed that it was all a caricature and my own invention! Then I saw what something whose spring is the soul and is a spiritual truth means, how frightening a sight it can be to a man when he is presented with shadows, and how much more threatening is *the absence of light*. From this time forward I began to think only of how to mitigate the painful impression which *Dead Souls* had produced. I have seen that many abominations are not worth anger; it is better to show all their insignificance, which must be their fate forever. Besides, I wanted to test what a normal Russian would say if he should be regaled with his own banality. Since the plan of *Dead Souls* had been adopted long before, for the first part I needed worthless people. These worthless people, however, are not simply portraits of worthless people; on the contrary, assembled in them are the traits of those who consider themselves better than others, like generals degraded to the ranks. Here, besides my own, are the traits of many of my friends, and yours too. I will prove this to you later in case you find it necessary; until then it is my secret. I had to pick up from all the fine people I know everything banal and nasty that they had caught accidentally and to restore it to its legitimate owners. Do not ask why all the first part had to be *banality* and why every person in it had to be banal: the other volumes will give you the answer—and that is all! The first part, despite all its imperfections, has done the chief thing: in everyone it has inspired a loathing for my heroes and their worthlessness; it has caused me a certain necessary melancholy at the sight of it all. For the moment, this is enough for me; I am after nothing else. Of course, it would all have been more substantial if I had been less in a hurry to publish it and had polished it better. My heroes were still not completely detached from me, and therefore did not receive independence. I had still not lodged them firmly in the land where they were to exist, they had still not entered into the round of our customs, furnished with all the circumstances of real Russian life. The entire book is still no more than a prematurely born child; but its spirit is already invisibly spread abroad, and even its premature appearance may be useful to me in that it will force my readers to point out all my blunders concerning social legislation and particular usages in Russia. So if you, instead of posing empty questions to me (with which half your letter was stuffed, and which had no end other than the satisfaction of an idle curiosity), if you had instead assembled sensible observations on my book, both yours and those of other intelligent people, busy, like you, with experience and a sensible life, if you had been able to adjoin accounts of events and anecdotes such as have occurred either in your immediate neighborhood or throughout the province, in confirmation or denial of what is in my book, so that it would have been possible for me to tidy up tens of them on every page—then you would have done a good deed, and I would have given you hearty thanks. How my horizon would have been enlarged! How my mind would have been refreshed and how successfully my work would have gone forward! But what I ask no one fulfills; no one considers my questions important but only esteems his own; and some even demand sincerity and frankness of me, not understanding what it is they demand. And why this idle curiosity to know beforehand, and this idle haste without object and without goal which I notice is already beginning to infect you? See how in nature everything is performed decorously and wisely, by harmonious law, and how reasonably everything proceeds, one thing from another! Only we, God knows why, are confounded. Everyone is in a hurry. Everyone is feverish. Well, have you thoroughly weighed your words, "A second volume is now vitally necessary"? Solely because of the general displeasure with me I should hurry the second volume as foolishly as I hurried the first. Have I really gone entirely out of my mind? I need this displeasure; it is in his displeasure that a man will express something to me. And what led you to the conclusion that a second volume is necessary right now? Have you really stolen into my head? Have you sensed the existence of a second volume? For you it is needed now, but for me not for two or three years, because of the rapid movement of circumstances and times. Which of us is right? He who already has the second volume in his head or he who does not even know of what the second volume will consist? What a strange fashion has now been established in Rus! The very man who is indolent, too lazy for the matter at hand, hurries someone else, exactly as though the someone else should be overjoyed by his friend's indolence. Hardly is a man seriously occupied with something before he is immediately pressed on all sides and given a good rating if he does something foolish; they do not say to him, "Why all the hurry?"

But I have finished my sermon. I have answered your intelligent question and even said more than I have said to anyone else. Do not think, however, after these confessions, that I am just such a monster as my heroes. No, I do not resemble them. I love the good, and I search for it and burn with it; but I do not love my abominations and I do not hold their hands, as my heroes do; I do not love those meannesses of mine which separate me from the good. I struggle, and will struggle, with them, and with the help of God I will expel them. What the foolish, clever men of the world turn out is nonsense, professing that a man may be educated only in school and that afterwards it is not possible for his features to be changed: such a foolish idea could only be formed in a foolish, worldly noddle. I have already got rid of many of my abominations by transmitting them to my heroes, I have turned them to ridicule in them and compelled others to laugh at them as well. I tore myself away from many things because, having deprived them of the fine airs and chivalrous masks under which our loathsomeness struts, I put them beside all the abominations which are apparent to everyone. When I confess myself before He Who commanded me to come into the world and free myself from my faults, I see many vices in myself; but they are already not such as they were but a year ago: a holy power has helped me to tear myself away from them.

I advise you not to ignore these words but, after having read my letter, to remain alone for a few minutes and, far away from everyone, look at yourself thoroughly, passing all your life in review in order to verify the truth of my words. In my answer you will find an answer also to other questions, if you look more intently. It will also explain to you why up to now I have not offered the reader consoling scenes and have not chosen virtuous people for my heroes. They are not invented by the mind. As long as you still somewhat resemble them, as long as you have not acquired constancy and firmly established some good qualities in your soul—all that your pen writes will be a dead thing, as far from truth as earth is from Heaven. As for inventing nightmares, I have not invented any either; these nightmares weigh on my soul: what was in my soul is what issued forth from it.

1843

4

The second part of *Dead Souls* was burned because it was necessary. "Lest the seed die, it will not live again," says the Apostle. It is first necessary to die in order to be resurrected. It was not easy to burn the work of five years, produced with such painful effort, where each line was the result of a shock, where was much of what had constituted my best thoughts and had occupied my soul. But all has been burned, and, further, at that very time when, seeing my own death before me, I desired so much to leave after me something which would be a better reminiscence of myself. I thank God for having given me the strength to do it. Immediately that the flame had carried away the last pages of my book, its content suddenly was resurrected in a purified and lucid form, like the Phoenix from the pyre, and I suddenly saw in what disorder was what I had considered ordered and harmonious. The appearance of the second volume in the form in which it was would sooner have done harm than good. It is necessary to consider not the enjoyment of some lovers of art and men of letters, but all the readers for whom *Dead Souls* was written. To describe some fine characters who are supposed to demonstrate the nobility of our race would lead to nothing. It would only arouse empty pride and vanity. Many of us today, especially among the young, have begun to pride themselves immeasurably on our Russian virtues and do not in the least think of deepening and cultivating them in themselves, but rather of putting them up for show and saying to Europe, "Look, foreigners; we are better than you!" This boasting is the destroyer of everything. It irritates others and will cause harm to the boaster himself. The best deed may be turned to dirt if you simply boast of it and swagger about it. And among us, even before something is done, it is boasted of! Boasted of in anticipation! No, in my opinion a temporary despondency and melancholy is better than presumption. In the first case, a man at least sees how contemptible he is, sees his base insignificance, and, in spite of himself, he remembers God who draws all things out of the depths of nothingness; in the second case, he runs away from himself straight into the arms of the devil, the father of presumption who deludes man by illusions of his own virtues. No, there are times when it is not possible to turn society, or even one generation, towards the beautiful, so long as it is not shown the depths of its present abasement; there are times when one may not even speak of the sublime and the beautiful, if the way and roads to it for everyone are not shown clear as day. This last circumstance was badly and weakly developed in the second volume of *Dead Souls,* where it should have been the chief thing, and therefore it was burned. Do not judge me and do not draw conclusions: you would be in error, like those of my friends who, having made their ideal writer out of me, according to their idea of a writer, began to demand that I answer to their created ideal. God created me and did not hide my purpose from me. I was not at all born to produce an epoch in the sphere of literature. My business is simpler and lower: my business is above all what every man must think about, not just myself. My business is *the soul and the durable things in life.* That is why the form of my actions must be firm, and what I write must be firm. There is no need for me to hurry; let others hurry! I burn when it is necessary to burn, and, probably, I act as I must, because I never start anything without prayers. Your apprehensions concerning my weak health, which would not perhaps allow me to write a second volume, are pointless. It is true that my health is very weak; at times it weighs so heavily upon me that without God I could not bear it. To the exhaustion of my strength is added so much sensitivity to cold that I do not know how I will ever get warm: I should move about a good deal—I have not the strength. I hardly have an hour in the day for work, and I am not always fresh for it. But my hope is not a bit diminished. It is He Who by pride, ailments, and obstacles has quickened the development of my powers and my thoughts, without which I would never have conceived my work, it is He Who has formed the greater half of it in my brain, it is He Who will give me the strength to accomplish the rest—and put it down on paper. I am decrepit in body but not in soul. In my soul, on the contrary, everything is getting stronger and becoming firmer; my body also will get stronger. I believe that, if the right time comes, in several weeks I will accomplish that on which I have spent five sick years.

1846

XIX

IT IS NECESSARY TO LOVE RUSSIA

From a letter to Count A. P. Tolstoy

Without the love of God no one can be saved, and you have not the love of God. It is not in a monastery that you will find it; only those enter a monastery who have been called there by God himself. Without the will of God, one cannot love him. Besides, how can one love Him Whom no one has seen? By what prayers and what efforts can we implore this love of Him? Look about you—how many good and fine people there now are in the world who evidently strive for that love and feel only hardness and futility in their souls. It is hard to love One Whom no one has ever seen. Christ alone brings and proclaims this mystery to us: that it is in love for our brothers that we obtain love for God. It suffices solely to love them as Christ has commanded, and the love of God will come of itself. Go into the world and acquire love for your brothers.

But how can we love our brothers, how can we love men? The soul desires only to love the beautiful, and poor men are so imperfect, there is so little beauty in them! How shall we do it? Thank God, above all, that you are a Russian. For the Russian, at the present time, there is a way; that way is Russia herself. If only the Russian loves Russia and everything there is in Russia! It is to this love that God Himself now directs us. Without the maladies and sufferings that have accumulated in such numbers

111

in her, and of which we are guilty, not one of us would feel compassion for her. And compassion is already the beginning of love. The cries against the outrages, the lies and the bribes are not simply the indignation of noble men against blackguards, but the wail of all the earth on learning that a foreign enemy has broken in in great numbers, is scattered among our homes and lays his heavy yoke upon every man; those who benevolently took these terrible enemies into their homes already want to be free of them and do not know how to do it. Everything merges into one tremendous wail and already those who were indifferent are moved. But still no sincere love is perceived in all that, and besides, it is not in you. You still do not love Russia: you still know only how to grieve, to feel your ears irritated by all the badness committed in her; all that produces only a stale vexation, a despondency in you. No, this is still not love, and you are still far from love, this is still only a portent of it, but at a great distance. No, if you will really love Russia, it is when this myopic thought, which has arisen among many honest and even highly intelligent people— that in our time they can do nothing for Russia, and that, besides, they are absolutely useless to it—disappears, it is then, on the contrary, that you will feel, in all its strength, that love is all-powerful and with it everything is possible. No, if you really love Russia, you will burst to serve her; you will be not like a governor but like a justice of the peace—the last post that anyone seeks in her you will accept, preferring a little activity in her to all your present lazy and idle life. No, you do not yet love Russia. And not loving Russia, you do not love your brothers, you are not burning with love for God, and not burning with love for God, you are not saved.

1844

XX

IT IS NECESSARY
TO TRAVEL THROUGH RUSSIA

From a letter to Count A. P. Tolstoy

There is no higher title than that of monk, and God honors some of us with a day when we can don the humble black chasuble, which is so desired by my soul that the very thought of it is a joy for me. But it cannot be done without the call of God. In order to acquire the right to withdraw from the world, one must know how to take leave of the world. "Distribute all your belongings to the poor and then step into the monastery"—this is what is said to everyone going there. You have riches, you can distribute them to the poor; but I, what have I to distribute? My riches are not in money. God has helped me to accumulate a few intellectual and spiritual goods; He has given me some abilities which are useful and necessary to others—consequently, I ought to distribute this property to those who do not possess it, and then enter the monastery. But you do not receive that right by the simple distribution of your money. If you had been attached to your riches and if it were painful for you to part with them, then it would be another matter; but they leave you cold, at present they are nothing to you—where, then, would be your exploit and your sacrifice? Or does throwing a useless object out of the window mean doing good to your brother, understanding good in the lofty Christian sense? No, for you as for me the doors of this desired cloister are locked. Your monastery is Russia! Mentally clothe yourself in the black chasuble and, completely mortifying yourself for yourself, but not for her, go forward to work within her. She now calls her sons more loudly than ever before. Her soul is ill and the cry she raises is that of her spiritual illness. My friend! either your heart is insensible, or you do not know what Russia is for a Russian. Remember that when misfortune came to her the monks left the monasteries and ranged themselves with others to save her. The monks Oslyabya and Peresvet, with the blessing of their Father Superior, took swords in their hands, which is loathsome to a Christian, and died on the bloody field of battle,[1] while you do not want to take up the career of a peaceful citizen. And where? In the very heart of Russia. Do not excuse yourself by your lack of ability; you possess much of what is now needful and necessary for Russia. A former governor of two entirely different provinces, you fulfilled your functions, despite your faults at that time, better than many, you amassed direct and positive knowledge about internal administrative matters, and you got to know Russia in its true light. But that is not the chief thing, and I would not urge you so to serve, despite all your knowledge, if I did not see in you one virtue which, in my opinion, is more meaningful than all the others—the virtue of knowing, without troubling yourself about anything, without working yourself, almost idling, how to compel all others to work. With you everything was set in motion quickly and lightly; and when someone asked you in amazement, "How did this happen?" you answered, "It is all because of the officials, I have happened upon good officials who give me nothing to do myself." And when the moment came for the presentation of rewards, you always helped your officials out, ascribing everything to them and nothing to yourself. That is your principal virtue, without speaking of your skill in choosing these same officials. It is not astonishing that

1. The monks Oslyabya and Peresvet were monks of the Trinity Monastery at Zagorsky whose Abbot was St. Sergius of Radonezh. They were heroes of the battle of Kulikovo Pole in 1380 against the Tatar Khan Mamai.

your officials strained all their powers for you and that one of them worked until he contracted consumption and died, although you tried to drag him away from his labor. What would a Russian not do when his chief treats him this way! This virtue of yours is only too necessary now, precisely now, in this time of selfishness, when every chief thinks only of how to advance himself and ascribes everything to himself alone. I say to you that this virtue makes you more than necessary to Russia . . . and it is your great sin that you do not perceive it! A sin would be mine if I did not show this virtue to you. It is your best property; those who have nothing ask it of you, and you, like a miser, lock it up and pretend you are deaf. Let us admit that it would now be indecent for you to occupy the same place you occupied ten years ago, not because it is too low for you—thank God, you have no ambition and in your eyes no service is too low—but because your abilities, having been developed, demand another food, a career of wider scope. But are there no places and careers in Russia? Open your eyes and look around attentively, you will find them. You need to travel through Russia. Ten years ago you knew it; this is no longer enough. In ten years more events have occurred in Russia than occur in half a century in another state. You yourself, living abroad, have noticed that for the last two or three years entirely different kinds of people have begun to come from her, in no way resembling those whom you knew not long ago. In order to get to know what present-day Russia is, it is indispensable to travel through it oneself.

Do not trust what anyone says. The only true thing is that never before in Russia has there been such an extraordinary variety and disparateness of opinion and belief among its people, never before has the difference in instruction and education so alienated one from another and produced such a discord in everything. Through all this a wind of scandal has blown, of empty, superficial deductions, of foolish gossip, of one-sided, worthless conclusions. All that has bewildered and confused everyone's opinions on Russia to the point that one cannot definitely believe anyone. It is necessary to get to know it oneself; it is necessary to travel through Russia. This is of particular importance for one who has lived for some time far from her and has returned with undimmed and fresh eyes. He will see many things a man does not see when he is in his own pond, excited by and sensitive to a burning concern of the moment.

This is how you should make your voyage: first of all, get out of your head all your opinions on Russia, whatever they may be; repudiate the conclusions that you have already drawn; present yourself knowing exactly nothing, and travel as though in a new land unknown to you up to that time. In the same way that a Russian traveler arriving in some celebrated European city hurries to see all its antiquities and famous sights, in the same way, and with even greater curiosity, after you have arrived in the chief town of a district or province, strive to get to know the sights. They are not in architectural works and antiquities but in people. I swear to you that a man is worth being considered with greater curiosity than a factory or a ruin. Only endeavor to look for him with a drop of brotherly love, and you will not be able to tear yourself away from him, he will appear so interesting to you. First make the acquaintance of those who constitute the cream of each town or region; there are two or three in every town. In many ways they will be like an index of the whole town, so that it will be apparent to you where and in what places to make the greatest observations on things as they are. By conversing with a progressive man in each class (they will all be willing to chat with you and unbosom themselves, or almost do so) you will learn what classes mean in their present form. An efficient and sharp merchant will immediately explain to you what the merchants in that town are; a respectable and sober petty bourgeois will give you an understanding of the petty bourgeoisie. From an administrative employee you will learn how business is going. And the general color and spirit of society you will perceive yourself. However, do not rely too much on progressive people, you will do better to seek to question two or three persons of

every class. Do not forget that these days everyone is at odds
with everyone else, and that they all lie and calumniate one another ruthlessly. You will be intimate with the clergy immediately, because in general you will make their acquaintance
quickly; from them you will get to know the others. And if you
travel in this fashion through the chief towns and places of Russia, you will see, clear as day, where and in what place you can be
useful and what position you should ask for. In the course of
your journey you can do much good, if you want to. During your
trip you will find more opportunities for Christian action than
you would meet in a monastery. Most important, in pleasant conversation, pleasing everyone, you will be able, as an outsider, a
newcomer, to be a third conciliating party. You know how important this is, how necessary it is today in Russia and what a
lofty action it is. Our Savior values this person higher almost
than all others; He frankly calls peacemakers sons of God. And
among us a career is open to peacemakers everywhere. Everyone
quarrels: the nobles among themselves like cats and dogs; the
merchants among themselves like cats and dogs; the petty bourgeoisie among themselves like cats and dogs; the peasants, if they
are not forced by some impelling force to work together, among
themselves like cats and dogs. Even honest and good people are
in discord among themselves; it is only among rogues that one
sees something like friendship and union, when one or another of
them has the police at his heels. There is a career for the conciliator everywhere. Do not be afraid, it is not difficult to conciliate. It
is difficult for people to pacify themselves, but as soon as a third
party comes between them he immediately pacifies them. That is
why, among us, the court of arbitration has always been so
strong; a true product of our land, this court up to now has succeeded more than all others. In the nature of man, and especially
of the Russian, there is a wonderful quality: immediately that he
notices that someone else is somewhat inclined to him or mani-
fests some leniency towards him, he is ready almost to ask his
pardon. No one wants to give in first, but it is enough for one to

make a magnanimous decision for another to long to outdo his magnanimity. That is why among us an end can be put more quickly than elsewhere to chronic quarrels and lawsuits, if only there is a truly noble man between the litigants, someone who is both respected by all and is an expert of the human heart. But, I repeat, it is the conciliator who is now needed: if just a few honest people, who because of their differences of opinion concerning some subject thwart each other's actions, would agree to hold out their hands to each other, how badly it would go for the rogues. Thus, these are some of the actions which can be offered at each step of your trip through Russia.

There are others no less important. You can render a great service to the clergy of those towns through which you pass by making them better acquainted with the society in which they live, by leading them to a knowledge of those things and those deceits of which contemporary man does not speak in confession, considering them to be outside the Christian life. This is of great necessity, because many of the clergy, as I know, dejected by the number of indecencies which have arisen these days, are almost persuaded that today no one listens to them, that their words and their sermons are dropped into a void, and that evil has pushed its roots so deep that no one can any longer even think of destroying them. That is unjust. The man of today sins, in effect, incomparably more than before, but he sins not by excess of depravity, nor by insensibility, nor because he wants to sin, but because he does not see his sins. Still not clearly revealed is the terrible truth of our century—that everyone, without exception, sins, except that they do not sin directly but obliquely. The preacher himself still does not entirely perceive this, which is why his sermon falls into a void and people are deaf to his words. To say: "Do not steal, do not make a show of luxury, do not trust in bribes, pray and give charity to the beggar," is now nothing and accomplishes nothing. Besides each person's saying "I know that quite well," he is justified in his own eyes and almost calls himself a saint. He says, "As for stealing, I never steal: leave your watch, ten rubles, anything you want, right in front of me—I will not touch them; I have even dismissed my servant for thieving; of course I live in luxury, but I have neither children nor kinsmen, I have no one for whom to save; through my luxury I even supply something useful—bread to workers, artisans, merchants, and manufacturers; I accept bribes only from the rich, who themselves ask about them, and it does not ruin them; as for prayer, I pray, and look at me, I am in Church, I cross myself and prostrate myself. As for help, I help: there is not one beggar who leaves my house without a penny, and I have never refused a donation to a charitable institution." In short, he considers himself not only right after this sermon, but he prides himself on his sinlessness.

But if the curtain before him is raised, and he is shown that he is a part of those horrors which he indirectly rather than directly causes, then he will speak otherwise. Say to the honest but myopic rich man that, by adorning his house and acquiring the habits of a great lord, he does harm: his temptation inspires others who are less rich with the desire to keep up with him, so that they will not only ruin their own substance but also the property of others, they will rob and ruin others utterly; then present to him one of those horrible spectacles of famine in Russia which will make his hair stand on end, one which would not occur if he were not living as a great lord, giving a tone to society and turning the heads of others. Also show everyone our dandies who do not like to appear anywhere in the same clothes twice, and who, before wearing out the old ones, pick out a pile of new ones, keeping up with the tiniest deviation of fashion—show them that they do not sin because they indulge in this vanity and waste money, but because they have made this way of life a necessity for others, that for it some woman's husband has extorted bribes from a brother official (let us assume that this official is rich; but in order to get the bribe he has had to perch on someone less rich, and he, in his turn, on some assessor or local policeman, and the local policeman, without wanting to, will have had to coerce the low and the indigent); then show all the dandies the spectacle of famine. Then their minds will no longer be preoccupied with hats or fashionable clothes; they will see that they have not saved themselves from their terrible responsibility before God, neither by the penny thrown to a beggar nor even by the philanthropic institutions which they have established in the towns for the ravaged provinces. No, a man is not insensible, a man may progress, if you only show him things as they are. He may now progress further than ever before, because his nature has softened, half his faults come from ignorance, not from depravity. He will kiss as a savior the one who compels him to turn his eyes upon himself. Only let the preacher gently raise the curtain and show him but one of the crimes that he commits at every instant, and he will immediately be divested of the instinct to flatter himself that he is sinless; he will no longer seek to justify his luxury by base and wretched sophisms, pretending that it is necessary so that artisans may procure bread. He will then realize that to ravage half a village or half a district in order to furnish work for some cabinetmaker is an idea which could be formed only in the empty head of a nineteenth-century economist and not in the sane head of an intelligent man. And what if the preacher brings up the whole chain of innumerable indirect crimes that are committed by imprudence, by pride and presumption, and shows all the danger of the present time, in which a person can at once ruin many souls as well as his own; in which, without being dishonorable, it is possible to compel others to be dishonorable and scoundrelly by his imprudence alone; in short, what if he shows just a little of how dangerously everything is going? No, people will not be deaf to his word, not a word of his preaching will disappear into thin air. And you can bring many priests to this by giving them an account of all the deceits of people of our time that you learn on your way. But it is not only for priests, you can work the same benefit for other people. This information is now needed by everyone.

Life must be shown to man—life, from the angle of its present problems and not those of the past—life, looked at not with the superficial gaze of a worldly man but weighed and appraised by an expert who has gazed at it with the lofty gaze of a Christian. Great is the ignorance of Russia within Russia. Everyone lives in foreign reviews and newspapers, not in his own land. Town does not know town, man man; people living separated only by a partition live as though separated by seas. In the course of your voyage you can get to know them and have mutually beneficial exchanges of information, like an efficient merchant: the information you imbibe in one town you can sell in another at a profit, enriching everyone and at the same time enriching yourself most of all. Exploit after exploit is proposed to you at every step, and you do not see it! Wake up! A blindfold is on your eyes! Do not be enticed by love for yourself in your soul. What servant can be attached to a master who is far away from him and for whom he has not yet worked personally? The child is so strongly loved by his mother because she carried him so long inside herself, did her best for him, and endured everything for him. Wake up! Your monastery is Russia!

1845

XXI

WHAT THE WIFE OF A PROVINCIAL GOVERNOR IS

A letter to Madame A. O. Smirnova

I am glad that your health is better; as for my health—but let us put our health aside: we must forget it just as we must forget ourselves.

So you have returned again to your provincial capital. You must love it with new strength: it is yours, it is entrusted to you, it ought to be your native town. It is wrong for you to begin to think again that your presence in it is perfectly useless in so far as public activity is concerned, that the society is rotten down to its roots. You are simply tired—that is all. There is activity for the wife of a provincial governor everywhere, at each step. She even has an impact when she does nothing. You know yourself that action is not in bustle and precipitant rushing about. There are two living examples before you, whom you have cited yourself. Your predecessor Mme J———bequeathed a pile of charitable institutions and at the same time a pile of fussy correspondence, housekeepers, secretaries, larceny, confusion. She became famous as a benefactress in Petersburg, and caused a mess in K———. But the Princess O———, previously the wife of the governor in your very town of K———, bequeathed no establishments, nor asylums, she did not become famous outside the town, she did not even have any influence on her husband and did not mix in matters of government and officialdom; however, unto this very day, no one in the town can remember her without tears, and everyone, from the merchant to the last poor landless peasant, still repeats today, "No, there will never be another Princess O————!" But who repeats this? The very town for which you suppose it is impossible to do anything, this very society which you consider spoiled forever. Is it really impossible to do anything? You are tired, that is all! Tired because you were too ardent, you relied too much on your own strength, feminine haste carried you away. . . . I repeat to you what I said before: your influence is strong, you are the first person of the town, you will be imitated in everything, down to the last trinkets, thanks to the habit of aping fashion and our Russian habit of aping in general. In everything you will be the legislator. If you manage your own task well, you will exercise an influence, because you will compel others to accomplish their tasks better. Banish luxury (so long as there is nothing else to do), this is already a good action; besides, it requires neither effort nor expense. Do not miss one meeting or ball, go to them just to display yourself in the same dress; wear the same dress three, four, five, six times. Boast only of what is cheap and simple. In short, banish this nasty, foul luxury which is the ulcer of Russia, the source of bribery, of injustice, and of all the abominations among us. If you succeed in doing no more than this, you will already be of more vital benefit than Princess O————. And this does not even demand any sacrifice, does not even take any time.

My friend, you are tired. I see from your earlier letters that, to begin with, you have already succeeded in doing much good (if you had not been so much in a hurry, there would have been still more), rumors about you have already spread beyond K————; some of them have reached me. But you are still too much in haste, you are still too carried away, every annoyance and vileness still stirs and strikes you too hard. My friend, remember my words, of whose justice you say you are convinced: look at the town as a doctor looks at a leper hospital. Look at it in the same way, but add something further; namely, convince yourself that all the sick people in the leper hospital are in fact your kinsmen and people close to your heart, and then everything will change before you: you will be reconciled with people and will be at war only with their illnesses. Who told you that their illnesses are incurable? You told it to yourself, because you found no remedy at hand. So, are you really an omniscient doctor? Why did you not request help of someone else? Is it really in vain that I asked you to report everything in your town to me, to acquaint me with your town so that I might have a complete concept of your town? Why have you not done this, especially since you yourself are convinced that I could have more influence in many things than you; since you yourself have attributed to me an understanding which is not common to all people; since, finally, you yourself say that I have helped you more than anyone else in your emotional affairs? Do you really think that I would not be able to help your incurably ill people? You see, you have forgotten that I can pray, that my prayer can reach up to God, that God can send to my mind the gift of understanding, and that my mind, made understanding by God, can do something better than a mind which has not been made understanding by Him.

Up to this time your letters have given me only general ideas on your town, in general lines that could appertain to every provincial town; but even your *generalities* are incomplete. You have relied on my knowing Russia like my five fingers; but I know absolutely nothing of what is inside her. If I once did know something, it has changed since my departure. Meanwhile, changes have occurred in the very administrative structure of the provincial capitals: many places and officials have moved away from dependence on the governor and are under the jurisdiction of other ministers; new officials and positions have been established; in short, the province and its capital have many different sides and a different aspect; I ask you to acquaint me *absolutely* with your situation, not in some *abstract* way but in a *substan-*

tial way, so that I may see in small and in large everything that surrounds you.

You yourself say that in the short time since your arrival in K———you have learned more about Russia than in all your previous life. Why have you not shared your knowledge with me? You say that you do not even know where to begin, that the mass of information collected by you is still in disorder in your head (N.B.: a reason for failure). I will help you to reduce it to order, but only if you fulfill the following request conscientiously, not as your brother is accustomed to fulfill it but as far as possible like the impassioned woman you are who misses eight words out of ten and answers only to two, because somehow they went to her heart. Your brother is a cold, passionless man, or better, a business man, a sensible official who, while taking nothing particularly to heart, answers exactly at every point.

For my sake, you must once more begin an examination of your provincial town. First, you must tell me the names of all the important personages of the town, with their patronymics and their family names, of all the officials, every one. I need this. I must be their friend, as you must be their friend, to all, without exception. Secondly, you must write me the precise function of each. All this you must learn from them personally, not through someone else. When conversing with anyone you must ask him in what his function consists, so that he may name for you all its *objects* and define its *limits*. This will be the first question. Then ask him to clarify to you exactly what the function is and how much good he can do in this function in the state of present circumstances. This will be the second question. Then exactly how much evil it is possible to do in the same function. This will be the third question. Then betake yourself home to your room and immediately put it all down on paper for me. In this way you will do two things at once: besides giving me a way to be useful to you in the future, you will learn, from the answers of the official, how he understands his function, what is lacking in him, in short, by his answer he will delineate himself. He may even incite you to do something right away . . . but that is not the point: for the time being, it is better not to hurry; do nothing, even if it seems to you that you can do something and that you have the strength to help. It is better meanwhile to observe closely; content yourself with what you can transmit to me. Then on the opposite side of the same page, or on another piece of paper, put down your own observations—what in particular you noticed about every man, what others say of him, in short, every facet which could be added.

Then get me information on the whole feminine half of your town. You have been intelligent enough to visit all of them and know almost everybody among them. Nevertheless, you know them imperfectly—I am sure of it. In so far as women are concerned, you are guided by first impressions: she who has not pleased you, you leave alone. You seek out the special and select. My friend! for this I reproach you. You ought to love them all, especially those who have a few extra faults—at least in order to know them better, for much depends on this and they can have a great influence on their husbands. Do not hurry, do not hasten to admonish them, but rather question them simply; you have a gift for questioning. You will learn not only the affairs and occupations of each, but even their way of thinking, their tastes, what this one loves, what pleases a particular one of them, what is the hobby of each. I need all of this. In my opinion, in order to help someone it is necessary to know him through and through; without that I do not even understand how it is possible to give counsel to anyone. Whatever the counsel you give, it will be taken in bad part, it will not be easy to give it, and not easy to carry out. In short, all the women—through and through! so that I may have a perfect understanding of your town.

Beyond the characters and persons of the two sexes, note down every incident which might throw some light on the people or, in general, on the spirit of the province; note it frankly, as it is, or as trustworthy people have reported it to you. Note also two or three bits of gossip at random, as they first strike you, so that I may know what kind of gossip is current among you. Do it so that these notations become your constant occupation, and set aside a fixed hour of the day for them. Imagine in your thoughts, systematically and in all its extent, the totality of the town, so that you may see if you have not left out some note for me, so that I may finally acquire a complete understanding of your town.

And if in this way you acquaint me with all the persons and their functions, and how they understand themselves, and, finally, with the character of the events that have taken place among you; then I will be able to tell you certain things, and you will see that much of what seemed impossible is possible and unjust just. Until that time I will say nothing, because I could make a mistake, and I would not want to do that. I would like to speak such words as would strike the mark precisely, neither higher nor lower than the object to which they are directed, and to give such counsel that you would immediately say, "It is easy, it can be put into execution."

There is something else in the meantime, not for you but for your husband: beg him above all to take care that the counsellors of the provincial government be honest. This is the chief thing. As soon as the counsellors are honest there will be honest district police commissioners and assessors, in short, everything will become honest. You ought to know (if you do not yet know it) that the safest bribe, the one which escapes all pursuit, is the one one official receives from another official on orders from on high; this sometimes goes all the way up the ladder. The district police commissioner and the assessor often must act against their consciences and take because others take from them and they must have money to pay for their own posts. This buying and selling can be carried on before the eyes of anyone without his noticing it. God save you from being victimized. Only try that everything be honest at the top and everything below will be honest perforce. Until then, so long as evil has not ripened, do not pursue anyone; it is better to act morally at the right moment. Your idea that a governor always has the possibility of doing much evil and little good, that in the pursuit of good his actions are thwarted, is not entirely just. A governor can always have a *moral* influence, indeed, a great one, just as you can have a great *moral* influence, even though you do not have a power established by law. Believe me, if he does not pay a visit to some notable, the whole town will talk about it, will begin to ask what and why—and this same notable, solely because of his fear, will now be afraid to perpetrate a meanness that he would not have been afraid to accomplish in front of the legal authority before. Your action, that is, yours and that of your husband, in regard to the Justice of the Peace of N———, whom you purposely summoned to the town in order to reconcile him with the Public Procurator, honoring him with cordial entertainments and a friendly welcome for his uprightness, generosity and honesty, believe me, has already had an effect. I am very glad that on that occasion the judge (who would seem to have been a most enlightened man) was dressed so that he would not have been received, you say, in the antechamber of a Petersburg salon. At that very moment I would have wanted to kiss the hem of his worn dress coat. Believe me, the best way to act at the present time is not boldly and vehemently to arm yourself against the grafters and wicked people, not to persecute them, but rather to try to bring every honest trait to light, to be friendly, in the sight of everyone to shake the hand of a sincere, honest man. Believe me, only when it is known throughout the province that the governor really acts this way will all the nobility rally to his side. There is an astonishing trait in our nobility which has always amazed me—the sentiment of honor, not that honor with which the nobility of other countries is infected, that is, not honor of birth or origin, and not the European *point d'honneur*, but a genuine moral honor. Even in the provinces and the localities where, if one analyzes the nobility separately, it appears simply filthy, it is enough for you to challenge it to some really honorable action for everyone suddenly to rise up as though galvanized and for the people who do villainies suddenly to do the most honorable things. The governor should without fail have a moral influence on the nobles; only in this way will he be able to move them to assume humble functions and to take unattractive posts. And this is necessary, because if the landed nobleman of this province accepts some post to show how needful it is to serve, whatever he may be, although he be lazy and in many ways not much good, nevertheless he will fulfill his task as no highly appointed official who has roamed through chancelleries for ages would have fulfilled it. In short, one must never lose sight of the fact that these are the same nobles who in 1812 sacrificed everything—everything except their souls.

When it happens that, owing to the villainies he has committed, an official is hauled to court, he must be *dismissed from office*. This is very important. For if he is hauled to court *without dismissal from office,* then for a long time the other employees will side with him, for a long time he will intrigue and will find means to confuse everything, so that the truth will never be attained. But if he is hauled to court after *having been dismissed from office,* he will soon be discouraged, he will frighten no one, evidence against him will come in from all sides, everything will clear up, and the whole affair will soon be known. But, my friend, for Christ's sake, never abandon an official who is down, as bad as he may have been: he is hapless. He should pass from the hands of your husband into your hands; he is yours. Do not have a talk with him and do not receive him, but follow him from afar. You did well to expel that superintendent of the insane asylum because she took it into her head to sell the bits of bread meant for those unhappy people—a doubly heinous crime when you consider that the madmen could not even complain, which is why her expulsion should be made public and open. But do not throw out any man, do not bar anyone's return, follow the one who has been dismissed: sometimes from bitterness, from despair, from shame, he can fall into greater crimes. Act either through your confessor, or, in general, through some intelligent priest who

would visit him and would constantly give you an account of
him; but chiefly, try that he not remain without some kind of
work and occupation. In this circumstance be not like the *dead*
law but like the *living* God who strikes man with all the
scourges of misery but does not abandon him until the end of
his life. Whatever the criminal may have been, the fact that
the earth still bears him and that the thunder of God has not
blasted him means that he clings to the world so that someone, touched by his fate, may help him and save him. If, when
you begin to make your description for me or during your own
investigations of our foes, our regrettable facets surprise you
too much and outrage your heart—in this case I counsel you
to talk about it more frequently with the bishop; from what
you say it appears that he is an intelligent man and a good
pastor. Show him your entire leper hospital and display before
him all the illnesses of your patients. Even though he is not
a great scholar in medical science, still you must not fail to
inform him constantly of all the fits, of the symptoms, and of
the appearance of the illness. Try to outline it all to him in
vivid detail, as though it were before his eyes, so that your
town may abide as vividly and continually in his thoughts as it
must continually abide in your thoughts, so that by this means
his thoughts may of themselves turn to incessant prayer. Trust
that, because of this, his preaching, from Sunday to Sunday,
will more and more wend its way into the hearts of his auditors:
he will then be able to put forward many things openly and,
without pointing out anyone, will be able to place each person
in the presence of his own abominations, so that the landlord
will himself spit on his possessions. Also, pay attention to the
town's priests, do not fail to get to know them; everything depends on them, our improvement lies in their hands and in the
hands of no one else. Do not neglect any one of them, despite
the simplicity and ignorance of many. It is sooner possible to
recall them to their duty than to recall any one of us. Among us
worldly men there is pride, ambition, vanity, self-confidence in

our own perfection, in consequence of which not one of us listens to the words and exhortations of his brother, however justified they may be compared with his own amusements. . . . A priest, whomever he may be, still more or less feels that he should be the humblest of all and the lowest of all; besides, every day he hears himself called to service—in short, he is closer than all of us to a return to his way and, returning himself, he can return all of us. Thus, although many of those you have met are not faultless, do not neglect them, but converse with them properly. Ask each one about his parish, so that he may give a full understanding of what his parishioners are like and how he himself understands and knows them.

Do not forget that up to now I have not known the lower middle class and the merchant class of your town; that they have begun to follow the fashion and smoke cigars—that happens everywhere; I must have someone *living* from among them, so that I may observe him from head to foot in all detail. So learn everything about them in detail. You will learn one side of the matter from the priests, another from the police commissioner, if you take pains to talk with them thoroughly on this subject, a third you will learn from them themselves, if you are not too squeamish to talk with some of them, even though it be on Sunday as they leave the church. All this information will serve to outline *a standard picture* for you of the lower middle class and the merchants as they really must be; in a monster you will recognize the ideal of that which, as a caricature, has become a monster. If you recognize this, you will summon the priests and discuss it with them; you will tell them precisely what they need: the essence itself of their entire vocation, that is, what it should be among us, and the caricature of this vocation, or rather, what it has become as a consequence of our abuse. And nothing more. Their minds will change, if only they begin to reform their lives. Our priests in particular need conversations with willing people who would know how, in few but bright and accurate strokes, to outline for them the limits and responsibilities of their whole vocation and position. Often, uniquely because of that lack of knowledge, one of them may not know how to behave with his parishioners and auditors, may express himself in general terms in no way directly addressed to his subject. Put yourself in his position, help his wife and his children if his parish is poor. Whenever one is coarse and choleric, threaten him with the bishop; but, in general, try rather to act morally. Remind them that their responsibility is terrible, that the response they give will be greater than that of people of all other vocations, that now the Synod and the Emperor himself are paying particular attention to the life of the priests, that everyone is being sifted, because not only the powerful in the State but every single person in the State is beginning to notice that the cause of all this evil is that the priests are fulfilling their function negligently. . . . Declare these terrible truths to them as often as possible, willy-nilly their souls will shudder. In short, do not neglect the urban priests. Helping them, the wife of the governor can have a great moral influence over the merchant class, over the lower middle class, and over the common people inhabiting the town, so much influence that you cannot now even imagine it. I will only cite to you a little of what it can do and indicate the means by which to do it: in the first place . . . but I recall that I have absolutely no understanding of the nature of the lower middle class and the merchant class in your town: my words may be beside the point, it would be better not to pronounce them at all; I say to you only that you will be astonished when you see how many exploits are in prospect for you in this domain, which in a short time will be of greater use than all those shelters and philanthropic institutions, exploits which will not only not require any donations or labors but will become a pleasure, a repose, a relaxation for your soul.

Try to persuade the most select and best people in the town to social action: every one of them will be able to accomplish almost as much as you. It is possible to persuade them to it. If you give me a full understanding of their character, their way of life and occupations, I will tell you in what way and how it is possible to instigate them: there are secret strings in the Russian, unknown even to himself, which you need but pluck for him to throb everywhere. You have already told me of some in your town who are intelligent, noble persons; I am sure that even more can be asked of them. Pay no attention to an antagonistic exterior, pay no attention to unpleasant manners, coarseness, callousness, awkward address, not even braggadocio, sloppy behavior and undue familiarity. In these latter days we have all acquired a presumptuous, unpleasant address, but with all that, there abide in the depths of our souls more good sentiments than ever before, even though we have encumbered them with all kinds of rubbish and even simply spit at them. Especially, do not neglect the women. I avow, women are much better than us men. There is more generosity in them, more courage for everything noble; pay no attention to the fact that they have been spun into a whirlwind of fashion and frivolity. If you only know how to speak to them in the language of their souls, if you only know how to sketch out for a woman the lofty career that the world expects of her today— her Heavenly career to be the source which propels us to everything that is right, noble, and honest, to summon man to noble aspirations, that same woman whom he esteems frivolous will suddenly blaze up, will look at herself, at her abandoned duties, will advance to everything honest, will push her husband to the honest fulfillment of his duty and, tossing her rags aside, will convert everyone to action. I avow, women among us will regain consciousness before men, nobly will they chastise us, nobly lash and drive us with the lash of shame and conscience, like a stupid flock of sheep, before any of us has time to look at himself and feel that he should long ago have broken into a run instead of waiting for the lash. You will be loved, and loved strongly; indeed, it will be impossible not to love you if your soul is known; but in the meantime, you will love them all to the last one, paying no heed if someone should not love you.

But my letter is becoming too long. I feel that I am beginning to speak of things which are perhaps not at all fitting to your town, nor to you as you are now; but the fault is yours, for you have not conveyed detailed information on anyone to me. Up to now I have been as though in a wood. I only hear about incurable illnesses and I do not know who is sick of what. But I have ordinarily not believed what is said by the incurable, and I never call a sickness incurable so long as I have not touched it with my own hand. So, for my sake, examine your town anew. Describe everything and everyone, sparing no one the three inescapable questions: in what his position consists, how much good he can do in it, and how much evil. Proceed like a diligent pupil: make up a notebook and in your explanations do not forget to be as detailed as possible; do not forget that I am a fool, decidedly a fool, so long as I have not been introduced to the most detailed knowledge. Imagine rather that a child or a kind of ignoramus stands before you, for whom you must comment upon everything, down to the last trifle; only then will your letter be as it ought to be. I do not know why you think me so omniscient. May it be vouchsafed me to predict something to you and that the prediction be fulfilled—that will only occur because you have put me in touch with the state of your soul at the time. It is of great importance to divine in this way! It is sufficient to observe the present more attentively, the future will take care of itself. He is a fool who thinks of the future and passes by the present. He is either a plain liar or speaks in riddles. By the way, I will scold you too for your following lines which I put before your eyes: *"It is sad and even mournful to see the state of Russia from close up, but let us not speak of that. We ought with hope and a clear regard to look at the future, which is in the hands of merciful God."* Everything is in the hands of merciful God: the present, the past, the future. All our misfortune comes only because, looking at the present, we remark something sad and mournful, in the past something simply foul; if it is not made as we would wish, we give it up as lost and stare at the future. That is why God does not give us prescience; that is why all the future is in suspense for us: some perceive that it will be good, thanks to a few progressive people who in their turn have perceived it while not believing it according to the laws of mathematical deduction; but how to achieve this future no one knows. The grapes are still too green. One trifle has been forgotten! Everyone has forgotten that the roads and ways to this bright future are hidden in the *dark* and *tangled* present which no one wants to know: each one thinks it low and unworthy of his attention and is even cross if it is exposed to the view of all. Bring me at least a knowledge of the present. Do not be troubled by abominations, serve every abomination up to me! I find nothing unusual in abomination: I have enough abomination of my own. So long as I was not myself sunk in abominations, each abomination troubled me, and I was overcome with melancholy at the great number of them, and I was terrified for Russia; since then, as I began to observe abomination more closely, my soul became more lucid; ends, means, and ways were revealed to me and I venerated Providence still more. And now above all I thank God for having honored me, be it only partially, with a knowledge of abomination, as much my own as that of my poor fellows. And if I should succeed in helping the spiritual state of someone near to my heart, in this case you, it is because I have observed my abominations more. And if I have finally acquired a love for people, substantial rather than dreamlike, it is always and in the end for the same reason—that I have observed every kind of abomination more. So do not be intimidated by abominations and especially do not be disgusted by those people who seem to you for some reason or other abominable. I assure you that a time will come when many *honest people* in Russia will weep bitterly, their faces buried in their hands, just because they thought themselves too honest, because they boasted of their honesty and of all their exalted aspirations, because of this thinking themselves better than others. Remember all this and, after having prayed, apply yourself anew to this matter with more courage and more freshness than ever before. Reread my letter five or six times, precisely because everything in it is haphazard, not in strict logical order. And yet the fault is yours. The substance of my letter must remain totally within you; let my questions become your questions and my desire your desire, so that each word and letter may haunt you and torment you, so long as you have not fulfilled my petition exactly as I wish.

1846

XXII

THE RUSSIAN LANDOWNER

A letter to B. N. B.

The chief thing is that you have arrived in the country and suppose yourself without fail to be a landowner; everything else will come of itself. Let your thoughts not be confused, as though the former bonds uniting landowners with peasants have disappeared forever. That they have disappeared is true; that it is the landowner's fault is also true; but that they have disappeared for good and all—spit on such words: only he can speak them who sees no further than the end of his nose. The Russian, who so knows how to be grateful for every good— which is something that you have not taught him—is it difficult to attach this Russian to yourself? It is so possible to attach him that afterwards you will only wonder how he could have been detached from you. If only you fulfill in detail everything that I now tell you, at the end of a year you will see that I am right. Conceive the business of the landowner as that of one who should take the Russian in hand, in the proper, lawful sense. First of all, gather the peasants together and explain to them what you are and what they are. That you are a landowner over them not because you wanted to command and be a landowner, but because you are already a landowner, because you were born a landowner, because God will make you answer if you should change this rank for another, because

137

everyone must serve God in his place and not in another's, just as they who were born under a power must submit to that power under which they were born, because there is no power which is not from God. Show them this in the Gospels, so that they may see it, every one. Then tell them that you are compelling them to labor and work not because you need money for your pleasures—and as evidence then and there before them deplore currency, so that they may really see that money is nothing to you,—but that you are compelling them to labor because it has been commanded by God that man must earn his bread in the sweat of his brow, and then read them a lesson in the Holy Writ, so that they may see it. Tell them the whole truth: that God will make you answer for the last scoundrel in the village, and that therefore you will take still more care that they work honestly, not only for you but for themselves, for you know, and, indeed, they know that the peasant, once having become lazy, is capable of anything—he becomes a thief and a drunkard, he ruins his soul, and he makes you render the account to God. And everything that you tell them, then and there confirm by the words of Holy Writ; with your finger show them each letter as it is written down; compel each one to cross himself before it, to bow down and kiss the book in which it is written. In short, let them see clearly that everything that concerns them you will consider with God's will, not with any kind of European or other fancy. The peasant will bear it in mind; he does not need a great number of words. Declare the whole truth to him: that the soul of a man is the dearest thing in the world, and that you will look after it above all, so that no one may ruin his soul and hand it over to eternal torment. When you reproach and reprimand anyone caught in thieving, idleness, or drunkenness, place him before the face of God and not before your face; show him that he sins against God and not against you. And do not reproach him alone but summon his wife, his family, assemble the neighbors. Reproach the wife because she has not driven her husband away from evil and has

not threatened him with the fear of God; reproach his neighbors because they have allowed their brother to live like a dog
in their midst and, through that, ruin his soul; prove to them
that they will all give an answer to God for that. Arrange it so
that the responsibility may lie on everyone and so that everyone who environs the man may be reproached and he not be too
much undone.[1] Give the strength of authority and responsibility to the model managers and better peasants. Shake them
up, so that subsequently they may not only live well themselves but so that they may teach others the good life, so that
drunkard may not teach drunkard, so that this may be their
duty. Assemble the scoundrels and drunkards, so that they
may be shown who is to be esteemed, be it the elder, the steward, the priest, or, indeed, you; so that, when they catch sight
of the model peasant and manager from afar, all the peasants'
caps may fly from their heads and they may all make way for
him; but whoever makes bold to show him some disrespect or
does not listen to his sensible words, give a good scolding in
front of everyone; say to him: "You, you unwashed bum! You
have always lived in such grime that your eyes no longer see,
you don't want to render honor to the honest! Down on your
knees and beg that he bring you to reason; he who does not
call on reason dies like a dog." After having called the model
peasants to yourself and, if they are old, having seated them
before you, have a little talk with them about how they can
edify others and teach the good to them, fulfilling it in just that
way that God has commanded us. Act so for the course of one
year only and you will see how everything will come into harmony; because of this even your property will become better.
Only take care of the chief thing, and all the rest will come creep-
ing along by itself. Not for nothing did Christ say, "Greater glory
shall be given to them." This truth is seen still more in the Chris-

1. It is interesting to note that this concept has been enshrined in the
Soviet Union in parental law (see Harold J. Berman, *Justice in the U.S.S.R.*,
Vintage Books, New York, 1963, pp. 277–384).

tian life than in ours; among them the rich landlord and the good man are synonymns. And in whatever village the Christian life alone has visited, the peasants mine silver with spades.[2]

However, here is my advice to you as regards your property. Only get to the core of it thoroughly and you will be better off. Two men are already grateful to me; one of them is your acquaintance K———. I will not tell you with what areas of your property you ought to occupy yourself, or how to occupy yourself. This you know better than I; besides, your village is not so well known to me as my own palm. You are capable so far as any innovations are concerned and you realize that not only ought all the old be adhered to, but also looked at thoroughly, so that things for improvement may be extracted from it. But I do give you advice concerning the contact of the landowner with the peasants in matters of husbandry and work, which for the time being is most necessary. Remember the attitude of nearby landowner-managers to their peasants: be a patriarch, the inceptor of everything, the vanguard of all things. Be the head, at the beginning of every general thing, that is: the sowing, the mowing, and the harvesting of the grain, let there be a feast for the whole village and on these days let there be a common table for all the peasants in your manor house, as on

2. The phrase is a quotation from Pushkin's *Eugene Onegin*, V, 8:

> *Tatiana curiously gazes*
> *At the prophetic waxen mold,*
> *All eager in its wondrous mazes*
> *A wondrous future to behold.*
> *Then from the basin someone dredges,*
> *Ring after ring, the players' pledges,*
> *And comes her ringlet, they rehearse*
> *The immemorial little verse:*
> *"There all the serfs are wealthy yeomen,*
> *They shovel silver with a spade;*
> *To whom we sing, he shall be made*
> *Famous and rich! . . ."*

(Translated by Walter Arndt, E. P. Dutton, New York, 1963, p. 118)

your namesday, and you should dine together with them, and go out to work with them, and in the work you should be the vanguard, inciting everyone to work robustly, praising the daredevil and reproaching the idler. When autumn comes and field work ends, celebrate the end of work with still more feasts, to the accompaniment of a solemn thanksgiving service. Do not beat the peasant. To slap his face betokens no skill. This a policeman, an assessor, and even a village elder can do; the peasant is used to it and simply reacts to it by scratching the back of his neck. But know how to get hold of him properly with a word; you are a master of the apt word. Criticize him in front of all the people, but in such a way that all the people may laugh at him; a bit of this will be more useful to him than all the cuffs and slaps. Keep in reserve a supply of synonymns for "brave fellow" for the one whom it is necessary to incite, and all the synonymns for "mollycoddle" for the one it is necessary to reproach, so that the whole village may understand that the mollycoddle and the blackguard is an idler and a drunkard. Dig up still more similar words; in short, name everything that the Russian does not want to be. Do not stay too long in your room but appear often at the work of the peasants. And where you appear, appear so that everyone, because of your arrival, is livelier and brighter, dodging about the work like brave fellows. Use powerful words: "Now let's get to it, lads, all together!" Take an axe or scythe in your hands; this will be good for you and more useful for your health than all the Marienbad medical tortures and langorous strolls.[3]

Your remarks about schools are absolutely just. To teach the peasant reading and writing so that he may attain to the possibility of reading the vapid booklets which European philanthropists publish for the people is really nonsense. Mainly because the peasant has no time for it. After so much work, no booklet will creep into his brain; after returning home dead

3. It was the custom of many Russians to take the baths at various of the German spas. Marienbad was one of the more popular spas.

tired, he will fall into a sound sleep. You yourself will do the
same when you engage in work more often. The village priest
can much more truly say what is needful to the peasant than
all these booklets. If there be one in whom a desire for reading
and writing has really been engendered, not for the end of being
a swindling clerk, but in order to read the books in which the
law of God for man is inscribed—that is another matter. Educate him like your son and for him alone use everything that
you would use for an entire school. Our people is not stupid;
it runs, as from the devil, from all documents. It knows that
there lurk all human confusions, chicaneries, and intrigues. For
the present it ought not to know that there are any other books
than the holy ones.

To return to the priest. In vain do you worry about changing
him and do you venture to ask the bishop to give you a more
knowledgeable and experienced one. He will not give you such
a priest, because such a priest is needed everywhere. Indeed,
get it out of your head that a priest who is fully conformable
to your ideal may appear. No seminary and no school could so
educate a priest. In the seminary, he receives only the elemen-
tary foundation of his education, he is fully formed by life itself. Be his guide, you understand the responsibilities of the
rural priest so well. If the priest is foolish, it is almost always
the landowner who is at fault. Rather than treating him kindly
in his home, like a relative, inspiring in him the desire for better conversation, which could teach him something, he throws
him among the peasants, young and inexperienced as he is,
when he still does not know what a peasant is; he puts him in
such a situation that he must be indulgent to them and play up
to them, rather than beginning to have some power over them,
so that after this the landowner wails that he has a foolish
priest, that he has acquired peasant manners and differs from
the peasants in nothing. I ask you, who, even of the prepared
and educated, may not become coarse?

But do it this way: arrange for the priest to dine with you

every day. Read spiritual books with him; this reading occupies you now and nourishes you more than anything else.
But the chief thing—take the priest everywhere with you,
wherever you are at work, so that from the beginning he may
be with you in the capacity of your assistant, so that he may
see everything you do with the peasants for himself. Then he
will clearly see what a landowner is, what a peasant is, and
what the relations between them should be. Meanwhile, he will
gain more respect from the peasants when they see him walking
arm in arm with you. Act so that he stand in no need of a home,
so that he be provided with everything in his own household,
and therefore have the possibility of being with you constantly.
Believe me, he finally would be so accustomed to you that it
would be lonely for him without you. Having become accustomed to you, he will insensibly accumulate a knowledge of both
things and men from you, and a great deal of good, because in
you, glory to God, there is a sufficiency of it all, you know
how to express yourself so clearly and well that each person
willy-nilly adopts not only your thoughts but even the form of
their expression and your words themselves.

As for the sermon, which you suppose necessary, this is what
I say to you: I am rather of the opinion that it is better for the
priest who is not fully trained in this matter and is not acquainted with the people around him not to give sermons. Have
you thought of how difficult it is to deliver an intelligent sermon, especially to the peasant? No, a little patience is better,
at least until the priest looks about more, and you too. Until
that time, I give you the same advice as the advice I gave someone else, which it seems he has already profited by. Take up the
Holy Fathers, and especially St. John Chrysostom—[4]I say Chrysostom because Chrysostom worked with the poor, who had
adopted the popular Christianity which remained in the hearts of

4. St. John Chrysostom (c. 345–407), one of the greatest Fathers of the
Church, venerated by Orthodox and Roman Catholic alike, had long been
considered a master of eloquence and a great moral teacher.

the rough heathens. He tried to be especially accessible to the understanding of the simple, rough man, speaking in such a vivid language about necessary and even very lofty subjects that it is entirely possible to deliver a passage out of his sermons to our peasant, and he will understand. Take up Chrysostom and read him together with your priest, with a pencil in your hand in order to mark all such passages; there are tens of such passages in every one of Chrysostom's sermons. In these passages he tells the way to the people; they need not be long: a page or even half a page—the shorter the better. But the priest, before pronouncing them to the people, must read them through several times together with you, in order to pronounce them not only with animation but in a persuasive voice, as though he were petitioning for his own advantage, on which the welfare of his life depends. You will see that this will be more effective than his own sermons. Little need be said to the people, but it must be accurate—they cannot become accustomed to the same sermons as the highest circles have become accustomed to, those who go to listen to famous European preachers in the same way that they go to an opera or a spectacle. At K———the priest does not deliver sermons, but, knowing all the peasants thoroughly, simply awaits their confessions. And they confess so that they come out of church as though out of a bath. Z———sent thirty workers from his factory to him expressly to confess, first-rate drunkards and swindlers, and he himself stood at the church porch, so that he might look at their faces as they came out of church; they all came out red as lobsters. It seems the priest had held them back a bit for confession; in four or five minutes a man would suddenly begin confessing. After that, according to what Z———himself said, for two months not one of them showed himself in the pot house, and the neighborhood tapsters could not understand what had happened.

But enough. Work diligently just one year, and then everything will be operating so well that you will not have to apply your hand. You will grow rich as Croesus, contrary to those weak-sighted people who think that the advantage of the landowner is different from the advantage of the peasants. You will prove the point, and not with hazy words, that if the landowner simply regards his obligation with the eye of a Christian he can not only strengthen the old bonds which were being discussed as though they had disappeared forever, but bind them with new, stronger bonds—the bonds in Christ, than which nothing can be stronger. And you, who have not hitherto served zealously in any special career, will deliver such service to the state in your rank of landowner as no other great official has delivered. Whatever you say, to enlighten eight hundred subjects who are all as one and can be an example to all your neighbors of a truly exemplary life—this is not an idle thing, it is a truly lawful and great service.

1846

XXIII

THE HISTORICAL PAINTER IVANOV

A letter to Count Matv. Yu. V.

A. A. Ivanov (1806–58) was a Russian painter whom
Gogol first met in Rome in the winter of 1838–39.
Ivanov was already at work at this time on his "Christ
Appears to the People." I have been unable to
identify "Count Matv. Yu. V." Chuzeville gives his
name as N. U. Veligoursky, on what grounds I
do not know. Gogol was, however, acquainted with the
Vyelgorsky family (I have found no "Count Matv.
Yu." among them) whom he first met during the winter
of 1843–44 in Nice. During this decade he became
particularly close to the youngest member of the
family, Anna. Indeed, many of Gogol's biographers
think he proposed marriage to her and was
refused. In any event, it appears that Gogol's relations
with the Vyelgorsky family broke off in the spring
of 1847.

I am writing to you about Ivanov. How incomprehensible is
the destiny of this man! It is already the time to explain his
work to everyone. Everyone is convinced the picture he is working on is an unprecedented phenomenon, interest in the painter
has been taken, on all sides they bustle about so that the means
to finish it may be given him, so that the artist may not die of
hunger—I say it *literally,* die of hunger—and so far not a
sound from Petersburg. For Christ's sake, find out what this

means. Absurd rumors are abroad here, as though the painters and all the professors of our Academy of Arts, afraid lest Ivanov's picture do away with everything our art has thus far produced, are striving out of envy to prevent the means being given him for finishing it. It is a lie, I am convinced of it. Our painters are generous, and if they knew everything poor Ivanov has endured because of his unexampled selflessness and love for his work, at the risk of really dying of hunger, in brotherly fashion they would divide their own money with him, instead of suggesting such brutality to others. Besides, what is there to fear from Ivanov? He goes his own way, he is an obstacle to no one. He is not only not seeking a professorial post and worldly advantage, but he seeks absolutely nothing, because for a long time he has been dead to everything in the world except his work. He is pleading for a beggarly salary, for the salary given to a beginning apprentice for his work, not for what he ought to have as a master with so tremendous a task that no one has undertaken it up to this hour. And this beggarly salary which everyone tries for and petitions for he cannot get, despite everyone's trouble. By your leave, I see in all that the fixed will of Providence that Ivanov must endure, suffer, and bear everything: I can ascribe it to nothing else.

Up to now he has been reproached for his slowness. They all said, "What! He has worked eight years on his picture and the picture is still not finished!" But now this reproach has faded away, when we see that not a bit of the artist's time has been wasted, that his preparatory studies for the picture alone fill a whole hall and could constitute a separate exhibition, that the extraordinary magnitude of the picture itself, which has not its equal (it is larger than the pictures of Briulov and Bruni),[1] has demanded an exorbitant amount of work, especially con-

1. K. P. Bryulov (1799–1852), one of the most important romantic-emotional painters of the time. He was a Professor at the Academy of Art. F. A. Bruni (1799–1875), born in Italy, studied at the Academy of Art in Petersburg, became Professor of the History of Art in 1836, and was rector of the Academy from 1855 to 1871.

sidering his lack of financial means, which deprived him of the possibility of having several models concurrently and of having those whom he would have liked. In short, now everyone recognizes the absurdity of the reproaches for slowness and laziness addressed to a painter like this, who has spent his whole life in work and, like a toiler, has even forgotten that any other pleasures than work could exist in the world.

Still greater will be the shame of those who reproached him for slowness when they learn the other secret cause of this slowness. To the production of this painting was joined the artist's personal spiritual state—an extremely rare phenomenon in the world, a phenomenon in which there participates not the arbitrary will of man but the will of Him Who is above man. It was predetermined that in this painting the education of the painter himself would be accomplished, both in artistic technique and in the ideas guiding his art to a lawful and lofty purpose. The subject of the painting, as you know, is most meaningful. The most difficult of the passages of the Gospels has been taken for execution, one which has never before been chosen by any artist, even during the early centuries of devout artists, namely, the first appearance of Christ to the people. The picture depicts the desert at the bank of the Jordan. In the foreground is John the Baptist, preaching and baptizing in the name of Him Whom none of the people has yet seen. A crowd of people clusters around him, some naked, some undressing, some redressing, some dressed, some leaving the water, and some ready to plunge into the water. Future disciples of the Savior himself also stand in this crowd. All, while performing a diversity of bodily motions, are turning an inner ear to the speech of the prophet, as if grabbing each of his words from his lips, and expressing on their varied faces their varied feelings: on some—a faith already complete; on others —still a doubt; a third group is wavering; a fourth have hung their heads in contrition and penitence; there are still others in whom the crusty insensibility of their hearts is seen. At the very moment that everything is moving with such varied motions, in the distance the very One in Whose name the baptism has just been accomplished appears—and this is the moment of the picture. The Precursor is seized just at that instant that, indicating the Savior with his finger, he is pronouncing: "Behold the Lamb of God, behold him who taketh away the sin of the world."[2] And the whole crowd, without losing the expressions on their faces, turns in look or thought towards Him Whom the prophet has indicated. Along with the first impressions, which have not had time to vanish from their faces, new impressions run all across all their faces. The faces of the foremost elect are illumined by a lovely light, while others are still seeking to penetrate the sense of the incomprehensible words, perplexed as to how one can take upon himself the sins of all the world, and a third group dubiously shake their heads, saying, "Prophets do not come from Nazareth." And He, in celestial calm and wonderfully remote, with tranquil and steadfast step already draws near to the people.

A trifle—to depict on these faces the course of *man's conversion to Christ!* There are people who are persuaded that everything is within reach of a great artist. The earth, the sea, man, a frog, a brawl and a carousal, a card game, and the supplication of God; in short, everything can easily be accomplished by him, provided he is a talented painter and has been lectured to at the Academy.

An artist can depict only what he *has felt* and a complete idea of which has been formed in his head; otherwise the picture will be a dead academic picture. Ivanov has done everything that another painter would consider sufficient for a finished picture. All the material part, everything pertaining to the intelligent and strict distribution of the group in the picture has been fulfilled to perfection. The persons themselves have received a typically Gospel-like air, together with an Hebraic air. You immediately perceive by their faces in what land it is

2. *John,* 2:29 (D.V.).

all occurring. Ivanov went everywhere expressly to study Jewish faces. Everything down to the harmonious distribution of colors, to the clothing of a man and its careful outline on the body has been studied with so much care that every crease arrests the expert's attention. Finally, the landscape, to which the historical painter usually pays little attention, the view of the whole picturesque desert surrounding the group, has been executed so that even the landscape painters of Rome are astonished. For this Ivanov spent many months in the unhealthy Pontine Marshes and in the desert regions of Italy; he brought into his sketches all the wild out-of-the-way places around Rome; he studied every pebble and arboreal leaf; in short, he did everything he could do, depicted everything for which he found a model.

But how can the artist depict something for which he has no model? Where could he find a model to depict the principal thing, that which constitutes the problem of the whole picture—to represent in persons of all kinds human behavior in regard to Christ? Whence would he take them? From his head? Create from imagination? Perceive by thought? No, this is nonsense! Thought is too cold for this and imagination worthless. Ivanov strained his imagination as much as he could; he endeavored, in the faces of all the people he met, to catch lofty emotional expressions; he lingered in churches to watch men at prayer—and he saw that it was all impotent and insufficient, that it did not confirm his soul in a complete idea of what was necessary. This was the reason for his great spiritual grief and the reason that the picture was delayed so long. No, so long as there is not an authentic movement towards Christ in the artist himself he cannot represent it on canvas. Ivanov prayed God to grant him such a complete movement; he wept tears in silence, begging Him for the strength to fulfill his inner thought, and all this time he was accused of slowness and was hurried on! Ivanov begged God that He might in the fire of His Grace reduce to ashes the cold callousness with which many of the best and finest people struggle today and to inspire him so to represent that movement that non-Christians might be softened at the sight of his picture.

And all this time even his acquaintances, even his friends, reproached him, thinking that he was simply lazy, they seriously wondered whether it would not be possible, through hunger and the deprivation of all means of support, to force him to finish his picture. The most compassionate of them said, "It is his fault; let the huge picture go its own way, and in the intervals he could work on small pictures, earn money with them and not die of hunger." They said that, not knowing that it was impossible for the artist whose work had become, by the will of God, a spiritual matter, to busy himself with any other work, and that he had no intervals, his thought could not even turn to something else, however he might coerce and constrain it. In the same way a faithful wife who truly loves her husband will not love another, will not give her caresses to anyone for money, even though by this means she might save herself and her husband from poverty. This was the state of Ivanov's soul. You will say, "But why has he not stated all that on paper? Why has he not clearly described his real position? Then we would immediately have sent him some money." Nothing of the sort. Let one of us who has not yet demonstrated his powers, who has not yet proved himself, attempt to explain himself to people in other walks of life who could not—and this is quite natural—even comprehend that his art can be of an elevation well beyond that now in fashion! Can he say to these people, "I am working along on something which will soon astonish you, but which I cannot now tell you about, because much of it is still not comprehensible even to me. So while I am at work, wait patiently and give me money for my support."? Then there is no doubt that one amateur will appear after another, and they will speak in the same way—and madmen will give them money too. Let us even suppose that Ivanov, during his vague period, could have expressed himself clearly and had said, "A haunting thought has been inspired in me by something superior—with my brush to depict the movement of man to Christ. I feel that I cannot do this without being truly changed myself. So wait until this movement is produced in me, and in the meantime give me the money necessary for my support and for my work." Then we would all cry out with one voice, "Hey, you, what nonsense are you talking? Do you take us for fools? What connection is there between a soul and a painting? A soul is one thing, a painting another. What! We should wait for you to change! You should be a Christian without that; and we are all of us true Christians." That is what we would all say to Ivanov, and each of us would almost be right. If he had not had those painful circumstances and that inner agony of soul, which compelled him to turn towards God with more ardor than others and gave him the ability to resort to Him and live in Him like no other contemporary lay painter, and by dint of his tears to acquire those feelings which he once attempted to obtain by meditation alone, he would never have depicted what he is now beginning to depict on his canvas, and he would really have deceived both himself and others, despite all his desire not to deceive.

Do not think it is easy to explain oneself to people while a spiritual transition is going on, when, by the will of God, a process is beginning in the very nature of a man. I know it because I have experienced it myself. My works are strangely connected to my soul and to my inner education. For more than six years I could do no work for the world. All my work was done within myself and for myself alone. And I then existed—do not forget it—uniquely on the income from my works. Almost everyone knew I was in need, but they were persuaded that it had come about through my own obstinacy, that all I had to do was dash off some little thing in order to obtain more money; but I was in no state to produce a single line, and when, having listened to the counsel of a senseless man, I took it into my head to force myself to write some articles for a newspaper, it was so difficult for me that my brain refused, all my feelings ached, I scribbled and tore up the pages. After two or three months of such torment I had so compromised my health, which was bad to begin with, that I had to take to my bed, and with the addition of nervous ailments and the ailments resulting finally from my inability to explain my position to anyone in the world, I was so exhausted that I was on the edge of the grave.

Approximately the same thing happened twice. Once, in addition to everything else, I found myself in a town where there was no soul close to me, without any resources, at the risk of dying not only of sickness and spiritual suffering, but even of hunger. This is all a long time ago. I was saved by the Emperor. Help from him came to me unexpectedly. Either he perceived in his heart that his poor subject dreamt of serving him in his useless and unknown career with no less honest a service than others in their useful and well-known careers, or it was simply the effect of his habitual mercy. But this help soon restored me. I was happy at that moment to be obliged to him and to none other. To the reasons impelling me to take up the work with new strength was joined the thought—if God should vouchsafe to make me a man really close to many people, really worthy of the love of all those whom I love—to say to them, "Do not forget that perhaps I would no longer be in the world if there had not been the Emperor." That is what my position was! In addition, I say to you that, during this very period, I had to listen to accusations of egoism: many could not forgive my lack of involvement in various problems which they took up, according to them, for the common weal. My statement that I could not write and ought not to work for any newspapers or reviews they took for a fiction. The life I led abroad was attributed to a Sybaritic desire to enjoy the beauties of Italy. I could not even explain to any of my close friends that, ill health aside, I needed some time away from them, just in order not to fall into artificial relations with them and not to inflict annoyances upon them—I could not even explain this. I myself felt that my spiritual state had become so strange that I would not even have been able to tell it plainly to one man in the world. When I tried to reveal but one part of myself, I soon saw that the many listening to me became gloomy at my words and shook their heads, and I bitterly regretted even the desire to be candid. I swear, there are situations so difficult that they can only be compared with the situation of a man who finds himself in a lethargic sleep: he sees himself being buried alive and cannot stir a finger or make a sign to show that he is still alive. No, God keep you, at these moments of spiritual transition, from seeking to explain yourself to any man whatsoever: you must have recourse to God alone and to no one else. Many have become unjust to me, even people close to me, and nonetheless they were innocent: I would have done the same had I been in their place.

This is exactly the case of Ivanov: if he should happen to die of poverty and want, a cry of indignation would soon be raised against those who had allowed it; there would be accusations that other artists were insensible and envious of him. A dramatic poet would make a sentimental drama out of it, one which would touch the spectators and move them to anger against his enemies. And it would all be only a lie, just because no one would really be guilty of his death. Only one man would be dishonored and guilty, and that man is—I; I have experienced just about the same condition, I have experienced it in my own body, and I have not explained it to others! This is why I write to you now. Take the whole business in hand; if you do not, the sin will be on your soul. I have already removed it from my soul by this letter; it now hangs over you. Do it so that not only would Ivanov be accorded the wretched support he solicits, but besides that a lump sum for having worked so long on his picture while he did not want to work on anything else, as other people would compel him, and as his own need would compel him. Do not skimp! The money will earn interest. The worth of this picture is already beginning to be discovered by all. All Rome, just judging from the picture's present form, in which the complete thought of the artist is still far from evident, is beginning to say openly that a like phenomenon has not appeared since the time of Raphael and Leonardo da Vinci. The picture will be finished—the poorest court of Europe will gladly pay for it a sum equal to that now spent on the newly found pictures of the great masters, and their value is not less than one or two hundred thousand. Do it so that the reward be given not for the picture but for the artist's selflessness and unparalleled love for art, so that it will serve as a lesson to other artists. This lesson is necessary so that all the others may see how necessary it is to love art: that it is necessary, like Ivanov, to die to all the enticements of life; like Ivanov, to instruct oneself and consider oneself an eternal student; like Ivanov, to refuse oneself everything, even an extra dish on feast days; like Ivanov, to wear a simple pleated jacket when at the end of one's resources and scorn vain conventions; like Ivanov, to endure all, despite one's lofty, delicate spiritual makeup; despite one's great sensibility to everything to bear all galling defeats, even when some choose to proclaim you mad and set the rumor afloat in such a way that you can hear it at every step. For this exploit he must be given a reward. This is particularly necessary for young artists who are setting out on the career of art, so that they may not be thinking about how to acquire cravats and dress well, about how to run into debt so that they can cut a figure in society; so that they may know in advance that subsidies and governmental aid await, not those who dream about dressing well and carousing with their comrades, but those who dedicate themselves to their work, as the monk to the monastery. And it would even be good if the sum given to Ivanov were large enough for all the others to scratch their heads. Be calm, he will not take this sum for himself; perhaps he will not take a kopek of it for himself—this sum will be entirely used for the relief of truly

laboring artists whom he, as a painter, knows better than any official, and the directions will be better carried out than by the officials. With an official you never know: there might be a woman of fashion at his house and friends whom he has to treat to dinner; the official is responsible for the luster of the establishment; he will even maintain that, for the maintenance of the Russian nation, it is necessary to throw dust in the eyes of the foreigner, and for that he will demand money. But he who has already pursued his career and who now needs help, he who has heard the wail of need and a real, not fake, necessity, he who has himself suffered and seen how others suffer, he who has pitied others, divided his last shirt with an indigent worker when he himself had nothing to eat nor clothes to dress in, as Ivanov has done—for him it is a different matter. One could boldly trust him with a million and sleep calmly —not one kopek of this million will be wasted. Treat him justly, show my letter to others who are, like me, your friends, especially to those who are entrusted with some administrative employment, because workers like Ivanov can occur in all domains, and still it is not necessary to let them die of hunger. If it happens that one of them, different from all others, should acquit himself of his business better than anyone else, even if it be personal business which he says—despite all appearances that it is his personal business—is nevertheless necessary for everyone, then consider him as having been of service and give him the vital nourishment. But in order to make certain that there is no deceit, because on this pretext idlers could make their way while doing nothing for mankind, observe his life; his life will tell you all. If he, like Ivanov, has spit on all worldly conveniences and conditions, wears a simple jacket and, having driven away from himself the thought not only of pleasures and feasts but even the thought of one day acquiring a wife and family or some property, leads a truly monkish life, sweating day and night over his work and praying constantly— then there is no longer anything to discuss; he must be given the means to work; there is no need to hurry him and urge him—leave him in tranquillity: God will urge him without you; your business is to see that he does not die of hunger. Do not give him too much support; give it to him frugally and even beggarly, and do not tempt him with the temptations of the world. There are people who ought to remain beggars all their lives. Beggary is a bliss that the world has still not got to the heart of. But he whom God has favored so that he may taste its sweetness, he who has really fallen in love with his beggar's bag, he would not sell it for all the treasures of this world below.

1846

XXIV

WHAT A WIFE CAN DO FOR HER HUSBAND IN SIMPLE DOMESTIC MATTERS, AS THINGS NOW ARE IN RUSSIA

For a long time I have thought about which one of you to attack —you or your husband? Finally I decided to attack you: the wife is sooner capable of coming to her senses and getting herself moving. Your situation is different from what you think: although you consider yourself at the height of bliss, according to me not only is it not blissful, but it is even worse than the situations of those who consider themselves in grief and misfortune. In you both there are many good, spiritual, tender, and even intellectual qualities; only missing is that without which all this serves for nothing—inner control. Neither of you is master of himself. You have no character, and by character I mean *strength of will*. Your husband, feeling this lack in himself, married for the purpose of finding stimulation in his wife for his every action and deed. You married him so that he might be your stimulus in all life's actions. Each expected from the other what was in neither. I say to you: your situation is not only not blissful, it is even perilous. You both are dissolving, melting away in the midst of life, like soap in water; all your merits and good qualities are disappearing in confused activities, which is what is happening to your character— you are becoming weakness personified. Pray God for *strength*.

It is possible to implore God for everything, even strength, which, as is well known, a weak and feeble man can by no means obtain. Only act intelligently. "I offered prayers and I reached the shore," says the proverb. Say to yourself in the morning, in the afternoon, in the evening, at every hour of the day, "God, make me whole and strengthen me!"—and act for a whole year as I now tell you, without arguing about why and to what end.

All the finances of the household depend on you; receipts and expenditures should be in your hands. Do not keep general account books, but at the very beginning of the year first make an estimate of everything, take all your necessities, consider first how much you can and how much you must spend in the year, in conformity with your circumstances, and reduce everything to round sums. Divide your money into seven almost equal piles. In the first pile will be the money for your quarters, including heating, water, firewood, and everything but the bare walls of the house and keeping the courtyard clean. In the second pile—money for the table and for all the victuals, together with the salary of the cook and foodstuffs for everyone [servants][1] who does not live in your house. In the third pile— money for the carriage: coach, coachman, horses, hay, oats, in short, everything that is concerned with this part. In the fourth pile—money for your wardrobe, that is, what you need both to appear in the world and to stay at home. In the fifth pile will be your pocket money. In the sixth pile—money for any extraordinary expenses you may meet: a change of furniture, buying a new carriage, even assisting one of your relatives if he should suddenly be in need. The seventh pile—for God, that is, money for the church and for the poor. Do it so that these seven piles do not get mixed up but remain separate as though they were the separate budgets of government departments. Handle every expense personally; on no pretext take from one pile for another.

1. Most domestic serfs lived in, of course, but even those who did not were the responsibility of the manor.

During this time—no matter what bargains may be offered you, however their cheapness may entice you—do not buy. This you can venture when you are stronger. Now do not forget for a minute that you are doing all this to buy a firm character and for the present this buying is more necessary to you than any other buying, and that is why you will be obstinate in it. Ask God for obstinacy. Even if a need to help the poor should occur, you cannot use more than what is in that particular pile. Even if you should be the witness of a picture of misfortune, of a lacerated heart, and you should see that monetary assistance could help, do not dare to touch other piles, but go through all the town, to all your acquaintances, and try to incline them to pity: ask, pray, even be prepared for humiliation, so that this may remain a lesson to you, so that you may remember eternally how you were led to the cruel necessity of displaying misfortune, how because of this you had to be subjected to humiliation and even to public derision; so that this may not leave your mind, so that through this you may train yourself to prune the expenditures of every pile and plan it out beforehand, so that at the end of the year there may remain a residue in each for the poor, not only balanced accounts. If you will keep this in mind constantly, you will never drop into a store without a strong need and unexpectedly buy for yourself some adornments for the chimney piece or the table, for which not only the women but the men among us have such a weakness (in essence, the former are rather peasant women than gentlewomen). Your caprices will unwillingly and insensibly be shrunk and will finally settle on what you yourself recognize, that you do not need more than one coach and a pair of horses, more than four courses at table, that people at a dinner party can be satisfied with a simple service, with the addition of one extra dish or a bottle of wine, carried in without every nicety in simple wine glasses. You will not only not burn with shame if the rumor runs through town that everything at your house is not *comme il faut,* but you will laugh at it yourself, being truly

convinced that the present *comme il faut* which is so demanding of a man he created himself; there is no system for dinners,
not even that of ephemeral etiquette, not even that of Madame
Sichler. Have a special book for every pile of money, place a
sum in every pile every month and the last day of the month reread it all, comparing everything, one with another, in order to
know how to recognize how many times one is more necessary
than another, in order to see clearly which it is first necessary
to deny in case of need, in order to learn the wisdom to comprehend what is most necessary.

Keep to this strictly for a whole year. Strengthen yourself
and be obstinate, and all this time pray to God that he
strengthen you. And you will grow in strength constantly. This
is important, so that something may be strengthened in a man
and become immutable; as a result of this, order cannot help
being established in everything. Strengthened in matters of the
material order, you will insensibly be strengthened in matters
of the spiritual order. Distribute your time: assume that every
hour is indispensable. Do not stay with your husband all
morning; send him to his job in his department, every minute
reminding him that he must give himself wholly to the common cause and to the property of the Empire (his own property is not his care; it must rely on you and not on him), that
he married precisely so that, freeing himself from trivial cares,
he might give his all to the Fatherland, that a wife was given
to him not as a hindrance to his service but to fortify him in his
service. Let you both work separately all morning, each in his
own occupation, and then meet merrily before dinner and you
will be happier together than you have been for several years,
you will talk to each other instead of regaling each other with
yawns. Recount to him everything that you have done in your
house in your domestic affairs, and let him tell you everything
that he has done in his department for the common weal. You
should constantly know all about him in his job—what his part
in it is, how he happened to manage affairs that day, of what

exactly they consisted. Do not neglect these things; remember that a wife must be a help to her husband. If only for the course of one year you listen attentively to everything he says, then in another year you will be strong enough to give him counsel; you will know how to encourage him when he encounters something unpleasant in his service; you will know how to compel him to bear and endure what might touch his spirit; you will truly arouse him to everything beautiful.

From this day onward begin to fulfill everything that I now say to you. Strengthen yourself, pray and ask God continuously to make you whole and keep you. Everything among us is now diffused and disunited. Every man has become a scoundrel, a spineless creature; he has turned into a base footstool for everything, and into a slave of his own vapid, trivial circumstances; nowhere is there now freedom in its true sense. A friend of mine, whom you do not know personally but who nevertheless knows all Russia, defines this freedom as follows: "Freedom is not arbitrarily saying '*Yes*' to one's desires, but in knowing how to say '*No*' to them." He is right, as truth itself. No one in Russia now knows how to say this stern 'No' to himself. Nowhere do I see a real man. Let a feeble woman remind him of this! Everything has now become so wonderful that the wife must command the husband, so that he may be her head and sovereign.

1846

XXV

RURAL JUSTICE AND PUNISHMENT

From a letter to M

"M" is probably K. I. Markov, a landowner
who was also a minor critic.

Do not neglect the investigation of legal problems and justice.
Do not delegate this matter to the steward or to anyone in the
village: this is the most important part of your activity as
landlord. Do the judging yourself. In this way alone will you
strengthen the broken bond of the landowner with the peasants.
Justice is a Godly thing, and I do not know what could be
loftier. Not for nothing do the people honor the one who
knows how to bring about true justice. Not only your villagers
will come to you in droves, but all the surrounding peasants
from other villages, for they will be aware that you know how
to deal with their legal problems. Neglect none of those who
come to you and judge everyone, even though the quarrel be
insignificant or foolish. You can say much to the peasant in
connection with it that may bring his soul to the good, and
which you would not have found to say at another time, nor,
having found it, what to tack it on to.

Judge every man with a double judgment, and give every
action a double decision. One judgment should be human. In it

vindicate the innocent and denounce the guilty. Try to do it before witnesses, that other peasants may be there, so that they may all see clear as day that one is innocent and the other guilty. Make the other judgment a divine one. In it vindicate both the innocent and the guilty. Clearly make the first admit what fault he committed for the other to offend him, and the second how he is doubly guilty, before God and before men; reproach the one because he did not forgive his brother, as Christ commanded, and reproach the other because in his brother he offended Christ himself; reprimand both because they did not make it up and came to court, and with both of them form the words for them to confess to the priest in their confession. If you pronounce such judgment, you will be like a representative of God, because God authorizes you. From this you will extract much good, much sincere and correct knowledge. If many people in the government began their careers not with paper work but with the verbal administration of business among the simple people, they would know the spirit of the land better, the temper of the nation and the general soul of man; they would then not borrow unseemly innovations for us from foreign lands. Justice among us can be fulfilled better than in all other states, because of all nations only the Russian has given rise to this certain thought—that no man is right, that only God is right. This thought, like an immutable belief, has spread everywhere in our nation. Even a simple, stupid man armed with it receives power in the nation and stops quarrels. Only we, people of a higher station, do not perceive it, because we have acquired an empty, chivalrous, European understanding of truth. Only we quarrel about who is innocent and who guilty; if each of our affairs is analyzed, you will come to the same meaning, that is, both are guilty. Look at how the highly reasonable commandant's wife treated this matter in Pushkin's tale *The Captain's Daughter*: she sent a lieutenant to judge between a garrison soldier and a peasant woman who had fought in the bathhouse over a wooden bucket; she gave him these instructions: "Look into who is innocent and who guilty, and punish them both."[1]

1845

---

1. There seems little doubt that Gogol twisted the meaning of this passage from *The Captain's Daughter*. It is more concerned with arranging peace in the household than it is with justice.

XXVI

FEARS AND DREADS IN RUSSIA

A letter to Countess
Gogol gave no further indication of the
identity of his addressee.

To your long letter, which you wrote in such fear, which you
asked me to destroy after reading, and to which you asked me
to answer only by the intermediary of trusted hands and not
by the post, I answer not only not secretly, but, as you see, in
a published book which perhaps half educated Russia will
read. I have been prompted to this by the consideration that
perhaps my letter will serve at the same time as an answer for
others who, like you, are disturbed by the same fears. What
you declare to me in secret is still no more than one part of the
whole problem; and, if I should tell you what I know (and
without doubt I am still far from knowing everything), then
your thoughts would really be muddied and you would consider fleeing Russia. But fleeing where? That is the question. Europe may be in a still more difficult situation than Russia. The difference is that there no one is fully aware of it;
everyone, not even excluding government personnel, abides for
the time being atop superficial information, that is, abides in
an enchanted circle of knowledge, premature deductions foisted
upon them by the press, precipitate testimony advanced through
the deceitful prisms of all their parties, never presented in a

true light. Wait, soon a great wave of dissent will rise from below, precisely in the states apparently well organized, those whose external luster enraptures us so as we try to adopt their ways and adapt them to ourselves, dissent that would put the heads of those same famous government personnel whom you so admire in the Chambers and offices in a whirl. Everywhere in Europe now they are brewing such disturbances that no human resources will help them when they burst forth; next to them the fears you now see in Russia will be an insignificant thing. The light still shines in Russia, there are still roads and routes to safety, and glory to God that these fears have come now and not later. Your words: "Everyone's spirit has fallen, as though in expectation of something inevitable," as well as the words: "Everyone is thinking only of preserving his personal advantage, of the preservation of his own profit, just as on the battlefield, after a defeat, each one thinks only of saving his own life—*sauve qui peut*" are really just; it is really like that now; so it must be: so has God willed it to be.

Each of us ought not think only of himself, of his own salvation. Another kind of salvation is offered. It is not to flee our land by sea, saving our despicable worldly goods, but, saving our souls, not going out of the state, each of us ought to save himself in the very heart of the state. It is on the ship of his position and service that each of us ought now escape the whirlpool, our eyes fixed on the Divine pilot. Even he who is not in the service now ought to join the service and grasp his position as a drowning man grasps his plank, without which no one will be saved. Each of us ought now to serve, not as he would have served in old Russia, but as he would in the celestial state, the head of which is Christ himself, and this is why we ought to fulfill all our obligations in the same way as Christ and no other has commanded, whoever may be the authorities over us, those equal to and surrounding us, as well as those below and under us. And certainly this is not the moment to pay attention to any slights to our vanity and self-love which may be inflicted on us by whomsoever it might be—let us remember only that our obligations are undertaken by the grace of Christ, and this is why they ought to be fulfilled as Christ and no other has commanded. Only by this means can each of us now be saved. And ill luck will befall him who does not reflect on this now. His intelligence will be dimmed, his thoughts will become clouded, he will find no corner where he may hide from his fears. Remember *the darkness of Egypt,* produced with so much strength by King Solomon when the Lord, wishing to punish only the Egyptians, sent mysterious and incomprehensible fears upon them. Blind night enveloped them suddenly in broad daylight; frightful forms were raised up before them on all sides; sinister scarecrows with dismal faces came before their fascinated eyes; a dread which had no need of iron chains locked them all and deprived them of all sense, all movement, they lost all their strength, only fear remained. This happened only to those whom the Lord had punished. The others, during this time, saw no terrors; for them it was day and light.

See that the same thing does not happen to you. Rather, pray and implore God that He make you understand that you ought to be in your position and in it accomplish everything in accordance with the law of Christ. This is now no joke. Before becoming confused because of the disorders surrounding us, it would be well for each of us to look into his own soul. Do you look into yours. God knows, perhaps there you will see the same disorder for which you abuse others; perhaps there dwells a troubled, disordered anger, capable at any moment of possessing your soul, to the greater glory of the enemy of Christ; perhaps there lodges a cowardly ability for falling into dejection at every step—pitiful daughter of lack of faith in God; perhaps, again, there is hidden a vain desire to chase after what glitters and to profit from worldly reputation; perhaps there dwells a pride in the personal qualities of your soul, capable of reducing to nothing all the good that we have in us. God knows what there can be in our souls. It is better and more worthwhile to be troubled by what is inside us than by what is beside and around us.

As to the fears and dreads in Russia, they are not without use: many have been educated by them with such an education as no other school could give them. The very difficulty of circumstances presents new resources to the mind, awakens the dozing abilities of many people, and, while in certain corners of Russia they continue to dance the polka and make up card games, in various occupations real sages ready for life and for action are already invisibly being formed. In some ten years you will see Europe no longer coming to us only to acquire skins and lard, but to acquire a wisdom which is no longer sold on European markets. I could name many to you who will one day shape the beauty of the Russian land and bring it eternal good; but, to the honor of your sex, I must say that women are the more numerous. I keep them in my memory like a necklace of precious pearls. I mean all of them, beginning with your daughters, who have vividly reminded me so many times that relationship of soul is superior to any relationship of blood (may God grant that these best of sisters fulfill the petition of their brother with the same readiness that they have fulfilled the least desire of my soul), beginning with them and continuing with others of whom you have hardly heard, and finishing with those of whom perhaps you have never heard but who are more perfect than all those of whom you have heard. Not one of them resembles any other, and each is in herself an extraordinary phenomenon. Only Russia could produce a like variety of character. And only at the present time of difficult circumstances, of enfeeblement and general corruption, of paltriness everywhere in society, could they be formed. But there is one who is far above all others, one whom I do not know by sight, and about whom only vague accounts have reached me. I did not think that a like perfection could exist on earth. To realize so intelligent and generous a work, and to realize it as she knew how to do; to do it so as to divert any suspicion of her part in it and to attribute all the merit to others, in such a way that these others have begun to boast of what she did as though it were their own, in the complete conviction that they did it. So intelligently to consider how to escape renown, since the thing itself of necessity must cry out and reveal her! To succeed in that and remain unknown! No, I have never yet met a like wisdom in our brothers of the masculine sex. It is at this moment that there palely appeared to me all the womanly ideals created by the poets: in comparison with this truth, they were the gibberish of the imagination in comparison with total reason. At this moment, all those women who chase after glittering fame appeared pitiful to me! And where has such a miracle occurred? In an inconspicuous out-of-the-way place in Russia, at exactly the time when it has become more difficult for a man to dodge away, when all circumstances are entangled and all the fears and dreads of Russia have come to frighten you.

1846

XXVII

TO A MYOPIC FRIEND

You have armed yourself with the sight of contemporary myopia and you think you judge events correctly. Your conclusions are rot; they were drawn without God. Why do you refer to history? History for you is dead—only a closed book. Without God you will not reach great conclusions; you will reach only insignificant and petty ones. Russia is not France: the elements of the French are not those of the Russians. You have forgotten the peculiarities of each people and you think that the same event can occur in the same way in each nation. When a hammer falls on glass it smashes it to smithereens, but when it falls on iron it tempers it. Your thoughts on finances are based on the reading of foreign books and English newspapers, and that is why your thoughts are dead. You should be ashamed, being an intelligent man, that you are not using your own intelligence, which could be developed in an original way; instead you are cluttering it up with alien muck.

I do not see any part for God in your projects; in the words of your letter I do not perceive, despite the brilliance of intelligence and wit throughout, that God was present in your thoughts when you wrote it; I do not see any consecration to Heaven in your thoughts. No, you are doing no good in your position, although you wish to; your actions will not yield the fruit you expect. One may do evil with the best intentions, as many have already done. In these latter days, stupid people have

171

produced less trouble than intelligent ones, and all because they relied on the strength of their native intelligence.

You are proud, and in what are you proud? If only it were in your intelligence, but no, you have encumbered your really remarkable and great intelligence with litter, and you have made it a stranger to yourself. You are proud of an alien, dead intelligence and you pretend it is yours. Look at yourself: you are proceeding dangerously. You aspire to be a bureaucrat, and you will be a bureaucrat, just because you have the ability for it; but now look at yourself more sternly. You will not acquire this advancement, with which your brain is so filled, before you enter upon your duties, and remember that every little indiscreet action can now produce more evil. Dread is sooner visible in your present projects than foresight. All your thoughts are directed to the avoidance of something threatening in the future. Fear not the future, but the present. God orders us to take care of the present. Whoever is darkened by dread of the future the sacred power has already renounced. Whoever is with God sees the light before him and in the present is the creator of a brilliant future. And you are proud: already you do not want to see anything; you are selfconfident: you think that you already know everything; you think that all the circumstances of Russia have been disclosed to you; you think that no one can teach you anything; with all your strength, you are trying to be like those bureaucrats who quickly flashed and quickly disappeared, who had in themselves everything to do a great deal of good, who even burned with the desire to do good, even worked like ants all their lives and with all that left no traces behind them; the very memory of them has been forgotten; like ripples disappearing in the water, their lives disappeared in Russia. And up to now, to our shame, the Europeans point out their great people to us, the wiser of whom sometimes visit us backward people: but although they have left something *durable* after them, and we are producing many things, like dust they sweep it all, together with us, from the earth.

You are proud, I say to you, and I repeat it once again; you are proud; guard yourself and save yourself from pride beforehand. Begin with the conviction that you are more stupid than anyone in Russia and it follows from this that you will grow wiser; listen attentively to every clever fellow as though you know exactly nothing and you want to learn everything from him. But my words are still a riddle to you; they will have no effect on you. You need either some misfortune or some shock. Pray God that this shock may occur, that you may meet some unbearable setback in the service, that a man may turn up who would strongly insult you and disgrace you in the sight of everyone, that you would not know where to hide yourself for shame, and that he would all at once explode all those oversensitive strings of your vanity. He will be your true brother and deliverer. O, how we need a public slap in the face, given in the sight of everyone!

1844

XXVIII

TO ONE WHO OCCUPIES
AN IMPORTANT POSITION

In the name of God, accept whatever position may be offered to you, and do not be disturbed by anything. You may have to go among the Circassians[1] in the Caucasus or, as before, accept the position of a governor-general—you are now needed everywhere. As for the difficulties of which you speak, everything is now difficult; everything has become complicated; there is much work everywhere. The more I investigate the substance of modern things, the less I can decide in what way a position is now more difficult, in what way easier. For one who is not a Christian everything has become difficult; for one who brings Christ into all the business and actions of his life, everything is easy. I would not say to you that you have become a complete Christian, but that you are close to it. Ambition does not move you, neither rank nor reward entices you, you are not thinking of showing off before Europe and making yourself an historic person. In short, you have reached the spiritual level necessary for one who wishes now to benefit Russia. What are you afraid of? I do not understand how anything can

1. The Circassians were tribal inhabitants of the Caucasus with whom the Russians were at war in the nineteenth century. They were not conquered until the reign of Alexander II (1855–1881). After the conquest of the Caucasus, about 200,000 Circassians emigrated to Turkey to join their coreligionists.

frighten one who already comprehends that it is necessary everywhere to act as a Christian. In every place he is a sage, everywhere a specialist.

Suppose you go to the Caucasus—first of all, you will get your bearings. Christian humility will not permit you any precipitancy. Like a beginning student, you will learn. You will not let one old officer pass by without asking about his personal participation in battles with the enemy, knowing that a knowledge of *the whole* can only proceed from a knowledge of the details. You will insist that everyone relate all his exploits in battle and bivouac life; ask an officer who served under General Tsitsianov or General Ermolov,[2] and the officers of the present epoch, and, when you have taken in everything that you need, imbibed all the details, unite all the separate data and find the result—in the result will appear a plan for the army commander; it will not be necessary to cudgel your brains; everything that you have to do will be clear as day. And when the whole plan is in your head, you will not then be in a hurry; your Christian humility will not allow it. Without announcing it to anyone, ask every notable officer how he would act in your place; do not leave one opinion unheard, not the advice of anyone whatsoever, even if it should be of someone of low position, knowing that God can sometimes inspire a simple man with an intelligent opinion. Do not bother with warring opinions, knowing that this is not a matter of disputes and quarrels; listen individually to each person who might want to speak with you. In short, listen to everyone, but do it so that your own brain remains in command of you; and your own brain will command you sensibly, because it listens to everyone. You will be in no condition to do an unreasonable thing, because unreasonable things are done from pride and confidence in self. But Christian humility everywhere saves you

2. Prince Paul Tsitsianov (1754–1806) was a Russian general of Caucasian extraction who was instrumental in the annexation of southeast Transcaucasia. General Alexis Ermolov was commander of Russian troops in the Caucasus between 1816 and 1827.

and drives away self-dazzlement, which is found in many even very intelligent people who, having learned only half the business, already think they know it all and fly headlong into action; while, alas! a whole half of that business which is apparently known to us may remain hidden in the unknown. No, God drives this crude dazzlement away from us. What is there for you to fear in the Caucasus?

You may, as before, happen to be a governor-general somewhere in Russia—and Christian wisdom will dawn upon you. I know very well that it is now more difficult to command in Russia than ever before and, perhaps, more difficult even than in the Caucasus. There are many abuses; graft has become so great that no human means can destroy it. I know that another lawless course of action has been set up side by side with the laws of the state, and it has already almost turned itself into a lawful one, so that the laws remain only for show; if we only look steadily at what others look at superficially, not mistrusting any fact, then the head of a more intelligent man than you will begin to spin. But act intelligently. Christian humility would compel you not to abandon yourself to the conclusions of prideful intelligence but to examine things patiently. Knowing how many outside influences every man is now subject to, and how they are all connected with carrying out his function, you will be curious first to learn the main job occupying each, to learn him from all sides, including his domestic and family life, the way he thinks, his inclinations and habits. For this you should not use spies. No, you would question him yourself. He would tell you everything and converse with you, because in your face there is something that inspires trust in you for everything; with the help of this you will learn what no high-handed shouter or name-calling scolder ever learns. You would not pursue anyone for injustice until the whole chain clearly appears before you, with the necessary links which the officials have not noticed. You already know that guilt has been so split up among everyone that it is now impossible to say at first who is the most guilty. There are the guiltlessly guilty and the guilty innocent. Therefore you will be incomparably more cautious and circumspect than ever before. You will scrutinize more firmly the soul of the man, knowing that the source of everything is in it. You must know souls, and do nothing without that. Only he can learn the soul of others who has begun to work on his own soul, as you have now begun to do. If you recognize a cheat not only as a cheat but also as a man, if you recognize all his spiritual strength, given to him for good but converted by him to evil or not used at all, then you will be able to reproach him so that he will find no place where he can hide from himself. The affair will suddenly take another turn, if you show the man how he is guilty to himself as well as to others. You will so shake him up that he will suddenly have the courage to be different, and only then will you realize how noble is our Russian race, even in the cheat.

Your present governor-generalship will be no different from the one before. The chief mistake of your former management, which nevertheless brought great benefit, despite the fact that you condemn and defame it, consisted, in my opinion, in your not really defining correctly the essence of your position. You took the position of a governor-general for the permanent head and business administrator of the province, whose beneficent influence could only be tangibly felt in the province as a result of his long sojourn in one place. One of our government men thus defined this position: "The governor-general is a minister of internal affairs pausing on the road." This definition is more in accordance with what the government expects of this position. This position is temporary rather than permanent. The governor-general is sent out in order to speed up the beat of the governmental pulse within the provinces, to bring into faster movement all governmental work in provincial places, both those combined and those independent under separate ministries, to give a push to everything, by his authority to ease the difficulty of many places in their dealings with separate ministeries, without bringing in any new elements and without introducing anything of himself, to compel everything to return more quickly to the laws and limits already pointed out and defined. You took this power, which is the supreme expression of what has been established, for the troublesome responsibility of a steward which should be left to him—he would take upon himself all such trivial matters; for yourself you seized that part which should belong to a governor but not to a governor-general, and by this you diminished the significance of your high position. You considered your position a lifetime sinecure. You wanted your establishment, by itself, to be the memorial of your sojourn. A fine aspiration, but if you had then been what you now are, that is, more a Christian, you would have seen to another memorial. To organize roads, bridges, and communications, and to organize them as intelligently as you have organized them, is really necessary; but to examine the many inner roads, which up to now have retarded the Russian in his aspiration for a full development of his strength and which have hindered him from benefiting from both the roads and all those other external forms about which we so zealously fuss, is still more necessary. Pushkin, when he saw the preoccupation not with the chief thing, but with what is derived from the chief thing, usually expressed himself in this proverb: "If there is a trough, there will be pigs." The bridges, roads, and all these communications are in fact the pigs, and nothing else. If there are cities, they will take care of themselves. In Europe they did not trouble overmuch about these things— as cities appeared, roads to them appeared: private persons built them without any government grants, and such a great number of them have now been developed that they have begun to propose seriously the following questions to one another: "Why this speed of communication? What has mankind gained by all these railroads, what has it acquired for its development as a whole, what use is it that one city now is impoverished and another has become a second-hand market place, while the number of lounge-lizards has been augmented through all the world?" Russia would have been screened off from all this trash and had such comforts as are unknown in Europe, if only many of us had bothered first about our internal affairs, as we ought.

First reflect on yourself, said the Savior, and greater glory will be given unto you. Your actions were much more meaningful morally. All those whom I have heard respectfully echoing your instructions say that you have eradicated many falsities, that you have created many truly noble and fine officials. I knew this, although in your modesty you did not tell me. But you would have done more if you had then remembered that your position was temporary: you should not have taken care only that everything be well during your tenure, but that everything be well after your tenure. You should constantly have imagined that after you a weak, untalented successor might come into this position, one who not only would not support the order arranged by you, but would corrupt it. That is why from the beginning you must think of acting so simply and strengthening what has been done so firmly that after you no one can undo what has once been established. You must cut down the crown of evil, not just its branches, and give such a push to the general movement of everyone that the machine will keep on working after you leave, so that there will be no need for a supervisor to stand over it, and an eternal memorial to your governor-generalship will be raised through it alone. I now know that you will not act otherwise and therefore will in no way neglect your position, if it should be offered to you anew. A governor-general has never been so important and needful as at the present time. I will name you some deeds that no one but a governor-general can do.

First, establish the legal limits of every position, and every official of the province in a full knowledge of his position. This is no trifle. In these latter days almost every provincial official has unnoticeably trespassed the bounds and limits prescribed by law. One has become too pared and constrained, another split up into operations damaging to others; some well-established positions were weakened and enfeebled through the introduction of innumerable others of temporary and related natures. In these latter days especially do we recognize a loosening of the hands of authority precisely where it is necessary *to hinder* action, and a binding of hands precisely where it is necessary *to assist* them. To restore every position to its legal circle has now become so difficult that the officials themselves have gone astray in their understanding of it. Receiving it as a legacy from their predecessors in the form that the latter had given it, they all more or less think of it in this form and not in the form of its prototype, which has already almost gone out of their heads. Because of this, many loyal and even highly intelligent chiefs wanted to destroy or quite transform those positions which ought simply to be reconstituted. Only a supreme and authoritative chief can accomplish this kind of thing, if he does not neglect to investigate the essence of every position himself. All our positions, in their prototypes, are beautiful and properly created for our land. Let us expressly look at the provincial administration.

The prime person is the governor. His power is manifested in several ways. He is the authoritative head and ruler of everything concerning economic and police administration throughout the province: all municipal matters except the internal organization of the cities; the maintenance of order between cities; everything of the rural administration produced in the country outside the cities: collection of taxes, distribution of duties, building of roads, construction and repairs of all kinds. In the first case, all the provincial city police commissioners and the town governors of all the towns are under his full and immediate command; in the second case, it is the captains of district police and the land assessors who are responsible to him through the provincial governments, which are formed in the spirit of joint-conciliar governments, not as individual chancelleries with their own secretaries, so that the responsibility for every important abuse, if the governor should desire, falls without fail on the advisors and officials and is limited by his authority.

He is more than a bureaucrat and a witness of the workings of other bureaus; they are all dependent on him and under the direction of his particular ministry; if these places are simply accomplishing some transaction and contract, whether it be concerning a return of something found or the leasing of public land or lake, or concerning business in general, fulfillment of contracts of purchase, he should be there. No running expenses and transactions can be made without his personal presence. In such a way, the offices, which are not at all compelled by him in so far as their internal workings are concerned, by his presence are cut off from all paths of abuse.

All the apparatus of the judiciary as, for instance, all town tribunals as well as courts of last resort are under him—the civil chambers which seem to be under the full jurisdiction of the imperial department appear independent of the governor, but in all instances of possible injustice are checked at every step by the governor, who at the time of his trips through all the province, which should occur not less than twice a year, has the right, since he oversees the courts, to demand a summary of two or three decided cases, so that he may examine them at his leisure along with his secretary; in this way he will keep them all in suspense. In short, while he has no authority over the offices which are dependent on other authorities, he has the right to put a stop to an abuse before it happens.

On the nobility he can have only a moral influence. In the performance of his duties that come in contact with the nobility, he arranges it so that he has dealings with their representative, in the person of the provincial marshal of nobility, in such a way that, by means of him alone, he can come to an understanding with them all; it is here that the legislator's wisdom is most apparent, because otherwise he would have no possibility of communicating with and getting on with them all, taking into consideration the differences of education, customs, ways of thought, and numberless diversities of character which not one of the European nobilities presents and which is contained only in us. Since the rank of marshal of nobility is almost equal in grade to the rank of governor, having a right to first place after him in the province, he already has an indication of the necessity for them to be friends; otherwise, they both would be uncomfortable in their secular relations and narrow in the execution of their functions. The very offices of district police commissioners and assessors, who are elected by the nobility, are later discovered to be fully dependent on the governor and thus indicate the necessity for each to reinforce the other. By threatening in the name of the governor, the marshal of nobility can do much where his own power is insufficient, just as the governor can operate on the nobility more successfully and powerfully by means of the marshal.

Blunders can occur everywhere; falsehoods can creep in everywhere; the governor himself can be sinful. And this is foreseen: there is a special official independent of everyone, whose function it is to keep himself apart from everyone, even from the governor himself. This is the government attorney, who is the eye of the law, without whom not one document can leave the province. Not one thing done in all the province can escape him. Nothing may be final if he does not mark on every page: "I have read it." He is not subject to anyone in the province; he gives an account to no one other than the minister of justice, with whom he alone is in direct contact, and he can always send in a protest on whatever is done in the province.

In short, everything is complete, and everywhere the wisdom of the legislators is perceived, both in the establishment of powers and in their contacts among themselves. I do not speak of those institutions where government provision has stretched still further; I refer only to the courts of conscientiousness,[3] whose like I do not know in other states. In my opinion, it is the best demonstration of love for mankind, for wisdom, and for spiritual knowledge. All those cases where the weight of the law is heavy and cruel; all matters connected with the minor and the insane person; everything which only human conscience can decide and where a just law can be unjust; everything that must be ended amicably and peacefully in a lofty Christian sense, without the delay of going the rounds of red tape—all this is this judge's [of conscientiousness] subject. And how intelligent it is that the choice of a judge of conscientiousness depends on the nobility, which usually selects for this position one whom the consensus agrees is a disinterested man who loves humanity. Also, how good it is that no salary is prescribed for him, no reward, and that there is no worldly enticement for a man here. I once desired very much to work in this office. How many confused, quarrel-making things it is possible to decide in it. Regardless of their own advantage, the litigants themselves will take the matter into the courtroom of the judge conscientiousness as the rumor gets about that the judge actually judges according to conscience and has become famous for the wisdom of his divine judgment. Which of us would not wish reconciliation?

In short, the more you look into the administration of the provincial governments, the more you are amazed at the wisdom of their founder: we perceive that God himself invisibly built it with the hands of the Emperor. Everything is perfect, sufficient; everything is organized just to promote men to good actions, to holding out their hands to one another and to stopping them on the paths to abuses. I cannot even think what an additional official is needed for; no new person has a place, every innovation is an unnecessary insert. As you know, how-

3. The office of the judge of conscientiousness had under its jurisdiction problems connected with estates, administration of the properties of minors, and some other matters.

ever, there are provincial rulers who have tacked innumerable varied officials on to special commissions, innumerable temporary investigative committees, distributed and parceled out the activities of every position and shook the officials so that they lost the least understanding of the exact limits of their functions. It is good that you did not do this, because you then understood this matter better than others. You know very well that to appoint a new official to limit his predecessor's thievery means to make two thieves instead of one. A general system of limitations is a very trivial system. It is impossible for a man to limit a man; in following years, a need to limit whatever is solicited for limitation will appear, and then there will be no end to limitations. This shallow and pitiful system, like all other limiting systems, can be formed only in a state with colonies[4] composed of the dregs of the people who have neither the national goals nor the national spirit, where selflessness and nobility are unknown and there are only mercenary personal advantages. It is necessary to show faith in the nobility of man; without that there will be no nobility. Who knows whether he will not be looked at suspiciously, as though he were a swindler, and overseers appointed on all sides of him, so that his hands cannot help being paralyzed. It is necessary to unbind every hand, not to bind them; it is necessary to emphasize this, so that everyone may keep himself in check, and not be checked by others; so that he may be several times stricter to himself by his own law, so that he may see how he is a scoundrel in the face of his position; in short, so that he may be introduced into the meaning of his lofty position. And only the governor-general can do this, if he does not neglect to comprehend every position in its actual essence and mentally put himself in the place of the official whom he wishes to introduce into the full meaning of his position. As a consequence of this, all your dealings with the officials will be personal,

4. Gogol's reference is probably to the Russian convict colonies, most of which were in Siberia.

without secretaries and lifeless memoranda, and because of this, your own offices will become smaller and will not at all resemble those monstrous, enormous offices which other chiefs acquire. As you know, these huge offices inflict a great deal of harm in that they cut officials off from their business, suddenly form new stages, and thus new difficulties, imperceptibly interject a new authority, sometimes not at all invisible, in the shape of a simple secretary through whose hands all business will begin to pass; a kind of mistress will appear among the secretaries, because of whom there will be intrigues, quarrels, and devilish confusions, which will become constant; and the affair will end, besides the outrages of new disorders and complications, in a quantity of public sums being devoured. God keep you from the establishment of offices. Do not be in touch with anyone otherwise than personally. How is it possible to neglect conversation with a man, especially if the conversation involves oneself, the fulfillment of one's obligations and duties, and thus involves one's soul? How is it possible to engage in such a conversation in the empty journalistic talk and lifeless speeches on every kind of nonsense plucked out of lying European journals? It is possible for both parties to converse about the duty of man so that it seems to both that they are chatting with angels in the presence of God Himself. Speak so with your subordinate, that is, instructing and nourishing his soul! Do not forget that the Russian language—I do not mean that language which is now shifting into everyday use, nor a bookish language, nor that language formed at the time of our abuses, but that actual Russian language which is invisibly carried through all the Russian land, despite our alienation in our land, which does not touch the business of our lives, but which everyone nevertheless perceives is the actual Russian language—this language the chief calls his father. Be with them as a father is with his children: a father does not employ red tape with his children, he expresses himself to each of them plainly. Acting so, you may introduce each one into a knowledge of his position and do a really great deed.

And here is another deed for you, which no one other than a governor-general can perform, which at the present time is even indispensable, not only necessary, namely, to lead the nobility to a real knowledge of its title. This estate in its really Russian kernel is beautiful, despite its strange husk. But the nobility does not yet perceive this. Many hardly suspect it, others abide in complete ignorance of it, a third group wishes to be the ideal nobility of foreign states, a fourth does not even pose this question to itself: is a nobility necessary in the world? If we find some among them who have some lucid thoughts on this, these thoughts are not distributed among the masses, and the masses do not hear them. In these latter days, aside from everything else, a spirit of distrust for the government has been established in some of the nobility. In these latter days of European disturbances and every kind of sedition, some malefactors have attempted to set a rumor afloat in our nobility that the government is seeking to weaken their importance and reduce them to insignificance. Fugitives, emigrants, and all kinds of ill-wishers of Russia have written articles that filled up columns of foreign newspapers with the precise intention of exciting enmity between the nobility and the government: on the one hand, showing the Emperor of Russia a party of some kind of fantastic boyars calling his power into question, and on the other hand, showing the nobility that the Emperor does not regard them with favor and does not like their rank as a whole. That is, they want to cook up trouble and turmoil in Russia, in the midst of which they might gain some advantage. Their calculation was that reciprocal peril and suspicion is a terrible thing and can in time really produce a break in the most sacred bonds. But, glory to God, the time has not yet come that a few madcaps can stir up the entire state. The project has remained a fantastic project, although not a few sparks of misunderstanding and reciprocal distrust have been lit, and

I know many nobles who are seriously convinced that the
Emperor does not like their estate and are even upset because
of it. Settle this matter for them and declare the whole truth,
hiding nothing. Say that the Emperor loves this estate more
than all others, but he loves the truly Russian meaning in it—
that beautiful form in which it should be according to the
spirit of our land. And it could not be otherwise. Who does not
love the flower of his nation? And among us, the flower of our
nation is the nobility, not an alien, foreign estate. But the nobility ought to put its best foot forward and define the meaning
of its rank, because in the form in which it now is, in the absence of unity in its general spirit, in this diversity of thoughts,
educations, lives, habits, in such a confused form of understanding of itself, it can give no one a real and complete idea
of what the nobility in our land is. Because of this, no wise man
can now know how he should be with it. It follows that the nobility should act in its actual and complete meaning. And here
you can really help them all, because, being yourself a Russian
noble and already understanding the lofty meaning of our
nobility, you have more powers than anyone to explain it.
Many words are not necessary for this, because the start of it
all is that you declare it to them in a group.

Our nobility presents an extraordinary phenomenon. It was
formed among us quite otherwise than in other lands. It began
not with a violent advent, with warrior vassals who were constant contenders for supreme power and eternal oppressors of
the lowest estate; it began among us as personal service to the
Tsar, the people, and the whole land, service based on moral
virtues, not on physical strength. In our nobility there is no
pride in the advantages of its estate, as there is in other lands;
there is none of the arrogance of the German nobility; no one
among us boasts of his family or of antiquity of origin, although
our nobility is the most ancient of all—only some anglomaniacs
really boast, those who have been infected during their trips to
England; perhaps now and then someone boasts of an ancestor

who served the Tsar and his land with a really loyal service; and he will also boast of a bad ancestor on whom an epigram made up by a noble was published. Only one thing excuses this boasting—the feeling of his own moral nobility, which God has put into his breast. And if it comes to displaying this inner lofty nobility by some action, not one of us is behindhand, although he may be worst of all and has lived in soot and grime. Among us the nobility is like a vessel in which this moral nobility is contained, needing to be spread, person by person, through all the Russian land, so that understanding may be given to all the other estates, which is why the highest estate is called the light of the nation. And if you only tell them what I now say, which is the real truth, and unfold before them that field of action which now presents all of them with the prospect of immortalizing their names in posterity; if you clearly show them that the whole Russian land calls for help and it is possible to help it by one noble deed, and the noble deed ought to show who has received nobility from birth, then their hearts will touch glasses with your heart, like wine glasses when hors d'oeuvres are served. Do not hide anything from them, declare the whole truth to them. Why compel them to learn from lying foreign newspapers and allow madcap ideas to spin around in their brains? Display the whole truth to them openly. Tell them that Russia is indeed unhappy, that it is unhappy because of plundering and falsehoods and they have still not raised the alarm against such insolence; that the Emperor's heart aches in a way that no one of them knows, nor hears, or can know. It is possible to be otherwise in the face of this whirlwind of confusions which have arisen, which have walled them all off from one another and almost taken away from each the scope to do good and really benefit his land, in the face of widespread obscurity and general diversion of everyone from the spirit of our land, in the face, finally, of these innumerable swindlers, salesmen of justice, and plunderers who, like crows, fly from all sides to peck at our living flesh and pick their profit out of our troubled waters. When you tell them this, follow it up by showing that now before them all is the prospect of giving really noble and lofty service to the Tsar, namely, as generously as once they stood in ranks against the foe,[5] so generously will they now occupy unenticing places and positions now disgraced by base *raznochintsi*.[6] Then you will see how our nobility is aroused. There will be no getting rid of those who desire to act in the service and take the most unknown places. And, having served, they will demand neither reward, nor honor, or even privilege and advantage, it will be sufficient that they have shown their lofty inner advantage. In short, only show them the eminence of their rank and you will see how generous their nature is.

You can point out a second great thing to them which they can do—it is the education of the peasantry, in such a way that they [the peasants] become a model of this estate for all Europe, because many in Europe have now seriously begun to think about the ancient patriarchal mode of life whose features have disappeared everywhere but in Russia, and, having examined the weakness of all the establishments and foundations of the present time, they are beginning to speak publicly of the advantages of our peasant mode of life for their improvement. And that is why you ought to persuade the nobility, so that they may consider more intently the real Russian relations of the landowner with the peasants, not those false lying ones which were formed in the time of their shameful carelessness about their own patrimony, which they gave into the hands of hired assistants and stewards, so that they may really take care

5. The reference is probably to the unity patriotic Russians thought Russia displayed in the face of the Napoleonic invasion of 1812. Indeed, 1812 became almost a mystic symbol for many of the nineteenth-century writers and thinkers.

6. *Raznochintsi* were persons of the lower classes who became educated but did not become members of the nobility. One might say that they were, by virtue of their education, classless. Many of them were to become cultural leaders of a more liberal persuasion. Belinsky is an example of a *raznochinets*.

of them [the peasants], as of their blood relatives, not as of alien people, and so that they may look upon them as fathers upon their children. By this means alone can they raise their estate to that condition in which it ought to abide, which purposely among us does not bear the name of free or slave but by Christians is called after the name of Christ himself.[7] All this a governor-general can fully explain to the nobility, if he thinks about it in advance and himself goes into the full meaning of our nobility. And this will be your second great deed.

And here is your third deed, which also can be done by no one but a governor-general. All European states are now ill of an extraordinary complexity of laws and resolutions. Everywhere one can see a remarkable phenomenon, namely, the laws properly civil have gone beyond their limits and have trespassed on areas that do not belong to them. On the one hand, they have trespassed on an area which for a long time was in the sphere of common law; on the other hand, they have trespassed on an area which should have remained eternally under the administration of the Church. This did not occur violently: the flood of civil laws proceeded of itself, everywhere meeting empty, defenceless places. Fashion undermined custom, deviation of the clergy from the true life in Christ abandoned to arbitrariness all the private relations of every man in his private way of life. Civil laws took these forgotten spheres— such as abandoned orphans—under their tutelage, and it is thus that they became so complicated. They did not extend of themselves, and if some things which by legal form belong to custom and other things which should be in the eternal possession of the Church revert to them, then only a book which embraces large-scale deviations from public order and relations properly governmental can deduce them. To a man we see that the num-

7. The Russian word for peasant is *krest'yanin,* that for Christian is *khristianin.* It was the habit for those of Slavophile inclination, like Gogol, to link the two together.

ber of suits, the abuses, and all the slanders occurred just because the European philosopher-lawgivers began beforehand to
define all possible cases of deviation, down to the least detail,
and they disclosed to everyone, even to the noble and good,
ways to endless and unjust litigations, dishonorable affairs
which formerly one might not have ventured but which one
now ventures boldly, seeing in some clause of some enactment
the possibility and the hope of sometime getting back a lost
property, or simply only the possibility of disputing another's
possessions. He walks like a hero, like a hero on the attack,
and he will not look at his opponent at all, although because
of this he may lose his last shirt, although it may mean he
wanders through all the world with all his family. The humanitarian now shamelessly produces a cruel thing in the sight
of everyone and even boasts of it, whereas he would be ashamed
of his very thoughts if a servant of the Church should present
both litigants in person to Christ, not merely their contemptible personal advantage; if it were handled as it ought to be,
so that in all cases of confusions, involvements, suspicions—in
short, in all matters where procrastination threatens from stage
to stage—the Church and not civil law would reconcile man
with man. But here is the question: how is it to be done? How
is it to be done so that to the civil law is restored only what
really ought to belong to the civil law; so that to common law is
restored what ought to remain in the power of common law;
and so that the Church is confirmed anew in what ought eternally to belong to the Church? In short, how may everything
be returned to its place? In Europe it is impossible to do this:
it is sick with blood, exhausted in vain battles, and has time
for nothing. The possibility is in Russia; it can insensibly be
accomplished in Russia—not by innovations, upheavals and
reforms, and not even by meetings, committees, debates, and
not by journalistic discussions and twaddle; in Russia every
governor-general can start it off by his administration of the
district entrusted to him, and as simply as this: by his own life.

By his patriarchal life and simple form of address to everyone he can extirpate fashion with its empty etiquette and strengthen Russian customs, which in this matter are good and can usefully be applied to present existence. He can have a strong effect on the relations both of the inhabitants of the cities among themselves and on making their relations with the landowners simpler; and the destruction of complex worldly relations such as the present ones will certainly lessen the quarrels and dissatisfactions which have sprung up like a whirlwind between the inhabitants of the cities. In the same way as he acts for the stabilization of customs, so can the governor-general act for the legal stabilization of the Church in the current life of the Russian: first, by the example of his own life and, second, by the measures he takes, which are not cumpulsory and forced, but are still several times stronger than all the forced ones. We will speak with you about this some time later, when you really have the position, but until that time I will say only this to you: if simple custom is stronger than all written law, then what is custom, if you examine it strictly? Sometimes it simply has no meaning in the present time, its basis is unknown, because it is not known from whence it came; its authority, its affirmation is not recognized; sometimes it has hung on from the time of paganism, in opposition to Christianity and to every element of the new life. Yet if, with all this, custom is so strong, why has it been so difficult to erase it through so many years? Why, if a custom based on reason is introduced, will it unanimously, with one voice, be recognized by everyone and be sanctified from on high by Christ himself and his Church? Such a custom continues forever and no power may smash it, however worldwide convulsions may ensue.

But this is a great subject; it is necessary to speak about it intelligently, and I am too stupid for it. Later, when God succors me and makes me understand, perhaps I will say something.

You will have much work. Be strong and trust firmly in the

position of governor-general, if only it is offered to you. Now you will fulfill it exactly as you ought and in conformity with what justice itself demands, that is, with your strength stimulated and refreshed, you will rush through all the district, arouse everyone, refresh everyone, excite everyone, give everyone a jolt, and then subsequently turn to another district in order to do the same thing there. You yourself will see that this position certainly ought to be temporary, otherwise it would make no sense, because the inner organism of the district is sufficient and complete, and there is no necessity for another steward besides the civil governor.

Be with God and fear nothing. But, although you may be busy in another position, follow these rules: nowhere forget that you are temporary. Arrange things so that they not only go well while you are there, but also after you, so that your successor can displace nothing, but cannot help acting in approval of your limits and keep to the legal directions you have given. Christ teaches you how to harden things firmly and forever. Be a real father to all the officials subject to you and help each one piously and honestly to fulfill his position. Lend everyone a brotherly hand, so that he may be relieved of his own vices and shortcomings. Have an influence on everyone, but an influence solely to compel each one to have an influence on himself. Also, see that no one be too dependent on you, using you for a crutch, like the Roman Catholic ladies who depend on their confessors, without whose permission they do not dare to step into another room and expect to go to confession if they do; but in order that a man may remember that a nurse is given to him for a time only and not for always, and that as soon as the tutor leaves him, he ought to guard himself more carefully than ever before, constantly remembering that now there is no one to look after him, and keeping sacred in his memory every word spoken to him. Also, seek that there be no weeping at parting from you, if you should happen to leave your post, but that every one look ahead more cheerfully and freshly, and therefore store up the admonitions that you may want to say to each one on the day of parting: all your words will be holy for them on that day, and what they have not accepted and fulfilled before they will accept and fulfill after you are gone. For me, the best moment is the time of parting from my friends; every one of my friends who now parts from me, parts gaily, his soul bright. All those who have parted from me in these latter days will confirm this to you. I am even confident that when I die all my loved ones will take leave of me gaily: none of them will weep; rather will they be brighter in soul after my death than during my life.

I will speak one word more to you concerning that love for and general inclination towards the self by which so many are driven. The courting of love for oneself is an illegitimate thing and ought not to occupy a man. Look to it that you love others, and not that others love you. He who demands payment for his love is mean and far from being a Christian. Oh, how thankful I am that from childhood God inspired me with a feeling—not understood by me—to shun all excessive effusions, even those of relatives and friends, as cloying and unpleasant. How right it is that a complete love ought not appertain to anyone on earth. It ought to be transmitted according to hierarchical order, and every authority, as he notes its tendency towards himself, ought immediately to turn it towards the lofty authority who has been established over him, so that in such a way it may reach its lawful source, and so that our beloved Tsar may solemnly transmit it, in the sight of all, to God himself.

1845

XXIX

WHOSE IS THE LOFTIEST
FATE ON EARTH

From a letter to U

The addressee is probably Count Sergey Uvarov
(1786–1855), Minister of Education, with whom Gogol
first entered into correspondence in 1833, when
he was seeking the post of professor of world history
at Kiev University. Before publication of
Selected Passages, Gogol had written to Uvarov to
assure him of Gogol's loyal intentions in the book.
See the "Introduction."

I can in no way tell you whose is the loftiest fate on earth, and
to whom is given the better lot. Before, when I was more foolish, I preferred one rank to another; now I see that the lot of
everyone is equally enviable. Everyone receives an equal requital—as one entrusted with one talent returned another in
addition to it, so another was given five talents and returned
another five in addition to them. I even think the lot of the first
is better, just because he did not enjoy fame on earth and did
not partake of the fascinating drink of earthly glory, like the
latter. Wonderful is the grace of God, appointing equal requital
to everyone who honestly fulfills his duty, whether he be the
Tsar or the last of the lowest. There will they all be made
equal, because they will all enter into the joy of their Lord and
will abide *equally* in God. Of course, Christ himself said in

another place, "In the house of my Father there are many mansions"; but as I think about these mansions, as I think about what the mansions of God must be, I cannot refrain from tears, and I know that I can in no wise decide which of them to choose for myself. If I should really be favored by the Heavenly Tsar and he should ask which of them I want, I know only that I would say, "The last, O Lord, only so that I may be in your house!" I am sure nothing would be more desirable than to serve in that assemblage which is already favored to contemplate His glory in all its grandeur. Only to lie at their feet and to kiss their holy feet!

1845

XXX

AN EXHORTATION

I will not now answer your letter; the answer will come later. I see and hear everything: your suffering is great. With such a tender soul to endure such coarse accusations; with such elevated feelings to live among such coarse, clumsy people as the inhabitants of the vulgar town in which you have settled, whose single insensitive, bungling touch has the power to smash, even without their knowledge, the best jewel of the heart, whose bearish paw slashes the finest strings in the soul, which were meant to strum celestial sounds—to shatter and explode them, to see, in addition to all this, the daily occurrence of abomination and to endure contempt from the contemptible! All this is grievous, I know. Your physical suffering is no less grievous: your nervous ailments, your dejections, and those terrible fits of anxiety which now obsess you—all this is grievous, grievous, I can say no more to you than—grievous!

But there is a consolation. This is but the beginning; you will be outraged still more: still mightier struggles are in prospect for you with bribe-takers, with scoundrels of all sorts, with shameless people for whom nothing is holy, who have not only the power to produce that vile thing about which you write, that is, to forge others' signatures, who dare to introduce such a terrible crime to an innocent soul, who see the penalty which is visited upon calumny and do not shudder at it—not only is this infamous, but there are other things many times more infamous; the story of any one of them would rob a tender-hearted man of his sleep forever. (Oh, it would have been better not to have been born among these people; all the host of heavenly powers shudders in terror of the punishments beyond the grave awaiting them, from which no one will deliver them.) You may expect to meet innumerable new defeats. In your almost defenseless vocation and inconspicuous position anything can happen. Your nervous attacks and ailments will also be stronger, your dejection will be more deadly, and your sorrows will be more shattering. But remember, we were not at all called into the world for celebrations and banquets. We were called here for battle; we will celebrate the victory *there*. And that is why we must not for a moment forget that we have entered into battle and choose something in which there is less peril; like good soldiers, every one of us must rush there where the battle is blazing. The Heavenly General views all of us from above, and our smallest deed does not escape his gaze. Do not shun the field of battle, and, when in battle, seek out not the enemy's weakness but his strength. You will not receive much glory for a battle which brings minor affliction and petty misfortune. It is no great glory for a Russian to fight with a peace-loving German when he knows beforehand that the German will run away. No! with a Circassian,[1] before whom everyone trembles, considering him invincible, to grapple with a Circassian and vanquish him, that is a glory one may boast of! Forward, my fair warrior! With God, good comrade! With God, my fair friend!

1. See note 1 to "To One who Occupies an Important Position."

1846

XXXI

ON THE ESSENCE OF RUSSIAN POETRY AND ON ITS ORIGINALITY

In spite of superficial marks of imitation, there is much in our poetry that belongs to it alone. Its native source was already in the breast of the people before its name was on anyone's lips. Its currents shoot through our songs, which have hardly any attachment to life and its objects, but many attachments to our propensity for boundless debauchery, to our aspiration to be carried no one knows where by their sounds. Its currents shoot through our proverbs, in which we may see a singular plenitude of the popular spirit, which knows how to make anything its instrument—irony, raillery, graphic accuracy of picturesque observation—so as to compose a thrilling language which thoroughly permeates the nature of the Russian, affecting all his life. Finally, its currents shoot through the words of the pastors of the churches—simple words, ineloquent, but marked by an aspiration to the height of that holy passivity to which a Christian ought to attain, by an aspiration to guide man not by captivating his heart but by the elevation, through reason, of his religious spirit. All that portended for our poetry something unknown to other peoples, a distinctive and original evolution.

But it is not in these three sources, already abiding in us, that our sweet poetry, now so charming to us, had its origin; just as the structure of our present civil order did not issue from elements already abiding in our land. Our civil order was not formed in a regular fashion, by a gradual march of events, by a measured and reasonable introduction of European customs —which would have been impossible, for the reason that the European enlightenment was already too mature, its flow too great for it not to burst into Russia sooner or later from all sides, and not to produce, without such a leader as Peter the Great was, much more dissension than really ensued—our civil order was born of a shock, of that Herculean shock of all the Empire which the Reformer Tsar produced when the will of God invested him with the thought of introducing his youthful people into the circle of European states and of suddenly initiating it into all that Europe had procured by long years of bloody struggles and sufferings. The Russian people needed an abrupt change and the European enlightenment was the flint on which it was necessary to strike with all our slumbering mass. The flint may enkindle the tinder, but, so long as you have not struck it, the tinder will not take fire. The spark suddenly flashed from the people.

This fire was an enthusiasm, the enthusiasm of an awakening, an enthusiasm at first unconscious: no one was yet aware that he had been awakened by the aid of the European light in order to examine himself more profoundly and not in order to copy Europe; everyone only felt that he was awakened. Indeed, this abrupt change of the entire state, produced by one man— who was, furthermore, the Tsar himself, who for a time magnanimously gave up his imperial title in the determination to learn every trade himself; axe in hand, he was foremost in every enterprise, so that no disorder might occur at the least change in governmental form—was a thing worthy of enthusiasm. A revolution, which as a rule floods the shaken state with blood for years, if it is brought about by internal party struggles, was carried out, in the view of all Europe, in such order that it seemed the brilliant maneuver of a well-trained army. Russia was suddenly clothed in a sovereign grandeur; she spoke with a voice of thunder and shone with the reflection of European knowledge. Everyone in the young state was enthusiastic, uttering the same cry of astonishment that a savage utters at the sight of glittering treasures brought before him. This enthusiasm was reflected in our poetry, or, to put it better, it created it. That is why our poetry, since the first piece of verse appeared in print, among us took on a solemn tone, attempting to express at one and the same time its rapture with that light which had been introduced into Russia, its astonishment at the great field of action at hand to it, and gratitude to the Tsar responsible for it. Since that time the yearning for light has become elemental to us, the sixth sense of the Russian, and it has set our contemporary poetry going, supplying a new civilizing principle which was not seen in a single one of the three sources we mentioned above.

What is Lomonosov,[1] if he is examined rigorously? A young enthusiast, attracted by the light of knowledge and the career in store for him. By chance he fell among the poets: the enthusiasm of our recent victory compelled him to draft his first ode. Hastily he studied the meter and form which at that time were in vogue among our neighbors the Germans, without examining whether they were proper for the Russian language. There is no trace of creation in his odes composed by rhetorical rules, but enthusiasm is immediately perceptible everywhere that he touched something similar to that science dear to his soul. He touched upon the Aurora Borealis, which was once an object of his researches, and the fruit of this contact was the ode "Meditation at Evening on the Divine Majesty," whose majesty, from one end to the other, is such that no one but Lomonosov could have written it. The same causes gave birth to the

1. M. V. Lomonosov (1711–1765), the "Leonardo of Russia," is often given credit for being the founder of modern Russian literature and culture. His importance to literature is enormous in that "he fixed the standards of the literary language and introduced a new prosody, which, despite numerous revolutionary attempts to dislodge it, still rules the greater part of Russian poetry." (Mirsky, pp. 44–45) Most of his original work was done in the didactic epistle and the ode.

famous message to Shuvalov,[2] "On the Uses of the Glass." All contact with that Russia dear to his heart, which he considered from the angle of its radiant future, filled him with a wonder-working energy. Into his cold strophes there suddenly slip stanzas which are such that you no longer know where you are. It is exactly as though he is describing himself in these lines:

> *The divine prophet David*
> *Sounds his sacred strings,*
> *And, his lips full of God,*
> *Enraptured Isaiah thunders.*[3]

He views all the Russian land from end to end as though from a luminous height, feasting his eyes on its infinitude and on its virginal nature without entering it. In his descriptions we perceive more the gaze of the naturalist than that of the poet; but the frank power of his enthusiasm turned the naturalist into a poet. It is most amazing that, while confining his versified speech to the narrow strophes of the German iamb, he did not at all cramp his own language: his language moves in these narrow strophes as majestically and freely as a deep river at ease between its banks. He is even freer and better in verse than in prose; it is not for nothing that Lomonosov has been called the father of our poetic speech. It is amazing that the inceptor should appear as the master and legislator of the language. Lomonosov stands in front of our poets the way a preface stands in front of a book. His poetry is the beginning of the dawn. In him it is like a flash of summer lightning: it does not illuminate all, only a few of his strophes. Russia itself only appears in general geographic outline. He seems only to care about sketching an outline of the huge Empire, marking the

2. Probably I. I. Shuvalov (1727–1797), a high nobleman and statesman during the reign of Elizabeth whose tendencies were generally conservative. While he was a supporter of Peter III, he did swear allegiance to Catherine when she usurped the throne.

3. These are lines 117–120 of Lomonosov's ode "On the Occasion of the Birthday of the Empress Elizabeth, 1757."

frontiers by points and lines, leaving it to others to fill in the colors; it is as though he were the original, prophetic outline of what is to come.

By the hand of Lomonosov, odes became customary among us. Festivals, victories, namesdays, even illuminations and fireworks became subjects for odes. The composers of them have expressed only an absolute lack of talent in place of enthusiasm. The only possible exception is Petrov,[4] who is not devoid of some power and a poetic flame: he was really a poet, in spite of the rigidity and staleness of his lines. All the others are reminiscent only of the cold rhetorical quality of Lomonosov's odes and exhibit, instead of the harmony of Lomonosov's language, twittering and confused words that torment your ears. But the flint had touched the tinder; poetry had already blazed up: Lomonosov did not have time to take his hand from his lyre before Derzhavin introduced his first songs.

It was in the epoch of Catherine, whose reign can be called a brilliant exhibition of the first truly Russian products, that in all fields Russian talents began to manifest themselves: out of battles, generals arose; out of domestic institutions, statesmen; out of negotiations, diplomats; and out of the philological and teaching academies appeared the poet Derzhavin, with that picturesque, stately mien found in all the personages of Catherine's time, still displayed with a certain savage freedom, with a good number of imperfections in its parts, still not quite trimmed, as happens with works somewhat hastily exhibited. The thought of a similarity between Lomonosov and Derzhavin, which comes to mind with the first glance at them both, disappears immediately that Derzhavin is looked at more attentively. In sum, even by his education, the second presents a complete contrast to the first. While the first was entirely given over to science, considering his verse only a diversion and re-

4. V. P. Petrov (1736–1799) was an imitator of Lomonosov who, while famous in his time, is no longer much read. He did, however, translate Alexander Pope, whom he greatly admired.

laxation, the second was entirely given over to his verse, considering a general education in science superfluous, unnecessary. In him we also perceive the autocratic, national grandeur of Russia; but it is no longer the geographic outlines of the Empire that we see: its people and life come forward. It is not the abstract sciences but the science of life that interests him. His odes are addressed to people of all estates and positions, and in them we discern an attempt to inscribe the law of man's moral actions, even that of his pleasures. In him art has appeared. There is in him something more gigantic and more soaring than in Lomonosov. The mind is at a loss to decide whence came the hyperbolic range of his speech. It may be a residue of our legendary Russian epic, which in the form of obscure prophecy has been transmitted to our own day in our land, prefiguring something higher awaiting us, or it may have been wafted to him from his distant Tatar ancestors, from the steppes where the wretched remains of the hordes wander, inflaming his imagination with tales of mile-high knights who lived on earth for a thousand years—be that as it may, this characteristic of Derzhavin's is amazing. Sometimes God knows how far he will go for his words and expressions, just so that he may come closer to his subject. Everything in him is wild, huge; but where the power of inspiration came to his aid, all this enormity contributes to vivify his subject with supernatural strength, so that it seems as though he is gazing with a thousand eyes. It is enough to run through his "Cascade,"[5] where it seems that a whole epic has been poured into one aspiring ode. In "Cascade," next to him other poets are pigmies. In it nature is as though superior to nature as we see it, men stronger than men known to us, and our ordinary life, next to the majestic life there portrayed, is like an anthill whose swarming is seen from afar. Derzhavin, it may be said, is the singer of grandeur. Everything in him is majestic: the grand figure of Catherine, grand Russia gazing round its eight seas, its eagle

5. Sometimes translated "The Waterfall."

captains; in short, everything in him is grandeur. Nevertheless, we notice that the constant object of his thoughts, which occupied him more than anything else, was to trace the image of a strong man, tempered in the work of life, ready for combat, not for some one time, but for all time; to present him as he must have been, in his opinion, when he arose out of the strength of our Russian race, fostered by the unshakable rock of our Church. Often, leaving aside the person to whom the ode was written, he puts in his place his own loyal, upright man. Then profound truths resound in a voice far loftier than the ordinary: a sacred, sublime significance is restored to what we were accustomed to call commonplace, and his eternal words are hearkened to as though they came from the very lips of the Church. In comparison with other poets, everything in him seems gigantic. His poetic images, not having a fully completed form, fade in a kind of spiritual outline, and because of this their grandeur is still greater. For example, the poet is depicting Old Man Caspian at a time when, angered by the tempest, he

> *Rises into the cresting waves:*
> *Now he leaps up sternly, now, rushing to Hell,*
> *His trident strikes against the ships;*
> *The grey ruler's hair stands on end,*
> *And his voice thunders in the mountains.*[6]

Here it seems that he wanted to create a *visible* image of Old Man Caspian, but the Old Man faded in a kind of spiritual *invisible* outline: the ear hears only the rumble of the thundering sea, and instead of the old man's grey rulers, it is the hairs on the head of the reader himself which stand on end, startled by the stern grandeur of the picture. Everything in him is on a large scale. His style is rougher hewn than that of any other of our poets. When it is dissected, we see that it is the result of an extraordinary union of the most noble terms with the lowest and simplest ones, which no one but

6. These are lines 66–70 of Derzhavin's ode "On V. A. Zubov's Journey from Persia through the Caucasus," written in 1797.

Derzhavin would venture. Who other than he would dare to express himself as he expresses himself in one passage about the majestic man at the instant that he has fulfilled his duty on earth:

> *. . . and he awaited death like a guest,*
> *Thoughtfully curling his moustache.*[7]

Who except for Derzhavin would be so bold as to associate a thing like death with such an insignificant act as curling a moustache? But how palpably visible is the man himself, and what a profound melancholy sentiment remains in your soul because of it! It must be said, however, that both this and all Derzhavin's other gigantic virtues, which have given him an advantage over all our other poets, are suddenly converted into indecorum and ugliness as soon as inspiration abandons him. Then everything is in disorder: diction, language, style—everything squeaks like a cart with ungreased wheels, and the poem is like a corpse abandoned by the soul. The traces of his incomplete self-education, both intellectual and moral, are visibly reflected in his creations. The man who preached to others about how to behave did not know how to behave himself, he was a long way from being himself and it took great effort for him to reach the inspiration to speak of what should be unbosomed freely in a poet. Add a complete education to such a man and there would have been no nobler poet than Derzhavin; now he remains like a huge desert rock before which no one can stop and stand for long; one would rather hurry to other, pleasanter places.

Derzhavin was still striking the strings of his lyre while everything around him was already changing: the century of Catherine, the eagle generals, manorial splendor, and the manorial life were passing away like a dream. The epoch of Alexander I ensued, neat, decorous, polished. Everyone buttoned himself up and, as though feeling they had been unbuttoned too

7. These are lines 99–100 of Derzhavin's poem "Aristipp's Bath," written in 1811.

long, they vied with one another to acquire an affected propriety and harmonious manners. The French became the models for everything, and, just as the Parisian fops for a long time captivated our society, so the clever French poets for a time captivated our poets. Nevertheless, to the honor of our real poetic sensibility, it must be said that La Fontaine alone passed for a model, exactly because he was closest to nature: Dmitriev, Khemnitzer, and Bogdanovich[8] began to produce works similar to his in simplicity of creation and in treatment of subject. The Russian language suddenly acquired the freedom and ease, unknown to Derzhavin, to fly from subject to subject. Instead of the ode, they began to attempt all sorts and forms of poetry. Dmitriev gave proof of much talent, taste, simplicity, and decorum in everything, by which means he killed the pomposity and grandiloquence which marked the untalented imitators of Derzhavin and Lomonosov. But a superficial epoch could not give rich content to our poetry: only social phenomena became its subject; it was like a clever man of the world showing his intelligence by sitting in a salon and leading the conversation, not at all openly to avow his spiritual position or to propose some important matter to others, but simply to start a conversation and flaunt his skill in all subjects. The last sounds of Derzhavin died away, as the last sounds of a church organ die away, and our poetry, leaving the church, suddenly found itself at a ball. Kapnist[9] is the only one in whom one scents a truly spiritual sentiment and a kind of special anthologic charm until then unknown. Here is his "Country House in Obukhovka":

Sheltering home with roof of thatch,
Neither too low nor too high for me;

8. I. I. Dmitriev (1760–1837), who tried to adapt Karamzin's elegant prose style to verse; I. I. Khemnitzer (1745–1784), a fabulist friend of Derzhavin's some of whose poems are still read; and I. F. Bogdanovich (1743–1803), a writer of Ukrainian origin whose adaptation of La Fontaine's *Psyché et Cupidon, Dushenka,* was highly regarded.

9. V. V. Kapnist (1757–1823), a polished practitioner of the Horatian ode and the author of the biting satiric comedy *Chicane* in 1798.

> *For friend a corner kept aside,*
> *And of the door, familiar to beggars,*
> *Idleness forgot to throw the bolt.*[10]

But our poetry could not long remain on this shallow worldly level. Its sensitivity was already strongly awakened by the torch lit by Peter from the European fire. Suddenly it observed that from the French, apart from dexterity, it could draw nothing for its improvement, and it turned to the Germans. At this time strange things were being produced in German literature. Vague reveries, mysterious legends, marvelous unexplained deeds, obscure indications of the invisible world, the dreams and terrors which had accompanied the childhood of man had become the subjects of the German poets. We might call such poetry pupils' pranks, if we did not perceive in it the infantile babbling that the immortal soul of man emits as he demands living nourishment for himself. Our sensitive poetry paused before this phenomenon with childish curiousity. Its slavic origins suddenly reminded it that there was something familiar there. But with all that, we would never have lit upon the Germans had there not appeared among us a poet who showed us all this extraordinary world in the clear glass of his own nature, which is more accessible to us than that of the Germans.

This poet is Zhukovsky, our most remarkable and most original author! By the miraculous will of the Almighty, from the days of his youth his soul was invested with a yearning for things invisible and mysterious which were incomprehensible to him. In his soul, just as in Vadim, the hero of his ballad,[11] there resounded a celestial bell ringing from afar. At this call, he rushed upon everything inexplicable and mysterious to him wherever he met it and began to reclothe it in sounds closer to

10. These lines for the second stanza of Kapnist's poem, which runs to 29 stanzas.

11. Vadim is the hero of Zhukovsky's ballad "The Twelve Sleeping Maids," written in 1817.

our soul. All things of this kind in him were taken from others, for the most part from the Germans—they are almost always translations. But the translations are so imprinted with his own inner aspiration, they are all so enkindled and animated by his own vivacity, that even Germans schooled in Russian admit that the originals appear to be copies and the translations true originals. One does not know what to call him—a translator or a real poet. The translator loses his own personality, but Zhukovsky has registered his more than all our other poets. Running through the titles of his poems, you see that one is taken from Schiller, another from Uhland, a third from Walter Scott, a fourth from Byron, and all most faithfully copied, word by word, the personality of each poet maintained, nowhere does the translator show himself; but, when you have read several of these poems, suddenly you ask yourself, "Whose poems have I been reading?" Before your eyes neither Schiller, nor Uhland, or Walter Scott appears, but a poet distinct from them all, worthy of a place not at their feet, but seated beside them, as an equal with equals. In what way his own personality came through the personalities of all these poets is an enigma of which we must all be aware. There is not one Russian who has not constructed for himself a faithful portrait of the author's soul out of Zhukovsky's works. Indeed, it must be said that in none of the poets he translated do we so strongly perceive an aspiration to pass beyond the clouds into a realm alien to human sight, in no other, indeed, do we see that firm acknowledgement of invisible powers everywhere keeping watch over man, so that reading him you feel at every step, as Derzhavin expressed it in these lines, that

> *You are given into the keeping*
> *Of invisible, immortal powers,*
> *And all the legions of angels*
> *Are ordered to watch to keep you safe.*[12]

12. These lines are from Derzhavin's poem "To the Conqueror," written in 1789.

While translating, still in his translations he somehow produced the effect of an original poet with his own personal color. Bringing in this new aspiration, until then unknown in our poetry, from the domain of the invisible and mysterious, he diverted our poetry from materialism not only in the ideas and in the images of its expression, but also in the lines themselves, which became light and incorporeal, like his vision. Translating, he left in his translations a lesson for everyone who would be original, embraced new forms and measures which all our other poets then began to use. A laziness of spirit prevented him from being a primarily ingenious poet—a laziness of invention but not a lack of creativity. He showed signs of this creativity from the very beginning of his career: *Svetlana* and *Lyudmilla*[13] for the first time conveyed the warming sounds of our slavic nature, much closer to our soul than those which resounded in other poets. The proof is that they produced a strong impression on everyone at a time when the poetic sentiment was still little developed among us. The elegaic genre in our poetry was created by him. There is a basic reason which gave rise to the laziness of spirit: it is the faculty of evaluation which, powerfully implanted in his spirit, forced him to linger lovingly over every finished composition. This is the reason for his fine critical sense, which so amazed Pushkin. Pushkin was very angry with him because he wrote no criticism. In his opinion, no one other than Zhukovsky could elucidate and define any kind of artistic work so well. This faculty of analysis and evaluation is reflected in his vivid descriptions of nature, which are all his own personal, distinctive works. Once he undertook a picture that fascinated him he did not leave off until he had entirely exhausted it, as though with a scalpel laying bare its most elusive details. The man who could write a poem like "A

---

13. Both *Svetlana* and *Lyudmilla* were written in 1815. The latter is Zhukovsky's adaptation of the *Lenore* of Gottfried August Bürger (1747–1794), whose publication coincided with the beginning of the *sturm und drang* school in Germany.

Report on the Sun,"[14] in which we see all the variations of the solar rays and the enchanting sights produced by them at divers times of day, with as much vivid detail as he depicts, in "A Report on the Moon,"[15] the enchantment of lunar rays, with the full range of nocturnal sights produced by them—that man, it goes without saying, must possess to a superior degree the faculty of *appreciation*. His *Slavianka*,[16] with its views of Pavlovsk, is a veritable painting. The reverential revery that imbues all his pictures fills them with a warm light that inspires an extraordinary calm in the reader. All your passions are quieted and something mysterious seals your lips.

In these latter days, we have begun to notice a crisis in Zhukovsky's poetic orientation. To the degree that that invisible light, which hitherto he had seen as vague, poetic, and remote in the distance, became more brightly clarified for him, to that extent was his passion and taste for the phantoms and ghosts of German ballads lost. Revery gave place to lucidity of spirit. The fruit of it was *Undine*, a work which belongs entirely to Zhukovsky. The German narrator of the legend in prose could not serve him as a model.[17] The entire creator of the lucidity of this poetic creation is Zuhkovsky. From this time forward, he acquired a kind of transparent language which rendered the object yet more visible than it was in the master from whom he took it. The former airy imprecision of his verse disappeared: his verse became solider and stronger; everything was arranged for the end of the transmission of a perfect poetic work, executed with all his feeling for the past and with such enlightenment, with the highest regard for life as to show the original, patriarchal essence of the ancient world in its nat-

14. Written in 1818 and entitled by Zhukovsky "Summer Evening."
15. Written in 1820 and originally entitled "A Detailed Report on the Moon."
16. Written in 1818. The Slavianka is a river which flows past Pavlovsk.
17. The German writer referred to is Friedrich Heinrich Karl, Baron de la Motte Fouquet (1777–1843), whose *Undine*, a classic of romanticism, appeared in 1811.

ural, most human light—an exploit as far as possible superior to all personal creation, which assured a universal meaning for Zhukovsky. Next to our other poets, Zhukovsky is like a jeweler in comparison with other masters, that is, a master whose task it is to give the finishing touches. It is not his business to discover the diamond in the mountains—his task is to mount the diamond so that it will play with all its fires and display all its quality before everyone. The appearance of such a poet could have taken place only among the Russian people, among whom the receptive genius is so strong that it was perhaps given to it in order to put in its finest setting everything which has neither been valued nor cultivated, everything neglected by other peoples.

When Zhukovsky was still at the beginning of his poetic development, detaching our poetry from the earth and from actuality and transferring it into the domain of immaterial visions, another poet, Batyushkov,[18] as though expressly in opposition to him, began to attach it to the earth and to the flesh, expressing all the fascinating charm of tangible reality. While the former lost himself in an ideal still vague to him, the latter drowned himself in the luxuriant loveliness of the visible world, which he perceived so clearly and felt so strongly. Everything beautiful, in all forms, even those invisible, he endeavored to convert into the palpable bliss of pleasure. He perceived, according to his own expression, "the voluptuousness of verse and of ideas." It is as though a kind of inner equilibrium abiding in the bosom of our poetry, preserving it from the excesses of afflatus, had created this poet just so that at a time when the sounds of the north European lyricists were beginning to be used, another might fan it with aromatic southern sounds, after having become acquainted with Ariosto, Tasso, Petrarch, and the tender echoes of antique Hellas; so that the

18. K. N. Batyushkov (1718–1855), like Zhukovsky, was a modernist in verse and language. His models, however, were southern rather than the German and English models of Zhukovsky—Latin, Greek, French, and Italian.

verse, which had begun to acquire an ethereal vagueness, might be executed like a quasi-sculptural relief, as we see it in the ancients, and with that blissful sound heard in the southern parts of modern Europe.

Two divers poets had suddenly introduced two divers principles into our poetry; out of these two principles a third was formed in a flash: Pushkin appeared. He is the focal point. He has neither the abstract idealism of the first, nor the abundant voluptuous luxuriance of the second. Everything is balanced, concise, concentrated, as it is in a Russian who is not overly verbal in the transmission of his sensations but keeps them and combines them in himself for a long time, so that after this long incubation they have an explosive power when he externalizes them. I will cite an example. Our poet was struck at the sight of the Kazbek, one of the highest mountains of the Caucasus, on the summit of which he saw a monastery which seemed to him like an ark soaring through the skies. In another poet there would have been an outpouring of ardent verse for many pages. In Pushkin it is all in ten lines, and he ends the poem with this surprising appeal:

> *Distant, desired shore!*
> *Thither, goodbye said to the gorges,*
> *May I be raised, to the mountain peak!*
> *There, in a cell beyond the clouds,*
> *Nearer to God, may I escape![19]*

This could be said only by a Russian, while a Frenchman, an Englishman, a German would give himself over to a detailed account of his sensations. No other of our poets was so sparing of words and expressions as Pushkin, no other examined himself so carefully, so that he might not speak immoderately and superfluously, fearing the over-sweetness of the one and the other.

19. These lines are quoted from Pushkin's poem "The Monastery on Kazbek," written in 1829

What was the subject of his poetry? Everything was his subject, but nothing specifically. Thought is dumbfounded before the infinite number of his subjects. At what did he not marvel and before what did he not pause? From the Caucasus peak lost in the clouds and the picturesque Circassian to the pale northern villager with his balalaika and trepak dancing[20] in taverns—everywhere, every place: a fashionable ball, a cottage, the steppe, a traveling sleigh—everything was his subject. Everything intrinsic to man, from his most sublime and grandest features to his least sigh of weakness and the most insignificant sign of his confusion, he responded to, just as he responded to everything in visible and external nature. Everything stands out like an isolated painting; everything is his subject; out of everything, the smallest as well as the largest, he forced the electric spark of that poetic fire present in all divine creation—its loftiest side, known to the poet alone, without applying it to life for the need of man, without revealing to anyone why this spark was extorted, without replacing it with a ladder for those who are deaf to poetry. This was not his business. He had no other care than to say, with his gifted poetic flair, "See how beautiful is the work of God"—and, without adding anything more, to fly to another subject, to say again, "See how beautiful is the work of God!" Because of this his works present an astonishing phenomenon through the contradictory impressions which they arouse in his readers. In the eyes of highly intelligent persons, who nevertheless do not have the poetic flair, they are unfinished, light, ephemeral, fragments; in the eyes of persons who are gifted with the poetic flair, they are complete poems, considered, finished, containing in themselves everything necessary to them.

To Pushkin were posed all the questions which had not previously been posed to any of our poets, and in them may be seen the spirit of an awakening century. Why, for what was his poetry? What new direction did Pushkin give to the world of

20. The *trepak* is still a popular Russian dance.

thought? What did he say that was necessary to his century? Did he act upon it auspiciously or destructively? Did he influence others by his particular personal character, by the errors of his genius, like Byron and like other secondary, lesser poets? Why was he given to the world and what has he shown in himself? Pushkin was given to the world to show in himself what a poet is, and nothing more—what a poet is not under the influence of a specific time or circumstance, not conditioned by a particular personal character, as a man, but independent of everything, so that later, if some supreme anatomist of the soul should want to give an account of and explain the essence of the poet (that sensitive creation who responds to everything in the world and has no response only to himself), he would be satisfied by seeing it in Pushkin. Pushkin alone was appointed to show in himself that independent being, that sounding echo that responds to all those separate sounds engendered in the air. In the thought of any poet his personality is more or less presented. To whom, at the thought of Schiller, will not appear that shining childish soul dreaming of the best and most perfect ideals, creating a world out of them for himself, and satisfied to be allowed to live in this poetic world? To whom, reading Byron, is not presented Byron himself, the proud man favored with all the gifts of Heaven and incapable of forgiving it for his negligible physical deformity whose grumbling is spread throughout his poetry? Goethe himself, that Proteus among poets, endeavoring to embrace everything, both in the world of nature and in the world of science, because of his pseudoscientific striving displayed his personality, full of a certain Germanic arrogance and of the pretension of a German theoretician to adapt himself to all times and all centuries. All our Russian poets—Derzhavin, Zhukovsky, Batyushkov—kept their personalities. Only Pushkin did not. What can you seize of him in his works? Just try to catch his character as a man! Instead of him, there will appear that wonderful image responding to everything, finding no response only to itself. All his works are an arsenal filled with the arms of the poet. Go, choose for your hand the one you desire and set off with it to battle; but the poet himself did not go to battle with it. Why did he not go? That is another question. He himself answers in these verses:

> *Not for worldly strife,*
> *Not for profit, nor for battle—*
> *We were born for inspiration,*
> *For sweet sounds and prayers.*[21]

Pushkin perceived his role better than those who posed questions to him, and he fulfilled it with love. Even at that time when he recklessly threw himself into the the smoke of passion, poetry was holy for him—really a kind of temple. He did not enter it carelessly and in disorder; he brought in nothing ill-considered, nothing rash from his own life; bedraggled reality did not enter it stark naked. However, his whole history is there. But it is not visible. The reader perceives only its fragrance; but what substances have been consumed in the breast of the poet so that he might exhale this fragrance no one may perceive. And how he cherished them in himself, how he nurtured them! Not one Italian poet polished his sonnets the way he worked over his light, apparently ephemeral creations. What precision in each word! What significance in each expression! How everything is rounded off, finished and sealed! They are just like pearls; it is difficult to decide which is the best. Like the sparkling teeth of that beauty just emerging from the baths whom Solomon compared to a young lamb,[22] each and all are equally beautiful.

21. These are the last lines of Pushkin's poem "The Poet and the Mob," written in 1828.
22. *Song of Sol.*, 4: 1, 2 (D.V.):
How beautiful art thou, my love, how beautiful art thou! thy eyes are dove's eyes, besides what is hid within. Thy hair is as flocks of goats, which come up from mount Galaad.
Thy teeth as flocks of sheep, that are shorn, which come up from the washing, all with twins, and there is none barren among them.

How would he have spoken of something necessary to present society at the present moment, since he wanted to respond to everything in the world and since each object called him equally? In *Onegin* he would have wanted to depict contemporary man and resolve a contemporary problem—and could not have done it. Eliminating his heroes, he put himself in their place, and, in their persons, he was startled by what would astonish a poet. The poem became a collection of disparate sensations, delicate elegies, caustic epigrams, picturesque idylls, and, reading it, instead of all that the marvelous image of a poet responsive to everything stands out. His most perfect works, *Boris Godunov* and *Poltava*, are a veritable response to the past. He did not want to say anything to his own time; he did not intend something useful to his compatriots by the choice of these two subjects; nor do we see that he was particularly in sympathy with either of the heroes he evoked, nor that he undertook the two poems (so masterfully and artistically worked out) because of them. He simply was struck by the singularity of two historic events and wanted others to be struck as he had been.

The reading of the poets of all nations and centuries engendered the same response in him. The Spanish hero Don Juan, that inexhaustible subject of numberless dramatic poems, suddenly gave him the idea of concentrating the whole affair into a short, personal, dramatic picture, where with great knowledge of the soul there is presented the irresistible allure of a debauchee, still more vividly the weakness of a woman, and more audibly still Spain itself.[23] Goethe's *Faust* suggested to him the idea of squeezing into two or three pages the principal thought of the German poet—and you marvel at how accurately it was understood and concentrated into one solid kernel, in spite of all its vague incoherence in Goethe.[24] The austere

23. The reference is to Pushkin's play *The Stone Guest*.
24. The reference is to Pushkin's *Scene from Faust*, a short dialogue between Faust and Mephistopheles written in 1825.

tercets of Dante suggested to him the thought of representing in identical tercets, and in the spirit of Dante, his poetic youth at Tsarskoe-Selo, personifying science in the form of a strict mistress assembling the children at school, and himself in the form of a schoolboy bursting out of class into the garden and stopping before the antique statues with lyres and compasses in their hands, speaking a more living language than science to him,[25] and we see how soon was awakened in him that sensitivity of response to everything.

And how sincere was his response, how sensitive his ear! You catch the smell, the color of the earth, of the times, of the nation. In Spain he is a Spaniard, with the Greeks a Greek, in the Caucasus a free mountaineer in the full sense of the term; with a man past his prime he breathes memories of the past; he looks at a peasant in his cottage—he is a Russian from head to toe; all the features of our nature were echoed in him, and everything was sometimes comprised in a single word, one delicately turned and accurately chosen adjective.

This quality grew in him little by little, and he would henceforth respond to the entirety of Russian life, as he had responded to each separate feature of it. The thought of a novel which would frankly tell a simple, plain tale of Russian life occupied him relentlessly during his last years. He had abandoned verse uniquely in order not to be diverted by anything and to be simpler in his descriptions, and he simplified his prose to the point that none of the qualities of his first tales is found in it. Pushkin was pleased, and he wrote *The Captain's Daughter,* decidedly the best Russian work of the narrative kind. In comparison with *The Captain's Daughter,* all our novels and tales are like saccharine mush. Purity and lack of artifice rise to such a high degree in it that reality itself seems artificial and a caricature next to it. For the first time, truly Russian characters come on scene: a simple fortress com-

25. The reference is to Pushkin's "I remember school when I was young," written in 1830

mander, a captain's wife, a lieutenant; the fortress itself with only one cannon, the confusion of the times, and the simple majesty of the simple people—it is all not only the truth itself, but like something better. It must be so: it was the calling of the poet to take us out of ourselves and then to return us to ourselves in purified and better form. Everything testified that Pushkin was born for and strove towards this end. Almost at the same time as *The Captain's Daughter,* he left masterful novelistic experiments: *The Manuscript of Gorokhin Village, The Negro of the Tsar,*[26] and the sketch done in pencil of a large novel, *Dubrovsky.* During these last years he collected a great deal of material about Russian life, and he spoke about everything so accurately and sensibly that each of his words should have been noted down: it was worth his best verse; but what was still more remarkable, he was forming his inner soul and preparing himself to illuminate still more the life in front of him. Echoes of this are perceived in the posthumous edition of his verse, where the flight from a city doomed to destruction and a part of the state of his own soul is represented in almost apocalyptic terms.[27] Much good for Russia was being prepared by this man. . . . But, having come to maturity, bringing together from every quarter the powers to handle great things, he did not think about how to handle insignificant and little things. A sudden death carried him away from us—and everyone in the Empire immediately perceived that it had lost a great man.

The influence of Pushkin as a poet on society has been minor. Society only considered him at the beginning of his poetic career, when his first youthful verses recalled the lyre of Byron; when he became himself and was at last not Byron but Pushkin, society turned away from him. But his influence on the poets was strong. Karamzin in prose only did what he had done

26. These titles should be *The History of Gorokhin Village* and *The Negro of Peter the Great.*

27. The reference is to Pushkin's poem "The Wanderer," written in 1835.

in verse. The imitators of Karamzin have served as pitiful caricatures of him and, from the point of view of style and ideas, they are sugary sweet. As for Pushkin, he has been for all poets contemporary with him a poetic fire dropped from Heaven from which, like tapers, other semiprecious poets caught fire. Their whole constellation was formed around him: Delvig,[28] the sybaritic poet who luxuriated in each sound of his almost hellenic lyre, and rather than toss down the nectar of poesy in one gulp, swallowed it drop by drop, like a wine connoisseur, paying attention to the color and inhaling the fragrance; Kozlov,[29] the harmonious poet in whom resound things hitherto unheard, sounds whose music touches the heart; Baratinsky,[30] a stern and gloomy poet, who so early showed the original yearning of his thoughts for the internal world and began to worry about their material realization before they had matured in himself; somber and withdrawn, he began to defy people and made himself an alien to everyone and was close to no one. Pushkin excited all these poets to activity; others he simply made. I mean by that our so-called anthologic poets, who have produced little; but if one makes a choice among these few fragrant flowers, then a book would appear on which the best poet would put his signature. It is sufficient to name the two Tumanskys, Krylov, Tyutchev,[31] Pletnyov, and several others who would not have revealed their poetic fire and deeply-moved reactions had they not been set on fire by the poetry of

28. A. A. Delvig (1798–1831), a close friend of Pushkin who edited the yearly poetic miscellany, *Northern Flowers,* from 1825 to 1831.

29. I. I. Kozlov (1799–1840), a minor sentimental poet of the time much influenced by Byron.

30. E. A. Baratinsky (1800–1844), according to Mirsky (p. 104), "Pushkin's worthiest rival among his contemporaries." The content of his poetry is largely intellectual within a romantic framework, while his style is classical.

31. For A. Krylov, see below, note 42; F. I. Tyutchev (1803–1873), often considered, along with Pushkin and Lermontov, one of the three greatest Russian poets, although he was largely ignored by the critics before 1850. Most of Tyutchev's poetry is metaphysical and pessimistic, based upon a Manichaean view of the universe.

Pushkin. Even earlier poets began to retune the register of their lyres. The famous translator of the *Iliad*, Gnedich; F. Glinka, who put the psalms to music; the partisan poet Davydov;[32] finally, Zhukovsky himself, the mentor and teacher of Pushkin in the art of versifying, later began to learn from his former student. Even some were made poets who had not been born poets and for whom another, no less lofty career was prepared, judging by the spiritual strength which they have shown even in their poetic experiments, for example: Venevitinov,[33] who passed away so early and Khomyakov,[34] who thanks to God, is still alive, apparently for some radiant future at present still unrevealed even to him. The strength of the influence exercised by Pushkin even injured a great number, especially Baratinsky, and another poet about whom I shall speak below—it injured them simply because they began prematurely to transmit the reactions of their souls, when their souls had not yet learned a poetry accessible to others, when it should have been their first task to accomplish their internal education, before which they should have kept quiet. The extraordinary artistic polish that Pushkin showed in his verses tempted them all. Forgetting society, forgetting everything that united them to mankind, forgetting the claims of their country, they all lived in a kind of poetic Hellas, repeating these verses of Pushkin:

> *Not for worldly strife,*
> *Not for profit, nor for battle—*
> *We were born for inspiration,*
> *For the sweet sounds of songs and prayers.*

32. N. I. Gnedich (1784–1833), a poet of the high classical style; F. N. Glinka (1786–1880), a religious poet who was a cousin of the composer; D. V. Davydov (1784–1839), a famous soldier and singer of the military virtues.

33. D. V. Venevitinov (1805–1827), a philosophical poet who was one of the great hopes of Russian literature until his death at the age of twenty-one

34. A. S. Khomyakov (1804–1860), who became far more important as a Slavophile and a theologian than as a poet. See note 28 to "Introduction."

Of the poets of Pushkin's time, Yazykov stands out most. With the appearance of his first lines a new lyricism was heard by all, a wildness and violent strength, a profundity of expression, a light of youthful enthusiasm, and a language of such power, perfection, and strictly controlled mastery as has not yet appeared in anyone. The name of Yazykov did not befall him for nothing.[35] He is master of the language the way an Arab is master of an untamed horse, so that he may vaunt his mastery. In whatever way he begins his sentence, by head or by tail, he develops it picturesquely, concludes it and locks it so that you stand defeated. Everything that expressed youthful strength, not limp but mighty, full of the future, suddenly became the subject of his verse. A youthful freshness springs from everything he touches. Here is his bath in a river:

> *Clothing away! Before our brows*
> *We stretch our arms far out,*
> *And—splash!*
> > *In a shining rain*
> *A spray of water flies.*
> *How strong is the wave!*
> *How fresh and cool!*
> *How voluptuous, how caressing*
> *Is the naiad's embrace to me!*

Here is his game of *svaika,* which he calls a simple Russian game.[36] The young people stand in a circle:

> *He drives a heavy peg tight and firm*
> *Into the ring—the ring jingles.*
> *The spring evening lightly,*
> *Invisibly, flies away.*

Everything that calls a young man to valor—the sea, holidays, the storm, banquets and raised glasses, brotherhood

35. The Russian word for language is *yazyk.*
36. *Svaika* is a game which took its name from the spike *(svaika)* driven into the ground in the center of the circle of players.

through work, a firm as flint hope in the future, readiness to fight for the fatherland—it is all expressed in him with extraordinary strength. When his poems appeared in a book of their own, Pushkin said in vexation, "Why did he call them 'Poems of Yazykov'? It would have been better simply to call them 'Intoxication!'" A man of ordinary powers will do nothing like this; the fury of nature is also necessary to produce something similar. I vividly remember his enthusiasm when he read to Davydov the verses of Yazykov that had been published in a review. That is the first time I saw tears on Pushkin's face (Pushkin never cried; he said of himself in his dedication to Ovid, "Stern Slav, I have never shed tears, but I understand them"). I remember some strophes which produced tears in him: the first is the one where the poet, addressing a Russia which was then considered powerless and feeble, calls forth thus:

> *The trumpet has sounded!*
> *Russia! for you the haughty call!*
> *Remember how once you met*
> *Invading enemies!*
> *Call your knights*
> *From your furthest borders,*
> *From the steppes, from the wide plains,*
> *From the great rivers, from the high mountains,*
> *From your eight seas.*

And also the strophe in which the unheard of self-sacrifice is described—when Russia set fire to its own capital with everything in it sacred for all the land:[37]

> *The flames rising to the sky,*
> *The fire of Moscow raged.*
> *Golden-domed, holy,*
> *Will you perish? Russia, arise!*
> *The thunder of the destroying storm be louder!*

37. The reference is to the burning of Moscow in 1812.

The courage of resistance be firmer!
This is the altar of salvation,
This is the flame of purification,
This is the pyre of the Phoenix!

Whom would tears not water after such strophes as these? His verses are really intoxicating; but in the drunkenness we perceive a superior power, forcing it to rise to the heights. In him, student carousing does not occur for the sake of debauchery and sottishness, but because of pleasure in the power of their arms and in the future before them, so that the students rush after "noble service and the fame of the pure and the good."

The only bad thing is that the drunkenness passed beyond measure and that the poet toasted the joy of his future too much, like many of us in Russia, and that everything was limited to the one mighty transport.

All eyes were turned on Yazykov. Everyone expected something extraordinary from this new poet in whose verses such heroic boasting arose as to promise the accomplishment of mighty things. But it ended there. Several poems, which were only feeble repetitions, appeared; then a severe illness visited the poet and affected his soul. In his last verses there was nothing that could stir a Russian soul. In them we heard of his boredom in German towns, his apathetic travel notes, the enumeration of his monotonous, long-suffering days. All this was dead to a Russian soul. We did not even notice the extraordinary polish of his last verses. His language, stronger than ever, served as evidence: it rested on skinny thoughts and povery-stricken content, like the armor of a knight on the puny body of a dwarf. We even began to say that there were no thoughts in Yazykov, only idle verses, and even that he was not a poet. These were still only rumors against him. Echoes of these rumors were absurdly given out by the press, but at bottom there was some truth in them. Yazykov, speaking of the poet, did not say, in the words of Pushkin:

Not for worldly strife,
Not for profit, nor for battle—
We were born for inspiration,
For sweet sounds and prayers.

For him, on the contrary, this is what the poet says:

When all in you is ready for deeds
Which are seen as a Heavenly gift on earth,
The light and heat of mighty thoughts
And fire-spitting words—
Go into the world, it will hear the poet.[38]

Let us admit that this is being said about the ideal poet, but he took his ideal from his own nature. If there had not already been this principle within himself he could not have presented such a poet. No, his forces did not abandon him, it is not poverty of talent that is to blame for the lack of content of his last verses, as self-assured critics have proclaimed, nor is it illness (illness is only given for the acceleration of work, if a man fathoms its meaning)—no, something else overpowered him: the light of love dimmed in his soul; that is why the light of poetry faded. Love what is needful and necessary to your soul with as much strength as you used to love the drunkenness of your youth—and your thoughts will be raised along with your verse, the word will resound and spit forth fire: you will show us the banality of our sick lives, but you will show it in such a way that men will shudder because of their lack of strength and thank God for their foe who has given them the power to feel it. It was not Yazykov's task to polish and round out his verses in imitation of Pushkin: he was born, not for elegies and anthologic poems, but for dithyrambs and hymns; everyone perceived this. It is rather from Derzhavin than Pushkin that he should have lit his lamp. His poetry only enters the soul when it is entirely in a lyric vein; his subject

38. These lines are quoted from Yazykov's poem "To a Poet," written in 1831.

only lives in him when he is either moved, or resounds, or is radiant, but never when he abides in calm. The lot of poets is not the same. One is appointed to be a faithful mirror and echo of life—and for that he is given a many-sided, descriptive talent. Another is commanded to be progressive, a power inciting society to noble and lofty actions—for that he has been given a lyric talent. Talent does not miss its proper path because the eyes of the great are not fixed upon it. Providence provides for man. Through misfortune, evil, and sickness, forcefully will it bring him to what he would not bring himself. And already, in the lyre of Yazykov, we note a striving for a turn into the right road. Not long ago we heard his poem "Earthquake," which in the opinion of Zhukovsky is our best poem.

Among the poets of Pushkin's time, Prince Vyazemsky[39] stands out. Although he began to write well before Pushkin, since his full development is in Pushkin's time we mention him here. Prince Vyazemsky is the opposite of Yazykov: just as the poverty of ideas is striking in the latter, so is it abundant in the former. Verse is used by him as the first instrument available: no external trimmings are his, nor any concentration and rounding off of thought in order to present it to his reader like a precious stone; he is not an artist, and does not care about it. His poems are improvisations, although for such improvisations one must have many gifts and a well-prepared mind. A profusion of unusual qualities of all kinds was brought together in him: intelligence, wit, visual clarity, keenness of observation, surprising deductions, sentiment, gaiety, and even melancholy; each of his poems is as variegated as a card game. He is not a poet by calling: destiny, having attired him with all its gifts, gave him, as though in addition, the poet's talent in order to form something complete of him. In his book *A Biography of Fonvizin*[40] the abundance of gifts possessed by

39. See note 17 to "Introduction."
40. Written in 1830, Vyazemsky's *Fonvizin* did not appear until 1848. But Gogol undoubtedly knew the book in manuscript.

him is still more evidently displayed. There we perceive at one and the same time the politician, the philosopher, the keen appraiser and critic, the positive statesman, and even the experienced administrator of the practical side of life—in short, all the qualities required to make a profound historian in the highest sense of the term. And if with the same pen with which he inscribed the life of Fonvizin he had written of Catherine's reign, a reign that already seems to us almost fantastic because of the great abundance of the epoch and the extraordinary efflorescence of extraordinary persons and characters, then we could almost certainly say that an historical work of like distinction has not been offered to us by Europe. But the absence of a large and full work is the sickness of Prince Vyazemsky; this we perceive in his verses. Noticeable in them is an absence of an internal harmonious accord among the parts: word is not matched with word, line with line, next to a solid, firm line, such as is not in any other poet, is placed another resembling the first in nothing; as soon as it makes your heart ache with a living cry, it immediately alienates you by a sound foreign to the heart, absolutely out of tune with the subject; we perceive a lack of cohesion, a life whose powers are incomplete; we perceive most of all a kind of sadness and depression. The lot of the man gifted with varied abilities who cannot bring them together is worse than the lot of the poorest man. Only the labor that compels a man to confront himself wholly and to descend into himself is our liberator. It is only in himself, as the poet says, that

> *The soul is sincere, the will firm,*
> *And our portion*
> *Plainly defined.*[41]

At the same time that our poetry so rapidly accomplished its evolution, being instructed by the poets of all centuries and

41. These lines are from Vyazemsky's poem "To Wolfe, Tyutchev, and Shepelyov," written in 1826.

nations, winnowing out the sounds of all political lands, testing all tones and chords, one poet remained aside. Having chosen the most unostentatious and narrow path for himself, he almost silently went his way, until he had passed all the others, as a strong oak outgrows all the grove which first hid it. This poet is Krylov.[42] He chose the form of the fable, scorned by all as obsolete, unfit for use and almost a child's game—and in the fable he knew how to make himself a national poet. This is our vigorous Russian brain, the very wit which is akin to the wit of our proverbs, the very wit which is the vigor of the Russian, the wit of inference, which is also called hind-thought. The proverb is not a received opinion nor an assumption about some fact, but the totality of an experience, the remainder, the deposit that remains of fermented and finished events, the finally extracted essence of the matter in all its facets and not on one side only. This is expressed by the saying that "A speech does not make a proverb." On account of this background of wit, or the wit to make final conclusions, which is the chief endowment, above all others, of the Russian, our proverbs are more significant than those of all other peoples. Beyond the plenitude of thought, their expression in images is a reflection of many of our people's characteristics; everything is in them: taunting, mockery, reproach—in short, everything stirring and pricking to the quick: like the hundred eyes of Argus, each proverb is aimed at man. All our great men, from Pushkin to Suvorov and Peter, have venerated our proverbs. Esteem for them is expressed in many sayings: "Proverbs are not spoken for nothing," or "Proverbs are never destroyed." We know that if you can end a speech adroitly with a tidy proverb, you can

42. I. A. Krylov (1769–1844), the greatest of the Russian fabulists whose work remains enormously popular and is endlessly quoted. There is no question but that Krylov is one of the brightest lights of nineteenth-century Russian literature. The best translation of his *Fables* is probably that of Sir Bernard Pares (London: Cape, 1926), unfortunately very difficult to obtain.

immediately explain to the people what was formerly beyond its understanding.

This is the origin of Krylov. His fables are by no means for children. It would be a grave mistake to call him a fabulist in the sense in which La Fontaine, Dmitriev, Khemnitzer, and, in last place, Izmailov, were fabulists.[43] His parables are a national property and constitute a very book of popular wisdom. His beasts think and act for the greater part in Russian fashion: in their pranks we perceive pranks and ceremonies with a "made in Russia" stamp. In addition to correct animal likenesses, which in him are so powerful that not only the fox, the bear, and the wolf, but even the pot acts as though it were alive, his beasts also show forth Russian nature. Even the ass—in him so well marked in its character that it is sufficient for it to poke its ears out of some fable for the reader to shriek, "This is one of Krylov's asses!"[44]—even the ass, despite its belonging to the climate of other lands, in him appears as a Russian. After having for so many years marauded in other people's vegetable gardens, it suddenly was smitten with ambition, it wanted a medal and put on terrible airs when its master hung a bell around its neck, without realizing that now every one of its thefts and dirty tricks would be exposed to everyone and would elicit blows on its sides from everywhere. In short, everywhere in him is Rus, it reeks of Rus; and each of his fables has historical origins. Despite his deliberateness and, it would appear, indifference to contemporary events, the poet has nevertheless observed every event in the state: he has lent his voice to everything, and in this voice is heard a reasonable middle way, a conciliating court of arbitration which is the strength of the Russian intelligence when it has attained its full perfection. By strictly weighed and rigorously used words, he defines a thing at a swoop, and he knows what its true essence is. When some excessively military people had gone so far as to maintain that

43. A. E. Izmailov (1779–1831) was a writer of picaresque fables
44. Krylov's fable "The Ass" appeared in 1830.

everything in the state should be based on military strength alone and that salvation is in that alone, and when state officials in their turn began to make fun of everything military, just because some have turned the military profession into an affair only of stripes and decorations, he wrote his famous argument of the cannon and the sail, in which he took both sides to their proper limits in a remarkable quatrain:

> *Every power has its strength,*
> *When organized for wise use:*
> *With an arsenal one menaces the enemy,*
> *While the power of the sail is civil.*[45]

What a neat definition! Without a gun you may not defend yourself, while without a sail you may not navigate. When some well-intentioned but short-sighted chief insisted upon the peculiar opinion that it is necessary to fear clever, intelligent people and deprive them of their posts only because some of them were once pranksters mixed up in a foolhardy affair,[46] he wrote a no less remarkable fable, *Two Razors.* In it he justly reproached those chiefs who

> *Fear intelligent people*
> *And keep fools about themselves.*

We especially note that he always keeps to the side of intelligence, that he pleads that the intelligent man not be neglected, but that one know how to appeal to him. This is reflected in the fable *The Musicians,* which he concluded with the words: "Drink if you will, but do the job!" He did not say this because he wanted to praise drunkenness, but because his soul was sick at the sight of how some, having gathered God knows what kind of people around themselves instead of experts, boast of it, saying they may not understand expertise, but, on the other hand, they do understand proper behavior. He knew that it is possible to do anything with an intelligent man

45. "The Cannon and the Sail" appeared in 1827.
46. This may be a reference to the Decembrists.

and that it is not difficult to convert him to proper behavior, if
you know how to speak to him intelligently, but it is difficult
to make a fool intelligent, however you speak to him. "A thief
is a thief, and a fool is sour milk," says our proverb. But he
makes tough remarks to the intelligent man, reproaching him
in the fable *The Stagnant Pond* for having allowed his abilities to doze off, and he sternly upbraids him in the fable *The
Composer* for his lewd and evil tendencies. In general, he
was occupied with important questions. There are lessons for
everyone in his book, of all levels in the state, beginning with
the Chief of State, to whom he says:

> *Does the Sovereign want to keep his subjects?*
> *Do not hold the reigns too tight, but keep them well in hand.*[47]

down to the last laborer working in the lowest ranks of the
state, to whom he points out his high destiny in the guise of a
bee who has not sought distinction in its work:

> *But honor to him who, in his hidden humility,*
> *For all his labors, for all his lost rest,*
> *Adulates neither power nor glory,*
>   *Only living with the thought*
>   *That he is working for the common good.*[48]

These words remain as an eternal proof of the nobility of
Krylov's soul. No other poet has known how to make his
thought so tangible and to express it in a way so accessible to
everyone as Krylov. The poet and the sage become one in him.
Everything is picturesque in him, from his fascinating, men-
acing, and even unsavory portrayals of nature down to his
transmission of the smallest nuances of dialogue in which sincere qualities are vividly rendered. Everything is so accurately
said, conceived so truly and so closely adapted to the object

47. Apparently Gogol's memory played him false, for this couplet does
not appear in Krylov's works.
48. These lines are from Krylov's fable "The Eagle and the Bee," written in 1813.

that one could not even define the character of Krylov's pen. You cannot name his style. The object, as though having no envelope of words, appears before our eyes as it is in itself in nature. Nor can you grasp his verse. There is no way to define its characteristics. Is it sonorous? Light? Heavy? It resounds when the object resounds in him; it moves when the object moves; it gathers strength when the idea gathers strength; and it suddenly becomes light when it gives way to the meaningless chatter of an imbecile. His speech is submissive and obedient to the thought and flutters, like a fly, now suddenly appearing in an elongated hexameter, now in a quick one-foot line; by the deliberate number of syllables it makes tangible the ineffability of its spirituality. It is enough to recall the sublime conclusion of the fable *Two Barrels:*

> *A great man is known only by his acts,*
> *He thinks his firm thought*
> *Noiselessly.*

By the placing of his words we almost hear the majesty of a man communing with himself.[49]

From Krylov we can proceed forthwith to another type of our poetry—to satiric poetry. There is so much irony in all of us. It is visible in our proverbs and songs and, most astonishing of all, it is often met where the soul apparently is suffering and is not at all disposed to gaiety. The profundity of this distinctive irony is still not completely revealed to us because, taught as we are by European teachings, we have deviated from our native source. Nevertheless, the inclination to irony has been maintained, although in another form. It is difficult to find a Russian in whom the ability really to revere something is not united with the faculty really to ridicule it. All our poets have possessed that faculty. Derzhavin scattered grains of its salt

49. In the Russian the lines read as follows:
  Veliki chelovek lish' viden na delakh,
    I dumayet svoyu on krepku dumu
      Bez shumu.

in the greater half of his odes. It is in Pushkin, in Krylov, in Prince Vyazemsky; we even perceive it in those poets whose characters are of a tender, melancholy inclination: in Kapnist, in Zhukovsky, in Karamzin, in Prince Dolgoruky, it is innate in them all. So it is natural that poets properly called satiric should have developed among us. Already, at the time that Lomonosov was tuning his lyre to the high lyrical mode, Prince Kantemir[50] found food for satire and with it lashed the folly of the nouveaux riches. In various epochs there has appeared among us a quantity of satires, epigrams, mockeries, which turned the most famous works inside out, caustic, spiteful parodies of all kinds, which probably will always remain in manuscript form and in which great power may everywhere be seen. It is enough to recall the parodies of Prince Gorchakov, the satire of Volikov on men of letters, *A House of Madmen,* and the talented parodies of Mikhail Dmitriev,[51] in which the bile of Juvenal is united with a kind of special slavic good nature. But satire soon demanded a wider field and passed into the drama. The theater, among us as everywhere, began with imitations; then original traits broke through. In tragedy appeared the moral strength and ignorance of man in the setting of a borrowed epoch and age; in comedy there is a light mockery of the ridiculous sides of society, without a glance at the soul of man. The names of Ozerov, Knyazhnin, Kapnist, Prince Shakhovskoy, Khmelnitsky, Zagoskin, A. Pisarev,[52] are re-

50. A. D. Kantemir (1704–1744), a satirist whose work was not published until twenty-eight years after his death, by which time Lomonosov's reforms had made his style obsolete.

51. M. A. Dmitriev (1796–1866), a minor writer of philosophical poetry and articles. He was a good friend of Zhukovsky, Batyushkov, Davydov, and Vyazemsky. Karamzin had visited his home when he was a boy.

52. V. A. Ozerov (1769–1816), a very successful writer of tragedies; Ya. B. Knyazhnin (1742–1791), a tragic imitator of Voltaire; A. A. Shakhovskoy (1777–1846), a prolific writer of minor classical comedies; N. I. Khmelnitsky (1789–1846), like A. I. Pisarev (1803–1828), was particularly well known as a writer of vaudevilles; M. N. Zagoskin (1789–1852) was a writer of comedies who later turned to writing novels imitative of Walter Scott.

membered with respect; but all that paled before two blazing
works: *The Young Hopeful* of Fonvizin[53] and *Wit from Woe*
of Griboyedov, which Prince Vyazemsky most acutely called
two contemporary tragedies. In them there is no light mockery
of the ridiculous sides of society; it is rather the wounds and
diseases of our society, the grave abuses within it that a ruthless, powerful irony exposes openly and shockingly. These two
comedies chose two different focal points. One displayed the
sicknesses arising from a lack of education, the other those
arising from a badly understood education.

Fonvizin's comedy strikes at the coarse brutality of man
which occurs because of the long, callous, shocking stagnation
in the farthest corners and Godforsaken places in Russia. It
exposes this crust of coarseness so terribly that you can hardly
recognize the Russian underneath it. Who could recognize anything Russian in that wicked creature, that perfection of tyranny, Prostakova, tormentor of her peasants, of her husband,
and of everyone except her son? Nevertheless, you feel that in
no other country, in neither France nor England, could such a
creature have been formed. This insensate love for our off-
spring is our powerful Russian love, which, in a man who has
lost all his dignity, is expressed in this perverted form, in this
incredible alliance with tyranny, so that the more she loves her
little one, the more she hates everything that is not her little
one. Then there is the character of Skotinin—another type of
coarseness. His awkward nature, which had never had any
powerful, violent passions, was turned into something calmer,
a love more artistic in its way for beasts instead of for man:
for him, his pigs become what for an art amateur would be a
painting gallery. There is also Prostakova's husband—a miserable, crushed creature, in whom such feeble strength as he
still possesses is beaten down by the urgings of his wife—the

53. D. I. Fonvizin (1745–1792), whose play, *The Young Hopeful*, which
appeared in 1782, marks him as the finest Russian playwright before
Griboyedov.

greatest degradation of all! Finally there is Mitrofan, who, while he has nothing wicked in his nature, no desire to make anyone miserable, insensibly will become, with the assistance of pleasures and indulgences, a tyrant over everyone, and above all over those who love him most, his mother and his nurse, so much so that inflicting insults on them becomes his pleasure. In short, it is as though these persons were no longer Russians; it is even difficult to recognize Russian qualities in them, with the sole exceptions perhaps of Eremeyevna and of the retired soldier. You perceive with terror that you may have no effect on them, neither by the power of the Church nor by the customs of the past, of which only the most banal is retained by them, and that the only thing to do is to put them in irons. Everything in this comedy seems a monstrous caricature of Russia. However, nothing in it is a caricature: everything has been taken from life as it is and verified by the knowledge of the soul. Such is the irrefutably terrible ideal of coarseness to which only a man of the Russian land and no other people can attain.

Griboyedov's comedy took another social area: it exposed the diseases arising from a badly understood education, from the adoption of foolish worldly trifles in place of important things, in short, it took the Quixotic side of our European formation, an incoherent mixture of customs which made Russians neither Russians nor foreigners. The type of Famusov is as profoundly comprehended as was that of Prostakova. As naively as Prostakova boasts of her ignorance does he boast of his self-education, which is both his own and that of the class to which he belongs: he boasts that his young upper-class Moscovite daughters can tap out a few notes on the piano, speak but two words, and do it all with a grimace; that his door is open to everyone, both people he knows and those he doesn't, especially to strangers; that his office is stuffed with relatives who never do anything. He is a decent, respectable man, a gallant, he reads moral philosophy, and he is such a master of eating that he does not surface for three days on end. He is even a free-thinker when he is at a reunion with friends of his own stamp, and at the same time he is not prepared to admit young free-thinkers within gunshot range of the capital and abuses by name those who have not submitted to the accepted worldly customs of his society. In essence, this is one of those self-effacing persons in whom, in spite of all their worldly *comme il faut,* absolutely nothing has remained, who are as detrimental to society through their sojourn in the capital and through their service as others are detrimental to it through their lack of service and through their coarse sojourn in the country. Detrimental first because, as possessors of domains that have been given into the hands of hirelings and stewards of whom they demand only money for their balls and dinners, for their invited and uninvited guests, they have destroyed the truly legitimate ties uniting landowners and peasants; detrimental second to the professional career, because, by furnishing employment only to their do-nothing relatives, they have deprived the state of real workers and scared away honest men's desire to serve; detrimental third and finally to the spirit of the government by their equivocal lives, in that, under the guise of zeal and loyalty to the Tsar, demanding sham morals from young people while at the same time leading a depraved life themselves, they have aroused the indignation of youth, its scorn for age and merit, and a propensity for free-thinking which operates on those who have weak heads and are capable of running to extremes. Another type no less remarkable is the inveterate scoundrel Zagoretsky, everywhere absurd and, to our amazement, everywhere received, a liar, a swindler, but at the same time a master at obliging any significant or powerful person by supplying him with his favorite sins, ready in case of need to play the patriot and the defender of morality, to light bonfires and give to their flames all the books in the world along with their authors, even the fabulists (because of their eternal ridicule of lions and asses), thus revealing that, while fearing nothing, even the most shameful abuse, still he fears ridicule as the devil fears the cross. No less remarkable is a third type: the liberal fool Repetilov, a knight of frivolity in every respect, running to midnight meetings, gladdened, as though by a God-given treasure, when he has joined up with a society that makes a fuss about things he does not understand, of which he can say nothing, but to whose nonsense he listens with emotion, certain that he has finally fallen into the right way and that he is really hatching some public business which, although it has not yet matured, will some time mature if only there is more noise about it, if the nocturnal meetings be more and more frequent and the disputations more heated. No less remarkable is a fourth type: the stupid front-line soldier Skalozub, who thinks of his job solely as a matter of skill in distinguishing different uniforms but retains a philosophic-liberal attitude towards the ranks, openly admitting that he considers them indispensable canals by which he may progress to the grade of general, after which he will not give a rap about anything; difficulties will be nothing to him and the conditions of the time and century will be an open book to him: he is sincerely convinced that the world will be tranquil once it has a Voltairean sergeant-major. No less remarkable as a type is old Khlestova, a pitiful mixture of the banalities of two centuries, retaining only the banal of the old age, with pretensions to the respect of the new generation, with demands of deference for herself from the very people whom she despises, ready to insult aloud anybody and everybody who has simply failed to address her as he ought; she feels neither love nor respect for anyone, but sees herself as a protectress of little dogs and people like Molchalin—in short, a rotten old blackguard. And Molchalin himself is also a remarkable type. This is a figure accurately caught: taciturn,[54] low, one who, while he quietly steals into people's houses, still, as Chatsky says, is preparing himself

54. Molchalin's name is derived from the Russian word *molchat'*, to be silent.

to be a future Zagoretsky. Such is the collection of social monsters, each of whom caricatures some opinion, rule, thought, perverts his very reason for being, and necessarily summons up his furthest extreme, which is clearly manifested in Chatsky. Annoyed and justly indignant with all of them, Chatsky too has gone to excess, without noticing that, thanks to his very intemperance of language, he has made himself both intolerable and ridiculous. All the personae of Griboyedov's comedy are badly brought-up children, like those of Fonvizin—badly taught children, miscarried Russians, transitional persons past their time, formed in a new, fermenting world. There is nothing of the true Russian type in them: you do not perceive the Russian citizen. The spectator remains in doubt on the subject of what a Russian is. Even the person who is apparently taken as a model, that is, Chatsky, shows only some yearning for something, expresses only indignation for the despicable and loathsome in society, but he does not in himself furnish a model for society.

Both comedies fulfill the requirements of the stage badly: in this connection, the most insignificant French play is better than they are. The substance, which is the intrigue, is neither securely tied up nor masterfully untied. It seems that the authors of the comedies did not bother much about it, using it as a pretext for another, loftier subject, considering it important only for the exits and entrances of their personae. Secondary characters and roles have been calculated less with the hero of the piece in mind than in regard to how much they can fulfill and clarify the thought of the author by presentation on stage, how much they can contribute to the wholeness of the satire. On the other hand, if they had fulfilled these indispensable conditions for all dramatic works and forced each of their persons, so accurately caught and perceived, to live the action before the spectators instead of speaking it—then these would be two masterpieces of our genius. As they are, it is already possible to call them truly social comedies, an expression which has not, so far as I know, been applied to the comedy of any other people. There are traces of social comedy in the ancient Greeks; but Aristophanes was guided rather by his personal temperament; he fell into abuse of a single individual and did not always have the truth in view: the proof is that he had the insolence to ridicule Socrates. Our comic authors have been moved by social rather than personal motives, they rose up not against a person, but against a whole crowd of abuses, against the deviation of a whole society from the right road. They made society something like their own bodies: the ruthless power of their satire was lit by the flame of lyric indignation. This was the continuation of that struggle between enlightenment and darkness introduced into Russia by Peter, which made every noble Russian an unwilling warrior of the enlightenment. Neither of these comedies is at all a work of art, nor do they belong to their composers' fantasies. Many disputes and quarrels within our land were necessary before they could appear in their proper function, in the form they took, as a kind of terrible purification. That is why nothing has appeared in our literature along their line, and probably nothing will appear for a long time.

Since the death of Pushkin our poetry has ceased to progress. Nevertheless, this does not mean that its spirit has died out; on the contrary, it is building up afar, like a storm; the dry and stuffy atmosphere itself announces its approach. Already somewhat talented people have appeared. But they are all under the powerful influence of the harmonious sounds of Pushkin; none is yet capable of tearing himself away from the enchanted circle traced by him and showing his own strength. Nobody has yet perceived that another time has succeeded to his, that the moods of a new life have been formed and questions posed that were never posed before; and that is why not one of them is a precious stone. It is not fitting even to name them, except for Lermontov, who went further than the others and who is already no longer among us. One perceives in him the marks of a first-rate talent: a great career might have awaited him, had

there not been an unfortunate star which he chose to take for
his own. Having got into a society which might justly be called
temporary and transitory, like a poor plant torn from its natal
soil, condemned joylessly to drift across the steppes, feeling
that it could not grow in any other soil and that its fate was to
wither and be lost—from his earliest age he began to express
that heart-rending indifference to everything that we have perceived in no other of our poets. Joyless meetings, careless part-
ings, strange, senseless liaisons, concluded for no reason and
broken for no reason, became the subjects of his verses and
furnished Zhukovsky occasion most correctly to define this
poetry by the neologism *unenchantment*. Thanks to the talent
of Lermontov, this was in fashion for a while. . . . As in former
times Schiller with a light hand diffused an *enchantment* which
became fashionable throughout the world, as then, under the
heavy hand of Byron, there was a run of *disenchantment,* born
perhaps of excessive enchantment, which also became fashionable for a time, so in turn there came *unenchantment,* the natural child of Byronic disenchantment. Its existence, it goes
without saying, was of shorter duration than the others, because in unenchantment there was no attraction for anyone.
Having evoked the power of some seductive demon, the poet
attempted more than once to depict its image as though wishing
to exorcise it by his verse. This image was not drawn definitively; it was not even invested with that seductive power over
man that he wished to give it. Apparently it was the degenerate
product not of his own strength but of the fatigue and indolence
of a man who had struggled with it. In one of his unfinished
poems, called "Story for a Child," this image is more definite
and sensible. Perhaps if he had finished this tale, which is his
best poem, he would have rid himself of this spirit, which is his
own, and of his dismal state (a mark of this shines forth in the
poems "Angel," "Prayer," and some others), if he had preserved a little more respect and love for his talent. But no one
has ever played with his talent so lightly, nor shown such

vainglorious disdain for it as Lermontov. In him we note no love for the children of his imagination. Not one line stands out in him, is carefully wrought, balanced, and concentrated upon itself; indeed, his verse has no solid personality; sometimes it vaguely recalls the verse of Zhukovsky, sometimes that of Pushkin; everywhere there is excess and verbosity. His prose works are more valuable. No one among us has written so correct, so beautiful, and so fragrant a prose. There is more of the depth and reality of life—a future great painter of Russian existence was being prepared. But strange is the fate of our poets. Only let one of them who has lost his principal vocation and purpose throw himself into another or sink into the slough of worldly considerations, where it does not suit him to be and where there is no place for the poet, and a sudden violent death tears him out of our midst. Three first-rank poets, Pushkin, Griboyedov, Lermontov, one after the other, in the sight of everyone, were stolen away by violent death in the course of a single decade,[55] when their maturity was just blossoming, in the full development of their powers—and it surprised no one; our frivolous breed did not even shudder!

It is time, however, to say, in conclusion, what our poetry is in general, why it exists, what it serves, and what it has done for all our Russian land. Has it had an influence on the soul of contemporary society, educating and ennobling each person in accordance with his place, elevating the concepts of everyone in general, in accordance with the soul of the land and the native strength of the people, all of which are necessary for the state to advance? Or has it simply been a verisimilar picture of our society—both a general and a detailed picture, a clear mirror of our existence? It has been neither the one nor the other; it has done neither the one nor the other. It was almost unheard and ignored by our society, which was at that time

55. Pushkin and Lermontov were both killed in duels, the former in 1837, the latter in 1841. Griboyedov was killed by a mob which attacked the Russian legation in Teheran, where Griboyedov had been sent to negotiate a treaty with the Shah, in 1829.

being educated by another education—under the influence of French, German, English tutors, under the influence of people originally from all countries, of all possible conditions, standards of thought, manners, and opinions. Our society—and this does not happen with any other people—was educated in ignorance of its country within its own country. The language itself was forgotten, so much so that our poetry was cut off from all access to our ears. If it did force its way into society, it was by unknown ways and country roads: either a fortunately accompanying melody brought the poetic work into the salon, or it was the fruit of an immature youthful poet, one of his insignificant and feeble productions which nevertheless was a reply to some alien, free-thinking idea dropped into the head of society by its alien educators, with the result that society recognized the existence of a poet in its midst. In short, our poetry has neither taught society nor expressed it. As though conscious that its lot was not for contemporary society, it constantly rose above society; if it sank down to it, it was really only in order to lash it with the scourge of satire, not to transmit the pattern of its life to posterity. A strange thing: we ourselves were all the subject of our poetry, but we did not recognize ourselves in it. When the poet shows us our best sides, they seem to us exaggerated, and we are almost ready not to believe what a Derzhavin tells us about ourselves. When the writer exposes our worst sides, we also do not believe it, and it appears to us to be caricature. It is as though in both cases there is a strong exaggeration, but there is really no exaggeration. The reason is, in the first case, that our lyric poets, possessing the secret of seeing clearly in the seed, which is almost imperceptible to the naked eye, the future magnificent fruit, have presented each of our virtues in more purified form. The reason for the second is that our satiric writers, bearing in their souls, although unclearly, the ideal of a better Russian man, saw more clearly everything ugly and low in the Russian as he actually is. The strength of a noble indignation gave them the strength to expose more clearly the thing which no ordinary man could see. That is why, in these latter days, mockery is more strongly developed than all our other virtues in us.

Everyone among us laughs; there is in our country something that laughs at everyone equally—at the old and at the modern, preserving reverence only for the unaging and eternal. Thus our poetry has nowhere fully expressed the Russian, neither in the *ideal* in which he ought to be, nor in the *real* in which he now is. It accumulates only innumerable little hints of our diverse qualities; it has brought together in one depository various unconnected sides of our many-sided nature. Our poets have perceived that the time has not yet come to paint us as a whole and brag about us, that we must still be organized, become ourselves and make ourselves Russians. Our nature is still too soft, still too unprepared to take the form fitting to it; we have still not had time to take in the total of that multitude of elements of all kinds and all origins brought into our land from every place, an incoherent concurrence of alien forces within us, an unwise result of a concatenation commanded by God. In consequence, they have simply taken care that the best part of our nature not disappear in the struggle. They have taken possession of this best wherever they found it and have hastened to expose it to the light of day without caring about where or how to put it. So does the poor owner of a house engulfed by flames try to rescue from them only what is precious to him, without troubling about the rest. Our poetry did not resound for our contemporaries, but in order to edify future times, when the ideal of the internal structure of man, in that image in which God commanded it to be made of His own nature at the creation of the world, would finally become common to all Russia and equally desired by all, so that we would see that there really is something in us better than us, and we would not forget to find room for it in our configuration. Our own treasures are more and more revealed to us in accordance with how carefully we read our poets. The better we recognize them, the more they will reveal to us other and loftier sides of themselves, which almost no one until now has noticed: we will see that they were not only our public treasure, but in part our builders, whether they really had the thought of being so or not, by revealing their superiority to our nature by their attachment to our national genius which in them is apparently more developed, in order that it may shine before us in all its beauty. That endeavor of Derzhavin to inscribe the image of an adamant, firm man in whom was a biblical grandeur was not an arbitrary endeavor: he had perceived its source in our people. In all the Russian land we perceive the broad traits of that man in all his grandeur, so strongly that even foreigners peeping into Russia are struck by it before they have even had time to know the usages and customs of our land. Not long ago one of them, who published his memoirs with the precise aim of showing the ugly side of Russia to Europe, could not hide his amazement at the sight of the simple inhabitants of our rustic thatched homes![56] As though thunderstruck, he stopped before our venerable white-haired old men seated on the thresholds of their thatched huts who appeared to him like the stately patriarchs of ancient biblical times. More than once he acknowledged that in no other of the European lands in which he had traveled was the image of man revealed to him with a majesty so close to that of the biblical patriarchs. And he repeated this thought on more than one page of a book which spreads such hatred for us. This virtue of *sensitivity*,[57] which is displayed to such a high degree in Pushkin, is our national virtue. Let us only recall the names by which our people

56. Gogol's note: "The Marquis de Custine." Custine's account of his travels through Russia, which he had undertaken in 1839, was published in 1845. A staunch monarchist before he left France, Custine's faith in this form of government seems to have been severely shaken by his observations in Russia.

57. The Russian word used here is *chutkost'*, while the word Gogol usually uses for sensitivity is *chuvstvitel'nost*. The former, however, also has connotations of quickness, delicacy, tact.

themselves characterize that virtue: the name of *ukho*,[58] given to a man whose every vein burns and speaks, who cannot stay still for a moment; *udacha*,[59] one who arbitrates anywhere and is successful everywhere; there are numerous other names among us defining distinctive details and variations of that virtue. This is a great virtue: the Russian sketched by Derzhavin emerges as incomplete and harsh if he does not have the additional ability vividly to respond to all objects in nature, to be amazed at each step at the beauty of God's work. That intellect capable of finding the valid core of all things, displayed in Krylov, is our *true Russian intellect*. Only Krylov reflects the real tact of the Russian intellect, which, while knowing how to express the true essence of everything, also knows how to express it so that no one will be insulted by the expression nor set against it or its idea, even those of different opinions—in short, that real tact which we have lost in the course of our worldly education and which has been preserved among our peasants. Our peasants know how to speak with those of the highest rank, even with the Tsar, as freely as any one of us, and not even one word is improper, while often we do not know even how to speak with our equals without insulting them by some expression. On the other hand, whoever among us really possesses this concentrated, sincere, true tact of the Russian intellect enjoys the respect of all; everyone allows him to say what no one else would be allowed; no one is angry with him. All our writers have had their enemies, even the gentlest and the most beautiful of soul (it is enough to recall Karamzin and Zhukovsky). But Krylov has not had a single enemy. That *youthful daring* and valor with which he rushed into a splendid action, which makes such a violent uproar in the poems of Yazykov, is the daring of our Russian people, a marvelous virtue belonging to it alone, which among us suddenly gives youth to an old man

58. *Ukho* means ear.
59. *Udacha* means good luck or success, or, in adjectival form, happy or felicitous.

and manhood to a youth, if the least occasion occurs for us to come together on a work impossible to other people—among us it fuses the heterogeneous mass, formerly at loggerheads, into one, so that the quarrels and personal advantages of each are all forgotten and all Russia is one man. All these characteristics, revealed by our poets, are our national virtues, more visibly developed in them: poets do not fall from the moon, they issue from their own people. They are fires bursting forth from it, advance messengers of its power. Besides, our poets have succeeded in carrying harmony to unprecedented heights. I do not know in what other literature the poets have shown such infinite diversity and nuances of sounds, which of course our poetic language itself has partly assisted. Each has his particular line and ring. The metallic, bronze-like line of Derzhavin has not yet been forgotten by our ear; the thick as resin, fluid as a hundred-year-old Tokay line of Pushkin; the radiant, festive line of Yazykov, shooting into the soul like a ray woven of light; the melting aromatic line of Batyushkov, sweet as the honey of mountain ravines; the light airy line of Zhukovsky, flitting like the distant sound of an Aeolian harp; the heavy, earth-bound line of Vyazemsky, sometimes penetrated with a caustic, aching Russian melancholy—all these, like differently toned bells or the innumerable keys of a magnificent organ, have carried harmony throughout the Russian land. Harmony is not such a small thing as is believed by those who are unacquainted with poetry. It is with harmony, as with the beautiful lullaby song of a mother, that the child-people lulls itself, even before it can penetrate the meaning of the words of the song, which insensibly calms it so that its wild passions die away. Harmony is as necessary as the incense of the censer in the Temple, which invisibly disposes our soul for the hearing of something better before the service itself has begun. Our poetry has tried all the chords, it was nurtured by the literature of all peoples, it lent an ear to the lyres of all poets, it obtained, thus, a kind of world-wide language, in order to prepare everyone for a more meaningful service. We cannot now speak of the trifles about which the youthful present generation of poets continues to prattle frivolously without knowing it; we cannot serve art—beautiful as the service may be—without having comprehended its loftiest goal and having defined why art was given to us; we cannot repeat Pushkin. No, neither Pushkin nor anyone else ought now to be our model: other times have come. Now you must forget yourself—no originality of mind, no picturesque personal character, no prideful poses; the poet must now be educated in a Christian, higher education. Other matters are now the concern of poetry. As in the time of the people's infancy it served to call them forth to battle, exciting a combative ardor in them, so now it is fitting for it to call man to another, higher battle, to a battle not for our temporal liberty, our rights and privileges, but for our soul, which our celestial Creator himself esteems the pearl of his creation. Much now is in prospect for poetry: to restore to society what is truly beautiful and what has been banished by its present senseless life. No, none of our former poets may be recalled. Their speech will be different; it will be closer and more familiar to our Russian soul. In it our national origins will appear. The original source of our poetry has still not burst forth in all its strength, although it was seething and beating in the bosom of our nature when the word poetry was not yet on the lips of anyone. No one has yet brought up from the depths those three sources that were mentioned at the beginning of this article. This is still the riddle, this inexplicable violence heard in our songs, which goes somewhere beyond life and the song itself, as if burning with the desire for a better fatherland for which man has pined since the day of his creation. There is still no one among us in whom is fully reflected the many-sided poetic plenitude of our intellect contained in our innumerable proverbs, which know how to draw such great conclusions from their poor, insignificant times when the Russian dodged about within such narrow limits and in such a turbid pool, and which speak only of the enormous advantages which the Russian of today could draw from our present open times, in which the results of all the centuries are strewn about and, like unsorted goods, are thrown into one disordered heap. Still a secret for many is this extraordinary lyricism—born of thoroughly sensible minds—which originates in our hymns and canons, which as unaccountably invade his heart. After all, our extraordinary language is itself a secret. In it are all the tones and all the shades, all the transitional sounds from the solidest to the tenderest and softest; it is unlimited and can, living like life, at each hour be constantly enriched, drawing, on the one hand, from the sublime terms of the biblical language of the Church, and, on the other, choosing to select accurate terms from the innumerable dialects scattered through our provinces, thus having the possibility in one and the same speech of ascending to heights inaccessible to any other language and of being lowered to a level of simplicity appreciatively felt by the dullest of men —a language already poetic in itself which was not without reason neglected for a time by our best society: it was necessary for us to blab this rubbish in alien dialects, so that it might not stick to us together with our alien education, so that all these vague sounds, these imprecise names given to things— children of obscure, confused ideas which darken languages— might not be so bold as to cloud the childlike lucidity of our language and so that we might return to it prepared to think and live as is fitting to our spirit and not to that of the foreigner. All these are still only instruments, only materials, only rocks; there are still precious metals in the ore, from which another more powerful speech will be distilled. This speech will pass into every soul, it will not fall on sterile soil. Our poetry will be imbued with an angelic passion and, having struck every string there is in the Russian, it will move the most hardened soul with a holiness with which no power and no instrument in man can contend: it will evoke our Russia for us—our Russian Russia: not the one jingoist patriots coarsely show to us, nor the one that foreign Russians display to us from abroad, but the one that has its root in ourselves and will display us in such a way that everyone, without exception, however different their ideas might be, of whatever education and opinions, will say with one voice: "This is our Russia; it is a warm refuge for us, and now we are really at home in it, under our native roof and not in a foreign land."

1846

XXXII

EASTER SUNDAY

The Russian has a special interest in the celebration of Easter. He feels it more vividly if he should happen to be in a foreign land. Seeing how everywhere in other countries this day is almost indistinguishable from other days—business is as usual, life is normal, there is a humdrum expression on people's faces, —he feels melancholy and cannot help turning to Russia. It seems to him that there this day is somehow celebrated better, and a man is more joyful and better than on other days and his life is somehow different, not normal. It suddenly appears to him—that portentous midnight, that universal sound of bells, as though the whole earth had fused into one ringing, that exclamation "Christ is risen!" which on this day replaces all other greetings, that kiss given only among us—and he is almost ready to exclaim: "Only in Russia is this day celebrated as it ought to be celebrated!"

Be it understood, this is all a dream; it vanishes suddenly as soon as he shifts to what it really is in Russia, or even as soon as he remembers that this day is a day of running and bustling about while still half asleep, of meaningless visits, of deliberate ignorings of one another instead of joyful greetings—if he is greeted, it is on the basis of the most mercenary calculations; if he remembers that ambition boils higher among us on this day than on all others and people speak not about the Resurrection of Christ but about who will get some decoration; if he remembers that this people whose glory is spread abroad,

250

as though it rejoices most of all, gets drunk in the streets immediately that the solemn mass ends and before the dawn illumines the land. The poor Russian sighs if he remembers all this, and he understands that it is really only a caricature and a mockery of the celebration, not the celebration itself. Some chief gives a smacking kiss on the cheek of an invalid only *pro forma,* desiring to show subordinate officials how necessary it is to love their brothers, like a reactionary patriot who, to the chagrin of the young who inveigh against our old Russian customs, contending that there is nothing among us, cries out angrily, "Everything is among us—family life and family virtues; customs among us are observed piously; we fulfill our duty like nowhere in Europe; we are a people who are a marvel to all."

No, not in outward signs, not in patriotic exclamations, and not in a kiss given to an invalid, but on this day to look at a man as at one's finest treasure—so to embrace him and clasp him to ourselves as our very own brother, to rejoice in him as though he were the best part of us, which we have not seen for several years and which has suddenly, unexpectedly returned to us. Still more strongly! Still more! Because the ties binding us to him are stronger than the earthly blood of our kin: we are related to him through our perfect Heavenly Father, who is many times closer to us than our earthly father; on this day we are in His actual family, in His very house. This day is that holy day on which all humanity, to the last one, celebrates its holy, heavenly brotherhood, from which not one man is excluded.

It is as though this day were fitted for our nineteenth century, when thoughts about the happiness of mankind have become the beloved thoughts of almost everyone; when to embrace all mankind like brothers has become the beloved dream of youth; when many dream only of how to transform all mankind, how to raise the inner quality of man; when almost half have already solemnly recognized that only Christianity has the power to bring this about; when they have begun to affirm that the law of Christ ought to be introduced more closely into both family and governmental ways of life; when they have even begun to talk about everything being held in common—both home and land; when deeds of compassion and help for the unfortunate have become topics of conversation even in fashionable drawing rooms; when, finally, our century has become crowded with humanitarian institutions, charitable houses and shelters.

One would think the nineteenth century should joyously celebrate this day which is so much at the heart of its magnanimous and humanitarian movements! But on this day, as on a touchstone, you see how pale are all its Christian aspirations and how they are all only in dreams and thoughts, not in deeds. If on this day one should embrace his brother as a brother, he does not embrace him. He is ready to embrace all humanity as his brother, and he does not embrace his brother. He is so separated from this humanity, for which he prepares such a magnanimous embrace, that one man who has insulted him, the one whom Christ commands him immediately to forgive, he does not embrace. Having been separated from humanity, alone, at variance with it over some insignificant human opinions, he does not embrace him. Having been separated from humanity, alone, clinging more conspicuously than others to the grievous sores of his spiritual unworthiness, more than all others demanding compassion for himself, he pushes him away and does not embrace him. He achieves an embrace only with those who have insulted him in nothing, with whom he has never come in conflict, whom he never knew and into whose eyes he never even looked. This is the kind of embrace a man of the present century gives to all mankind, and for that he thinks of himself as a real humanitarian and a perfect Christian! They have driven Christ into the street, into the leper houses and hospitals instead of summoning Him into their homes, under their roofs, and they think they are Christians!

No, the present century does not celebrate this brilliant celebration as it ought to be celebrated. There is a terrible obstacle, there is an insuperable obstacle, whose name is—*pride.* It was known in earlier centuries, but then pride was more childish—pride in physical strength, pride in riches, pride in birth and rank—but it had not attained to that terrible spiritual development in which it now appears.

Now pride appears in two aspects. Its first aspect is pride in one's purity. Rejoicing that it has in many things become better than its ancestors, the mankind of the present century has fallen in love with its own purity and beauty. No one is ashamed publicly to boast of his spiritual beauty and to consider himself better than others. He need only look attentively at how every one of us now acts like a knight of the nobility, how we judge others mercilessly and harshly. He need only lend an ear to our justifications for him to justify himself for not embracing his brother even on Easter Day. Without shame and without a quaver in his soul, he says, "I cannot embrace this man: he is vile, he is a debased spirit, he has soiled himself by innumerable actions; I will not allow this man even into my presence; I do not even want to breathe the same air as he; I will make a detour in order to go round him and not meet him. I cannot live with base and contemptible people— can I really embrace such a man as a brother?" Alas! the poor man of the nineteenth century has forgotten that on this day there are no base nor contemptible people, but that all people are brothers of the same family, and brother is the name of every man, no other. Everything is suddenly forgotten by him —forgotten, perhaps just because contemptible and base people have surrounded him, that after looking at them he might look at himself and might search in himself for that very thing that frightened him so in others. He has forgotten that he can at every step, even one not noticed by him, do a base thing, although in another way—in a way not discomfited by public disgrace, but which nevertheless, as the proverb expresses it, is the same pancake, only on another plate. Everything is forgotten. He has forgotten that it may be because of him that so many base and contemptible people have developed, that better and finer people have roughly and brutally pushed them away and thus have compelled them to harden even more. As though it were easy to endure the contemptible! God knows, perhaps this is the way a dishonorable man is born; perhaps his poor soul, feebly joining battle with temptations, begged and prayed for help and was ready to kiss the hands and feet of one who, moved by spiritual pity, would have supported him on the brink of danger. Perhaps one drop of love for him would have been enough to return him to the right road. As though it would be difficult for sweet love to reach his heart! Has his nature really been so petrified that no feeling can be stirred in him, when the robber is thankful for love, when the brute beast remembers a caressing hand! But man of the nineteenth century has forgotten everything: he pushes his brother away from him, as the rich man pushes the beggar with running sores away from his threshold. His suffering is nothing to him, so long as he does not see his discharging pus. He does not even want to hear his confession, fearing that the smell from the stinking breath of his miserable mouth might discomfit him, proud as he is of the fragrance of his purity. Does such a man celebrate the celebration of heavenly love?

There is another aspect of pride, yet stronger than the first—intellectual pride. Never has it grown to such strength as in the nineteenth century. We perceive it in the dread everyone has of being reputed a fool. The man of the century will bear anything: he will bear the title of cheat, of villain; give him whatever title you want—he will bear it—the only title he will not bear is that of fool. He will allow laughter at anything—he will only not allow laughter at his intellect. For him his intellect is sacred. Because of the smallest mockery of his intellect he is immediately prepared to challenge his brother to a duel and, without a quaver, put a bullet through his head. He trusts no one and in nothing; he trusts his intellect alone. Whoever does not recognize his intellect, for him is no one. He has even forgotten that the intellect advances when all the moral powers in a man advance, and it stands still, and even goes backward, when the moral powers are not exalted. He has forgotten that not all sides of the intellect are in one man; that another man can see just that side of things which he cannot see, and thus know what he cannot know. He does not believe this and everything that he does not see himself is a lie for him. Not a shadow of Christian humility can touch him because of his intellectual pride. He is summed up in many things: in the heart of a man whom he has known for many years past, in the truth, he is summed up in God. But he is not summed up in his intellect. Already quarrels and battles have begun, not for some essential right, not because of personal hatreds—no, not sensual lusts, but the lusts of intellect have begun: they fight bodily because of disparate opinions, because of contradictions in the mental world. Whole parties have already been formed, blind to one another, having no personal intercourse—and abhorring one another. It is amazing: at the very time that people had begun to think that they were driving malice out of the world through education, malice came into the world by another road, from another end—by the road of intellect and on the wings of journalistic sheets, like an all-devouring locust it attacks the hearts of people everywhere. It is almost not perceived by the intellect itself. Intelligent people already begin to tell lies against their own convictions, only in order not to yield to the opposition party, only because pride does not allow them to acknowledge a mistake before everyone—already pure malice instead of intellect ascends the throne.

And does the man of such a century know how to fall in love and feel a Christian love for man? Does he fulfill that bright, open-hearted, and angelic infancy that brings all people together in one family? Does he perceive the fragrance of our heavenly brotherhood? Does he celebrate this day? Even that

outwardly benign expression of the early simple centuries that
gave the appearance of man being closer to man has disappeared. The prideful intellect of the nineteenth century has
annihilated it. The devil already struts in the world without a
mask. The spirit of pride has already ceased to appear in various forms and to frighten superstitious people; it has appeared
in its own shape. Sensing that its supremacy is recognized, it has
ceased to stand on ceremony with people. With arrogant shame-
lessness it laughs in the face of anyone who recognizes it; it
gives the most foolish laws to the world, such as have never
before been given to it—and the world sees this and does not
dare to disobey.

What does this worthless, meaningless fashion mean, which
from the beginning man has tolerated as a trifle, as an innocent
thing, and which now, like the total proprietor, has begun to
give orders in our homes, driving out everything that is chiefest
and best in man? No one is afraid to transgress several times
on the day of the first and the holiest of the laws of Christ,
while we are afraid not to fulfill pride's least command, trembling before it like a timid little boy. What does it mean that
even those who laugh at it dance, like flighty creatures, to its
tune? What do these so-called countless proprieties mean, which
have become stronger than all native decrees? What do these
strange powers, formed beside the lawful ones, this foreign, col-
lateral ascendancy, mean? What does it mean that seamstresses
rule in the world, tailors and tradesmen of all kinds, while the
Lord's anointed have been left aside? Shadowy people, unknown to anyone, having no sincere thoughts and convictions,
rule the opinions and thoughts of intelligent people, and the
newspaper column, which everyone recognizes is deceitful, becomes an insensible legislator for the man who does not respect
it. What do all these illicit laws, which the impure power whose
origin is below openly draws up in the sight of everyone, mean—
all the world sees this, and, as though fascinated, does not dare
to stir. What a terrible mockery of mankind!

In the face of such a course of events, for what are the outward holy customs of the Church preserved, that heavenly master who has no power over us? Or is this a new mockery of the spirit of darkness? Why has the meaning of the celebration been lost? Why is it more silent each time it comes to call the people together into one family and why, after sorrowfully glancing over us all, does it leave like one unknown and alien to all? Is it really unknown and alien to all? But why have people somewhere escaped destruction, people who seem to grow brighter on this day and celebrate their infancy—that infancy whose heavenly kiss, like the kiss of eternal spring, inundates the soul, that beautiful infancy which prideful present-day man has lost? Why has man not forgotten this infancy forever, why, like a vision in a kind of remote sleep, does it still stir our souls? Why all this, what for? Why as though unknown? As though unseen, what for?

So that for those few who still perceive the springtime breath of this celebration, it may suddenly become so sad, so sad, as sad as to an angel in heaven. So that, having begun to wail with a heart-rending cry, they may fall at the knees of their brothers, praying that this day stand out alone from the round of other days, that this day be observed not by the customs of the nineteenth century, but by the customs of the eternal century, that on this day we may embrace and clasp mankind, as a guilty friend embraces the magnanimous friend who has forgiven him everything, although tomorrow we may push him away from ourselves and tell him that he is alien to us and unknown. If only we would desire this, if only we would by force compel ourselves to do this, if only we would grasp this day as a drowning man grasps a plank! God knows, perhaps for this single desire a ladder is being prepared to be thrown down to us from Heaven and a hand is being extended to help us to fly up by it.

But nineteenth-century man does not want to spend one day so! An incomprehensible melancholy has broken out in the land: life has become more and more callous; everything is becoming petty and shallow, and the gigantic figure of boredom increases in the sight of all, each day reaching a more immeasurable size. Everyone is deaf, everywhere a grave. God! how empty and terrible is your world become!

Why does it seem only to a Russian that this celebration is celebrated as it ought to be, and celebrated so in his land alone? Is this a dream? But why does this dream come to no one but the Russian? What does it mean that the celebration itself has disappeared, while visible signs of it are so clearly borne across the face of our land: the words "Christ is risen!" are pronounced, and kisses, and the holy midnight comes solemnly, and the boom of all-sounding bells rolls and rings through all the land, exactly as though they are calling us? Where the palpable signs are borne, they are not borne without a reason; where they call, they rouse from sleep. The customs that have been eternally fixed do not die out. They die out in the letter, but they live in the spirit. They fade temporarily, they die out in empty and evanescent crowds, but they are resurrected with new strength in the select, so that they may overflow with greater strength from their world through all the world. The kernel passed down by our ancestors, which is really Russian and has been sanctified by Christ himself, will not die. It is scattered in the sounding strings of the poets, it is proclaimed by the fragrant lips of the holy men, having grown dim, it blazes up—and the celebration of Easter is celebrated as it ought to be, among us before among other nations! Basing ourselves on what, depending on what facts contained in our heart can we say this? Are we better than other peoples? Is our life closer to Christ than theirs? In no way are we better, and our life is more unsettled and disordered than theirs. "We are worse than all others," is what we must always say about ourselves. But in our nature there is something which prophesies it to us. Our very disorder prophesies it to us. We are still a molten metal, not cast in the mold of our national form; it is still possible for us to reject, to push away from ourselves what is improper to us and to take into ourselves things impossible to other peoples, who have received their form and hardened in it. There is much in our native nature, forgotten by us, which is close to the law of Christ—the proof is that Christ came to us without the sword and the prepared soil of our hearts invoked His word; that there is a base for the brotherhood of Christ in our Slavic nature, and fraternization is more native to us even than blood brotherhood; that among us there is no irreconcilable hatred between estates and we do not have those bitter parties such as abound in Europe and constitute an insuperable obstacle to the unity of peoples and brotherly love among them; that there is among us, finally, a courage not innate to anyone else: if we have some task before us that is absolutely impossible for any other people, even if, for example, it is suddenly getting rid of all our faults, everything most shameful to the lofty nature of man, then, ignoring bodily pain, ignoring our property (as in 1812 we burned our homes and earthly belongings), everyone among us would rush to get rid of what is shameful and has stained us, not one soul would hold back from another, and in that very moment all quarrels, hatreds, enmities—all are forgotten; brother hangs on the breast of brother, and all Russia is one man. It is by basing ourselves on this that it is possible to say that the celebration of the Resurrection of Christ is celebrated among us before among others. My soul says this to me firmly; this is not a thought invented in my brain. Such thoughts are not invented. It is by the power of God that they are given birth in the hearts of many people who have never seen one another, who live at different ends of the land; simultaneously, as though from one mouth, they are cried abroad. I firmly know that any man in Russia, although I do not know him personally, steadfastly believes that and says, "In our country, earlier than in any other, will the advent of the Kingdom of Christ be celebrated."

INDEX

Abomination: daily occurrence of, 197; in Gogol, 104; knowledge of, 135; love of, 107; presence of, 130; of self, 135; source of, 123; spitting on, 88

Abuses: paths to, 181, 183; in Russia, 14, 176

Academies: ecclesiastical, 74; philological and teaching, 203

Action: Christian, 117; honorable, 128; law of, 40, 204; lawless course of, 176; moral, 132; social, 132

Activity: moral, xxi; public, 122

Actor, 77 ff.

Administration: economic and police, 180; provincial, 180, 183

Advantage: personal, 191; worldly, 147

Affairs: domestic, 161; internal, 179

Ailments: grave, 80; necessary, 19

Aksakov: family, 23, *n* 3; S. T., ix; identified, ix, *n* 8, xx

Alexander I, epoch of, 206.

Alexander II, 174, *n* 1

Ambition, 174

Analysis, faculty of, 210

"Angel," 240

Anglomaniacs, 187

Annichkov Palace, 54

Antiquity: life of, 33; men of, 36; treasures of, 35

Aphrodite, 35

Apostles, 34

Arabesques, xxiv

Arbitration, court of, 117, 229

Ariosto, 212

"Aristipp's Bath," 206, *n* 7

Aristophanes, 239

Arrogance, Germanic, 215

Art: career of, 155; love for, 155; as moral activity, xxiv; service of, 247

Art-for-Art's-Sake, xxiv

Articles, literary, of Gogol, 3

Artifice, lack of, in Pushkin, 218

Artist: relief of, 155–156; thought of, 155

Arts, Academy of, 147

Aspiration: Christian, 252; inner, 209; noble, 133; Russian, 178

"The Ass," 229, *n* 44

Atheists, 23

Attorney, government, 182

Aurora Borealis, 201

Authors, dramatic, 74

An Author's Confession, xii, *n* 20

Authority, all-powerful, 52

Awakening, enthusiasm of, 200

Ballads, German, 211

Balthazar, 86

Banality, 103–105

"Banquet on the Neva," 63

Baratinsky, E. A., 220; identified 220, *n* 30

Batory, 50

Batyushkov, K. N., 212; identified 212, *n* 18, 215, 246

Beaumarchais, 75

Beauty: of God's work, 245; spiritual, 253; sublime, 16; of women, 16

Belinsky, V. G.: anger of, x; attacks of, xii, xxi; critic of *The Contem-*